S0-AIM-168

THE LIBRARY

COLBY JUNIOR COLLEGE

BEN-GURION OF ISRAEL

David Ben-Gurion, first Prime Minister of Israel

BEN-GURION
OF ISRAEL

Barnet Litvinoff

Zionist
+
non-zionist

PRAEGER : NEW YORK

Published in the United States of America in 1954
by Frederick A. Praeger, Inc., Publishers,
105 West 40th Street,
New York 18, N.Y.

DS
125.3
B 37
L5

ALL RIGHTS RESERVED

LIBRARY OF CONGRESS CATALOG CARD NUMBER : 54–9526

PRINTED IN GREAT BRITAIN
BY WILLIAM CLOWES AND SONS, LIMITED
LONDON AND BECCLES

35496

To the memory of my son Michael

Contents

Illustrations and Maps

Acknowledgments

THIS BOOK OWES a great deal to the many people, in England and Israel, who freely allowed me to draw on their knowledge and experience. The biography does not claim to be comprehensive or official, and I hasten to point out that any opinions expressed are solely my own. My debt to Mr. Ben-Gurion, who, while still Prime Minister of Israel, gave so readily of his time, is obvious. No less valuable, though perhaps less apparent, was the assistance of Mrs. Ben-Gurion and Mr. Ben-Zvi, the President of Israel. They were particularly helpful in providing the background to some of the early pioneering years in Palestine.

Those who are not mentioned individually I hope will accept this grateful acknowledgment of their part in the composition of the story. I would, however, refer to a few of those who must have found my constant importuning with questions some strain on their patience, but who nevertheless volunteered much valuable advice and information. They are: Mr. Shlomo Zemach, a leading figure in the Israel literary world; Mr. Igal Yadin, formerly Commander-in-Chief of the Israel Forces; Mr. Joseph Serlin, Minister of Health; Mr. Ehud Avriel, one-time Minister to Czechoslovakia and Hungary; Mr. Zalman Aranne, Minister Without Portfolio; Mr. Zerach Wahrhaftig, Vice-Minister of Religious Affairs; Mr. David Hacohen, now Minister to Burma; Mr. Zeev Sharef, Secretary to the Cabinet; Mr. Moshe Sneh, Mr. Isaac Ben-Aharon, Mr. Aron Zisling, Mrs. Esther Raziel-Naor, all members of the Israel Parliament; Mr. Berl Locker, co-chairman of the Jewish Agency Executive; Mr. Theodor Kollek, Col. Nehemiah Argov and Mr. Isaac Navon, Aides to Mr. Ben-Gurion during his term of office; Mr. Levi Itzhak, Mr. Harry Sacher, Mr. Gershon Agron, Mr. David Zakkai, Mr. Eri Jabotinsky, Col. Lassya Galili and Mr. Lavy Bakstansky. I also found the Hebrew work on the early generation of pioneers, *David Ben-Gurion VeDoro*, by Miss Bracha

Habbas (published by Massada, Tel Aviv, in 1952), of great value in writing chapters two and three.

May I, finally, thank three people for their helpful stylistic suggestions. They are Mrs. Sonia Orwell, Mr. Nicolas Thompson, and my wife.

B. L.

London, July, 1954.

I

The Man, the People, the Idea

'Ben-Gurion Day' in New York – Zionists and non-Zionists – Rabbi Abba Hillel Silver – The nation independent – Jacob Blaustein – Raising funds for Israel – Unity of Jewry – Economic position of Israel – Bleak facts – Speech in Madison Square Garden – Mentality of the golden calf

ON TUESDAY, MAY 8th, 1951, newspapers in New York City carried this advertisement:

TOMORROW NEW YORK CITY WILL MAKE HISTORY

IT will greet Prime Minister Ben-Gurion of Israel with a memorable reception. For the first time in the 287-year-old history of New York, this great city will be host to a Prime Minister of Israel.

To the people of all races and creeds who make up the great metropolis of New York, tomorrow, Wednesday, May 9th, will be 'Ben-Gurion Day'. By proclamation of the Mayor of the City of New York, Prime Minister Ben-Gurion will be given the hospitality and welcome that befits the leader of the courageous new democracy of the Middle East and one of the world's greatest statesmen.

PRIME Minister Ben-Gurion is arriving tomorrow to pay tribute to the people of New York for the great moral and material assistance they have extended to the young republic of Israel.

ON Thursday, May 10th, Prime Minister Ben-Gurion will be the guest of honour at an historic mass rally at Madison Square Garden. This rally will celebrate the Third Anniversary of the independence of Israel and will mark the nation-wide launching of the Israel Independence Bond Drive.

HAVING watched with deep sympathy the birth of Israel and its valiant efforts to solve the problem of Jewish homelessness, New Yorkers will wish to take this occasion to salute Prime

Minister Ben-Gurion who symbolises the great devotion of the people of Israel to the ideals of human liberty and world peace.

The following day a million citizens left their homes and offices to line the streets of Manhattan and to give a frenzied welcome to the stocky, bronzed figure, of leonine profile, as he drove in an open car to pay his respects to their Mayor. At the centre of a triumphal procession which included 2,000 members of the American armed forces, the white-haired little man was carried to the sounds of martial music and past cheering crowds, as far as the tip of the island. Then the parade swung north again to City Hall. There 100,000 people saw him greet Mayor Impelliteri, just as a few days earlier General MacArthur, the great conqueror of the East, had done. This was Ben-Gurion of Israel, creator of the world's newest state, whose entire population was hardly larger than this welcoming, flag-waving crowd.

He had come to America on a mission which affected the survival of his young republic. But he was entitled to forget this for a moment (as indeed the woman by his side, Paula Ben-Gurion, was entitled to forget it) and steep himself in the fruits of victory, achievement, and recognition. Years of struggle had lined his face, but his eyes were uncynical and twinkled with pleasure at this taste of New World pageantry. He surrendered to it with unconcealed joy.

In the preparations for this visit nothing that might have contributed to the effect of grand climax had been omitted. Eight days before, two grey warships had steamed into Boston harbour, and were now cruising along the eastern seaboard of America, indicating that young though Israel was, she was nevertheless capable of serious business. Their crews marched through their various ports of call and the American public was made to realise the fuller possibilities, no less than the dangers, which statehood brought to the Jewish people on the narrow Asian shore of the Mediterranean. Several ministers of Ben-Gurion's Cabinet soon followed: among them his austere Finance Minister, Eliezer Kaplan, and Montreal-born Dov Joseph, one-time Governor of the beleaguered city of Jerusalem and now Minister of Commerce. When the Prime Minister himself arrived, it was by a Constellation plane that inaugurated the trans-Atlantic service of Israel's National Airlines, and as he touched down at Washington's airport its blue and white emblem was a further reminder of the significance of Jewish statehood, revived after two thousand years.

American newspapers during that week were deeply engrossed in an enquiry into General MacArthur's sudden dismissal from his Far Eastern Command, and by the evidence of administrative laxity which had been brought to light by Senator Kefauver; and since these matters usurped the headlines from the arrival of the Prime Minister, the advertisement announcing 'Ben-Gurion Day', stridently displayed over entire pages, did much to restore the event to national prominence.

What prompted Israel's envoy to turn at that moment from affairs of state in his homeland, from perilous party strife and the menacing situation on his borders? Bankruptcy was the spur, or rather the threat of bankruptcy. He had come to ask for money. Ben-Gurion was launching a gigantic drive for funds, a drive to raise 500 million dollars in bonds towards the 1,000 million dollars which the Israelis believed they must obtain from the outside world to lift themselves out of their economic difficulties. No one before had dared to seek such a sum in foreign investment from the American public. It called for a thoroughly worked out and pertinaciously implemented plan in every city of the United States; a vast propaganda campaign; a catalogue of public relations techniques; the sympathy of the United States government; the prayers of the Jewish clergy; and a lavish curtain-raiser in which one man alone was colourful and important enough to occupy the chief role —David Ben-Gurion.

"I am a happy captive of your city," Ben-Gurion told Mayor Impelliteri outside City Hall in his reply to a welcome that echoed through loud-speakers into the ears of the hundred thousand New Yorkers assembled before him. He must have been happy to be again among the people from whom in 1918 he had chosen a bride, who was now here beside him, and to stand upon the steps of the very building where they had been married. For years he had been guided by the knowledge that these New Yorkers would share the anxiety of his difficulties and the joy of his victories; that in the last analysis they would never let him down. And understanding emotions such as those he now saw massively stirring before him, he had tussled with the British Empire, confidently asserted his

nation's independence in 1948, waged successful war against overwhelming odds, and opened the gates of Israel to large numbers
of immigrants.

But a captive? A metaphor perhaps, chosen by the Premier to
voice sentiments far from uncharitable. Ben-Gurion is an expressive
orator, with a talent for the *mot juste* that has been sharpened by
half a century of polemical debate with his own wordy race and
against silvery-tongued representatives of the British government.
But this time he was not making a political statement, but rather
describing the spell cast over a workaday individual by the warmth
and the magnitude of his reception. Nevertheless, the expression of
surrender was not without its undertones of irony. During the
previous three years many of Ben-Gurion's actions had been
governed by what these people might think, or their Jewish leaders
say, or their government hint. Three years had changed him from
an ideological purist into a statesman. This transformation had
involved conflicts, had brought him defeats as well as victories; and
when seated in his Prime Minister's room in Jerusalem, or addressing his parliament there, or in private negotiation with colleagues
of the Zionist movement, his phraseology could be less generous.

When people have a great deal in common, their differences often
stand glaringly out. In the case of Ben-Gurion and his fellow-Jews
of New York their differences provided the substance of bitter
conflict. To the inhabitants of the New World he represented the
challenge of a newer one. The gulf dividing them was of time, not
of space. For the secret of Ben-Gurion is to be found in his satisfaction, which is free of arrogance, at being a man who has returned
home, who has gone back to the land whence his forefathers
wandered; but implied in that satisfaction is a contempt for Jews
who do not accept this homeland, who prefer, in fact, the hazards
and the desolation of dispersion. In the mind of the first Prime
Minister of Israel they are in *Galuth*, a Hebrew word meaning
exile and the spiritual 'incompleteness' that goes with exile. The
choice that has to be made between the hardships and the cultural
rawness of Israel and the comforts, richness and sophistication of
Galuth in the English-speaking world, where Jews now enjoy a
measure of equality denied in other ages and in other civilisations,
has become, since the extermination by Hitler of millions of
European Jews, the Jewish problem of our time.

In his role of recruiting-sergeant for his country Ben-Gurion spared neither individuals nor occasions to ram this problem home. In October, 1952, he was addressing a public dinner at the King David Hotel in Jerusalem in honour of Dr. Nahum Goldmann, the suave leader of American Zionists, whose clever negotiations with Germany had just resulted in an agreement to pay heavy material compensation to Israel for the Nazi spoliation of the European Jewish communities. One might have expected thanks in this case to be undiluted by criticism; that Goldmann, of all Jews, was fully justifying his continued existence in the Diaspora. Yet Ben-Gurion chose this moment to reprove his fellow-Zionist for not taking the plunge and returning 'home'. "He is a great Jew," said the Prime Minister, "but his one defect is that he is not fully identified with Israel. Here, and here alone, Jewishness and Zionism begin." It had many times been hinted to Goldmann that exalted office in the service of the new state was his for the asking, perhaps one day the Presidency itself. He continues to make many crossings of the Atlantic, but has refrained from crossing the Rubicon.

Ben-Gurion has made his own rough adjustments in his relations with the Jews outside Israel. Some are Zionists, and their place is in Israel. Others, the non-Zionists, are privileged to help Israel, but are under no moral compulsion to live there. Sometimes he had warmer praise for these than for the Zionists, who preach the political and spiritual renaissance of the Jewish people but exclude themselves from its joys and consequences. Not six months after his return home from his American mission, he told parliament in the course of a statement whose frankness he long had cause to regret: "American Zionist leaders went bankrupt on the establishment of this state. There were not five of them to get up and come to Israel. They might not have been followed by the masses, but this would have proved that Zionism was not void of meaning, at least for the leaders." While no Israeli could be found to demur, the American Zionists were goaded to fury, and long mellifluous telegrams had to be addressed to them before their resentment was assuaged. American Jews were privileged to help Israel, Ben-Gurion maintained, because they had been granted three hitherto unpossessed attributes: "a sense of pride, a place where they can learn to be unhyphenated Jews, and a link with the old country, such as other Americans have."

2

In New York the happy captive had to accord his favours equally between 'Zionist' and 'non-Zionist'. He had a word of greeting for Henry Morgenthau, banker, philanthropist, former Secretary of the Treasury, successful non-Zionist fund-raiser who was to lead the drive for bonds; and for Benjamin Browdy, Brooklyn textile merchant, of East European origin like himself and head of the Zionist Organisation of America. Nevertheless, the delicate balance of forces was disturbed. When David Ben-Gurion spoke on May 10th at the great bond rally at Madison Square Garden, 19,000 thronged the hall to hear him and to listen to words of praise about him from Governor Dewey and Mayor Impelliteri, and to soak in the rhetoric of Israel's brilliant Ambassador in Washington, the young British Jew Aubrey Eban. But none of these compensated for the man who was not there—Rabbi Hillel Silver of Cleveland, Ohio. His absence pointed to the perplexity which had been caused in America's powerful Zionist movement by the fruition of its work in May, 1948, when Ben-Gurion had called the new nation into being.

This rabbi from the Middle West, a Jewish brand of Senator Taft, had, by a careful adjustment of time-tables, avoided being in the same continent as Ben-Gurion, and at that moment was being fêted at a private parade of his own in Tel-Aviv. Curiously enough, this was his first visit to independent Israel since the heroic days of the Provisional Government and the Israel-Arab war, late in 1948. Yet to him more than any other individual was due the credit for the successful marshalling of the diplomatic case before the United Nations in 1947. Silver had stood with Weizmann and Ben-Gurion as one of the three best-known Jewish figures at the moment of independence. In those days politicians, wire-pullers, and orators had counted. Not so now. Silver had been sacrificed on the twin altars of Israel's present-day needs—man-power and money.

Silver clashed with Ben-Gurion because his mind refused to be adjusted to the realities of Jewish autonomy in Israel. He wanted, as the acknowledged leader of American Zionism, to have a hand in events which to him were world Zionist problems and which to Ben-Gurion were matters of state, pure and simple. Ben-Gurion would not hear of Silver's remote control from New York, or Cleveland, Ohio. He envisaged people like Silver automatically transferring themselves to Tel-Aviv after the completion of their political work for the establishment of the state, and that there the task of consolidation might have been pursued jointly. Because of their defection he sought out new allies in America, such as Morgenthau, who could be trusted to do an urgent non-political job without encroaching on the Jewish government's preserves.

There was another telling point in Ben-Gurion's argument. He was himself a socialist and leader of the strongest party in Israel. Rabbi Silver was a right-winger, a Republican in American politics and a devotee of private enterprise in Israel. Israel was now entering upon an era of vast development and economic doctrines mattered more than previously. Silver and the Prime Minister were in 1951 on different sides of the political fence, with the rabbi offering his powerful support to the opposition in Israel. Ben-Gurion did not approve of Zionists who did not immigrate to Israel themselves, and who were not in favour of encouraging other American Jews to do so, but who nevertheless insisted upon meddling in internal Israeli affairs.

Silver himself replied with counatercharges. The Premier, he said, was encouraging one American Jewish group against another. He was entrusting a specifically Zionist task—the collecting of funds for Israel—to a group that had stood on the side-lines for years, quite apathetic to Jewry's national aspirations. Now that the work had been crowned with success these people were usurping the prestige that others had earned in the establishment of Israel. But it was to him, Silver, and his colleagues, that Ben-Gurion had always been able to turn with confidence in the past, pledged as they were to the common ideal. It was they who should lead the fund-raising movement now, and direct its expenditure as before in the old harmony between the Jewish leaders of Palestine and of world Zionism.

Ben-Gurion won the day. Silver found to his sorrow that the voice of a prime minister, even of a tiny, under-developed, penniless state that he himself had helped to establish, counted for more than the voice of a private American citizen. He resigned the Zionist leadership in February, 1949, taking his following with him. Although Nahum Goldmann succeeded Silver and managed to cooperate with Ben-Gurion and still grow in stature, Silver was never forgotten by his own American friends nor by his Israeli supporters.

What was most illuminating in this conflict was the speed with

which Ben-Gurion pushed towards a breach. Gone were the interminable discussions of the days before 1948, gone the tender regard
for susceptibilities. He thought little of dropping an old soldier who
had outlived his usefulness. Ben-Gurion was the man on the frontier,
gambling at every pioneer step with the survival of a people; Silver
had nothing to lose but a career; and his miscalculation of the
changing forces in Jewish life proved fatal. Ben-Gurion came out
of the controversy as the most powerful individual in all Jewry and
it will be profitable to examine at this point the world he dominated
and to assess his strength within it.

"To be a nation answerable for its own destiny," he wrote some
months after his return from America, "is a precious ideal, and the
Jewish people had bided for that ideal with messianic longing
through jubilee upon jubilee. But it is also an ideal for which one
must pay very dearly, with unceasing effort and grim sacrifices. A
state is not manufactured by a mere declaration; it is set up anew day
after day, by incessant toil and by the labour of years, even generations. A people that is not fit and ready to bear that onerous duty of
being sufficient unto itself will not preserve independence even after
it has won it. This is so for every state, and it is pre-eminently so
for the State of Israel. From the start, the conditions of its survival,
its internal and its external aims, its place in the world, its security
and its relations with its neighbours, were coiled in difficulties of
which no other country has seen the like."

These sentences do not merely contain the kernel of Israel's
problems and aspirations. They also reveal a great part of the personality of their author. He had faith in the simplest of propositions:
that the Jewish world was at a great new dawn. He was anxious lest
his people might not be ready for, or equal to, the great opportunity
that was offered for self-transformation. He demanded in his own
actions unbending fixity of purpose, yet he was not sure of his
nation's readiness to follow him. Did Israel understand that this was
the era of the Messiah, requiring rigidity, self-abnegation, patience?
Or had it decided that statehood was 'a platter bearing the golden
calf'? His speeches after 1951 invariably expounded these alternatives.

Israel has proved capricious in independence. Decisions of great
urgency remain unmade while parties splinter on differences of
a hair's breadth. A readiness to accept heavy burdens has not been

accompanied by a full acceptance of their consequences. Controversy is acrimonious. Yet in all this Ben-Gurion's authority over the people he leads (and he remained their leader even after November, 1953, when, to the dismay of the Jewish world, he chose to leave the Prime Minister's room in Jerusalem for a hut in Israel's desert south) is unshaken. For six years he held unquestioned sway in a land-mass where the characteristic method of political change is the *coup d'état*, and it seemed as if Israel were a calm island in a sea of anarchy, which it is not. This was so because he is the embodiment of Israel's one desire ardently felt, but not yet achieved—national maturity. It is doubtful whether any other man in Israel, or any Jew outside it, could fulfil this role of leadership at the present time.

Ben-Gurion is a man bred from the working-class movement, and throughout his years of residence in Western capitals he never assimilated their intellectual atmosphere. Nevertheless, he had the philosopher's approach to his tasks and his speeches proliferate in historical allusion. When a junta of army officers brushed Farouk and the old-guard Egyptian politicians out of Cairo he extended the hand of friendship towards General Neguib with these words: "During the conflict between Egypt and Great Britain we did not attack Egypt in revenge, either for the Egyptian treatment of Israel 4,000 years ago in the days of Pharaoh, or for the Egyptian invasion of Palestine four years ago in the days of Farouk." Ben-Gurion's way is to set a current issue against the background of ancient history or in the context of general morality. He firmly believed he was carrying on where the Bible left off.

The Prime Minister's justification then for his trip in May, 1951, to America, involving as it did political implications that must have weighed heavily with him, lay in the moral he drew from two thousand years of Jewish history. This enabled him to seek his money with a majestic air, to cover the pauper's rags with the cloak of the conqueror. The country he governed is one of great physical weakness. In size it is as small as Wales; its population, in May, 1951, hardly larger than Glasgow's; rainfall varies from the excessive to the inadequate, so that after hundreds of years of neglect swamp alternated with desert throughout the land. Even in this, the seventh year of statehood, only a minority of the population speak and write the national language, Hebrew, with the fluency normally expected of a literate people. Some twelve per cent of the population are Arabs who enjoy a large measure of freedom but who have not yet been awarded complete political equality with the Jewish Israelis, and who maintain links across the border with the countries glaring resentfully at Israel on three sides.

As to the Jews themselves, practically all of them, apart from the native-born (perhaps 150,000), arrived through one form of compulsion or another. The 750,000 immigrants since May, 1948, came from places in Eastern Europe, Asia and North Africa where living conditions for Jews were intolerable; and, in the large majority of cases, no other government would accept them. Of the 650,000 constituting the Jewish population of Palestine at the end of the British Mandate, some 400,000 had been induced to make their homes there because the Zionist urge to return to the homeland of old provided them with an escape from the restrictions imposed upon Jewish minorities in other states; or from some personal experience, such as prompted those escaping from Nazi extermination. The number of Israelis who have chosen to live in their country purely from Zionist devotion alone is minute, less than 5,000 men and women. Most of these came from the United Kingdom or South Africa, a handful from the United States and Western Europe. Ben-Gurion himself was a Zionist who left his native Poland in 1906 with a young group intent upon a pioneering life on the land. It was a period of mass Jewish escape from Czarist oppression, with entire towns and villages packing up and going mostly to the new world, but also to Western Europe. Had Ben-Gurion been born in one of those western lands he might still have grown up with a belief in Palestine as the one hope for the Jews; but it is doubtful whether he would ever have emigrated there at all.

For such a conglomeration the word nation would hardly seem applicable. But in the case of Israel the designation is justified because the Jewish religion is a unifying force transcending the barriers created by widely differing environments. The word Zionism has in the past 70 years, and especially since Theodor Herzl wrote his *Judenstaat* at the turn of the century, taken on a political connotation, but in reality it is a spiritual need enshrined in the character of the people no less than in the prayers of the synagogue. This is one source of strength in the nation of Israel. There is also another: the strength of being the only centre of Jewish life in the world free of dilemma. Its people are sure of where they are going, and are therefore blind to the hurdles every one else sees in their way.

To David Ben-Gurion the word Israel does not represent merely the national structure of the 1,500,000 assembled inside the state. It is synonymous with the whole Jewish people. "The Zionist movement, the Jewish people and the State of Israel now constitute one cohesive unity impossible to break," he told an international conference of key Zionist politicians in Jerusalem in May, 1952. This is not the view to which the bulk of Jewry in the Diaspora would subscribe, and more often than not such an assertion disconcerts even the Zionist faithful who consider their own stake in Israel deeper and stronger than that of other Jews. It also explains Ben-Gurion's haughtiness towards those who do not recognise what he considers the essential facts of Jewish existence today.

This concept of the unity of the Jewish people as expressed in the emergence of the state has been enlisted in the search for economic expedients; and economic expediency absorbs at present much of the emotional energy of Israel's leaders. For in a country whose population doubled in four years, but which is without considerable sources of raw material and whose industrial development is in its infancy, economic problems stand out as the greatest hurdle of all. The enunciation of this principle of unity, and adherence to it, has been Ben-Gurion's most considerable contribution to the survival of his state since, as commander of his army, he repulsed the Arab invasion of 1948-9.

We have to go back to the year 1950 to find this principle first adapted to serve the needs of the state. That year can now be seen as a minor watershed in the development of new-born Israel. From the middle of 1948 until 1950 events there had stirred Jewry to hitherto unknown enthusiasm and self-confidence. Internationally, the young country's position was rapidly consolidating. It became the 59th member of the United Nations, and the armistice following the brief war with the Arabs augured well for an early peace settlement. During 1949 some 240,000 Jews were ingathered, more than half of them from European backgrounds, and administrative frailties, housing shortages and constitutional ills could legitimately be ascribed to this extraordinary and unparalleled expansion. In the year 1950 the 'honeymoon' period ended with unpleasant abruptness. The country discovered its woeful lack of technical skill; most of the newcomers were by western social standards retarded; the economy grew steadily worse and the much hoped-for capital investment did not flow in. Grumbling among the immigrants themselves added fuel to the fires of opposition, stoked up by a right-wing element which blamed the economic low water-mark on Ben-Gurion and his socialist colleagues, rather than on the time-lag between the arrival of newcomers and their full integration. Rations dwindled catastrophically, while to everyone's consternation and disillusionment, a black-market spread to the collective settlements, Palestine Jewry's most striking social achievement. Where there had once been talk of moral fervour, now more was heard of moral crisis. And Zionist solidarity was waning as men in the vanguard of the national struggle in Britain and America became despondent when they observed the results of their efforts.

Despite the seriousness of the country's economic situation, Ben-Gurion and his Cabinet felt that neither world Jewry nor the inhabitants of Israel fully comprehended the dangers. The new and unexpected apathy, reflected abroad in the decrease of Jewish voluntary contributions, threatened to bring the national experiment to disaster. Only a drastic and comprehensive scheme could save it, a scheme addressed to Israel's most reliable and potent ally, America's five and a half million Jews. The Cabinet was divided on the prospects of a giant loan in the United States, but Ben-Gurion's enthusiasm finally won over the dissenters, chief of whom was Eliezer Kaplan, his Minister of Finance.

There was, however, a grave obstacle to the successful launching of a loan commensurate with their needs: Israel's fundamental misunderstanding of the psychology of American Jewry. The Cabinet was reminded by Mrs. Golda Myerson, the Minister of Labour who had grown up in Milwaukee, that they must woo the American Jews (four times as many as the Israelis then were) and reassure them about Israel's aspirations. American Jews, she pointed out, were generously disposed towards Israel but had no great estimate of its economists' efforts to make the country a going concern. They were not exhilarated either by Israeli attempts at seducing young men and women from their country of birth to settle in Israel 'because you have anti-Semitism in America, and Hitler can happen here too'. Another reason for the hardening of American Jews' hearts was their suspicion of socialist intentions in foreign policy. They were not sure that Israel was completely in the western camp; Mr. Sharett, the Foreign Minister, had elaborated a policy of 'non-identification' with both East and West, and this had pleased nobody.

Once the bold decision had been taken, Ben-Gurion effected a radical change in Israel's external relations. In the face of the menacing realities of the country's situation, he maintained, the continued separation of Jews abroad into Zionists and non-Zionists was meaningless. He could not abolish the word Zionism, but he defied a large body of Jewish opinion by declaring that its old-fashioned precepts no longer applied. For they were fighting old battles, these veteran Zionists, unaware that a 'catastrophe' had befallen them, now that there was nobody left for them to fight. (This was a reference to the thirty-years' struggle against the British Mandatory Government.)

"In those days," he said in the presence of comrades of that hard old school, of those men who had drained marshes with him in the Vale of Jezreel when Palestine was still a Turkish province, and had suffered imprisonment or exile for the cause, or of those who were still entrusted with keeping the fire of enthusiasm burning in far-away countries, "in those days there was an ideological, emotional, and spiritual barrier between the Zionist movement and the Jewish people as a whole. That barrier exists no more. Zionism is no longer a group contending for the soul of the people!" His hearers returned to their homes and their organisations perplexed. It was something new for them to be told that men running department stores or textile factories in Manchester and Tennessee were as useful, if not more useful, in solving the problems of statehood than they, with their knowledge of the Hebrew language, their faithful attendance at Zionist congresses, and their die-hard devotion to the memory of Theodor Herzl.

The Prime Minister needed to make a gesture, so that in one concrete act he could terminate the old controversies and demonstrate the outlook of his new young world. As it happened, there was a man in America ready to give his friendship and support if Israel could only grant him peace of mind on precisely those three points made by Mrs. Myerson. He wanted fiercely to help Israel, because he was a Jew and intelligent enough to see the significance of recaptured statehood. Nevertheless, he was also a good American, proud of the freedom of religion and opportunity in his own country, believing in it devoutly both for coming generations of Jews and for the future of mankind. This was Jacob Blaustein, of Baltimore. To the arched eyebrows of conventional Zionists the world over, Ben-Gurion issued a warm invitation to Blaustein to visit Israel.

Jacob Blaustein, the soft-spoken president of the American Jewish Committee, had made a fortune out of Texas oil. He commanded one of the most powerful Jewish organisations in the United States, and was frequently consulted by Washington, where the State Department often availed itself of the Committee's knowledge of conditions in foreign countries. The organisation as a body has no politics, but works entirely for the protection of Jewish rights in America, and the continuance of Judaism as a faith and a way of life within the national framework. It accepts responsibilities towards overseas Jewish communities in need of help, though its own forte is intercession at government level rather than the doling out of relief. Its membership is drawn from the well-to-do, not the masses, and on its executive are to be found bankers, publishers, industrialists of all kinds, including Senator Herbert Lehman and Judge Joseph Pros-kauer, two men who link it closely with other important sectional interests. The Committee no longer looks for its support only to the American Jews descended from the central European exiles of 1848, as was once the case. Its character has undergone changes with the years, and today it finds sympathisers among the much larger body of Jews who came to America in the great East-European influx that began in the eighteen-eighties, and who have themselves become as typically American as any citizen of that country. But because of its lack of Zionist faith and its general aloofness, its activities, even after the establishment of Israel, incurred the hostility of bodies like the Zionist Organisation of America. Ben-Gurion received Blaustein in August, 1950, after listening to his Foreign Minister telling their annual party convention that "*Mapai* (the Israel Labour Party) must launch a vast collective effort for the political and moral education of the masses of newcomers so as to prepare them for the moral ordeal they might be required to endure."

Demonstrating to his guest the validity of his principle of the essential unity of the Jewish people, he showed how this did not prejudice the loyalty or nationality of Jews in their various countries of residence. Ben-Gurion knew the importance of winning the American Jewish Committee's backing for the extension of the fund-raising movement which was necessary to raise the projected loan. Blaustein returned home eminently satisfied, for only the year before he had expressed alarm at a statement of Ben-Gurion's that foreshadowed an agitation for the large-scale immigration of young American Jews. Thenceforward, no one would outdo him and his associates in obtaining the finance needed to put the state on a firm footing.

The agreement between the two men epitomised the new David Ben-Gurion: his renunciation of ideology in the search for expedients. For forty years he had lived and thought as a doctrinaire socialist, anchored to his conviction that the Promised Land would be redeemed through collective labour; now he found himself in a situation which only a great capitalist, or rather many of them, could save. For years he had scorned the help proffered by Jews who were themselves heedless of the call to Zion; now he was more than ready to respect their viewpoint and to placate them from the very pinnacle of Zion. Soon after statehood had been won, he had endeavoured to steer his country clear of entanglements with either of the great power blocs; now he was speaking warmly of an organisation whose orientation was determined by American politics. But he had vindicated his proud claim that the creation of Israel affected Jews of every nation and opinion. From the moment Ben-Gurion converted Blaustein his co-religionists throughout the world knew he could convert anybody.

Only a few voices persisted in urging the Americans to come and make their homes in the Jewish state. One of these was Eliahu Dobkin, a member of the Zionist executive (known as the Jewish Agency) charged with settlement problems. He warned the departing Blaustein of his intention to continue his propaganda in America, and cited a Zionist Congress resolution as his authority for doing so. The full tragedy of the situation was to be found in this man's pathetic challenge. He was a European working in Israel to build a European state; but, looking into the future, he saw his state transformed into a Levantine unknown quantity as the sources of European immigration dried up and were replaced by Arabia and North Africa, where Jews were impoverished, illiterate and socially

primitive. Soon these Orientals would outnumber the others, unless
the balance of immigration could be redressed in favour of the
Europeans. Dobkin knew of only one remaining pool of European
Jews upon which he could draw—America. How could he command
their coming? Only by calling to his aid the pious resolution of a
body, the international Zionist Congress, whose *raison d'être*, since
Israel was created, had become a matter of history. He refused to
face the harsh fact that America was now out of Zionist earshot.

Blaustein kept his word. Ten days after his departure fifty men
crossed the Atlantic at the urgent request of Ben-Gurion and they
went with a blessing from this hitherto frigid quarter. They were
the assembly of businessmen, fund-raising executives and Zionist
leaders whom the Premier and Berl Locker of the Jewish Agency had
summoned to hammer out with them an overall estimate of costs
for the coming three years.

Ben-Gurion related the bleak facts: a disastrous balance of payments position, with imports eight times as large as exports; a dire
lack of productive enterprises to absorb labour in either industry
or agriculture; and the manifold related problems caused by the
arrival of (up till then) half a million newcomers. Having stated the
problem, he proceeded to formulate a solution. Israel, if she was to
survive, must have from America a thousand million dollars within
three years. She herself, in partnership with the Jewish communities
of other free countries, would reinforce this sum with an additional
five hundred millions. The astronomical price of preservation was
not a figure of rhetoric. It was based on previous experience and the
current immigration situation. Economists had worked out that to
bring an immigrant into the country, to sustain him until he was
settled in work, to house him and to provide him with the tools to
do a job—i.e. capital installations, irrigated land, electricity, farming
gear and industrial equipment—would average £900 or $2,500.
This figure took into account the cost of making him self-supporting
and of closing his personal balance of payments gap. The country
dared not estimate for less than 200,000 immigrants a year for the
next three years, and the computed figure was therefore produced—
to terrify, awe, chasten and embarrass, the assembled Americans.
It was a period when the quality of immigration was low and the
cost of raw material and equipment high. Yet they went home, it
might be said, docilely, to see what they could do.

Some weeks later Ben-Gurion went to the microphone to announce to his own people far-reaching measures to control imports, stimulate exports and fight the black-market. He drew a sombre balance-sheet of two-years' statehood—£163 millions spent on imports, £20 millions earned by exports. The early lustre of the ideal had been dimmed, he admitted, by administrative inefficiency and a lack of departmental co-ordination in the government. Corruption and inconsiderateness on the part of officials towards the public came in for round condemnation. But these were not the main source of their woes. Mostly to blame were the need to import food, raw materials and equipment, the crippling expenditure on security, and the cost of immigration. Then he spoke resentfully of the two important party groups, the left-wing socialists and the right-wing 'General Zionists' who declined to join the government at this time of acute internal crisis. The solution to their ills, he said, lay in increased productivity, more honesty, unity and discipline; and in order to obtain them he hinted that he would seek extraordinary powers.

Parliament surrendered practically all authority to the Prime Minister within a week. The lawyers went back to the file of ordinances introduced during the Mandate and picked from them the Defence Regulations under which the last British High Commissioner had ruled in Palestine. For three months Ben-Gurion did the governing while his parliament did the talking. Profiteers were rigorously dealt with, and in the published list of miscreants there appeared collective settlements as well as private enterprises. New immigrants were cleared out of transit camps and put to work on the land. Consumer goods disappeared from the shops. Senator Claude Pepper was visiting Israel at the time, and Ben-Gurion asked him bluntly to have Israel grouped with Greece and Turkey, both then countries not belonging to the Atlantic Pact but qualifying for military and economic aid from America.

Such was the man in the spotlight at Madison Square Garden. The climax of the day was a 'roll-call of the 48 States', as a representative from each announced the quantity of bonds immediately purchased within his own State. Television took the scene to every corner of America. Nevertheless, the great hall could not contain all those wishing to participate in the proceedings. Traffic was closed on 49th Street and the crowds swarmed to an overflow meeting to hear the speeches by radio.

Amid cheers Ben-Gurion spoke of the ties uniting his country with America. "We shall never forget the long and unbroken support which the Zionist idea enjoyed in this country, and we shall always remember that it was America which was the first to recognise our status as a free and independent nation," he said. Then came a reference to the purpose of the establishment of Israel, a theme that is central to Ben-Gurion's outlook and which differentiates him from all other prime ministers, past and present. The State of Israel was created to belong to Jews throughout the world. It was a political skeleton, whose flesh and blood depended upon the steady inflow of new immigrants.

"We never regarded independence as an ideal in itself. The Jewish people at all times rejected the idea that statehood in and for itself was the purpose of its strivings. We maintained that this was merely an instrument for the achievement of Jewish immigration and settlement in Israel. We have used our independence to attain this purpose. We have not yet attained it. Our work in Israel will not be accomplished until we have created the economic conditions which assure the stability and independence of our country, and until we have absorbed in our midst those many hundreds of thousands of Jews who look to us for deliverance."

Ben-Gurion then went on to review Israel's requirements in terms of foreign currency. The five hundred million dollars loan would be honoured, maturing with profits for the investor. This was but a third of the need. The balance must be obtained from donations, given freely and unreservedly, through the United Jewish Appeal, the vast community treasure chest to which American Jews gave nearly a hundred million dollars each year for all philanthropic purposes; by the stimulation of private economic investment in new industries and the development of Israel's natural resources; and by grants-in-aid of the American government, through one or other of the agencies created during the Truman administration to assist the under-developed areas of the world.

His plea was supported by an impressive panel of speakers. Mayor Vincent Impelliteri said: "This is not the first time a foreign movement has come to America to strengthen its economy, but it is the first time any nation has approached us for investments with which to finance the rehabilitation of 600,000 newcomers in a country pledged to create a better world for them." Before the evening was through the State of Israel was the richer by 35 million dollars, a figure probably equal to any foreign issue till then handled by Wall Street. Two years afterwards Morgenthau could publicly announce the purchase by 400,000 individuals of bonds worth 140 million dollars.

On emerging from Madison Square Garden, Ben-Gurion was confronted by a picket-line distributing leaflets charging the Israel Government with destroying religious freedom. The Jewish religious conscience, powerful, unpredictable, as yet untested, had come to interrupt the story he must perforce bring to America, the story of a compact, sturdy nation confident and proud as it embarked upon its career of independence. The story that won applause and dollars was only one part of the reality at home. There the prophet was to some a figure of oppression, outraging the traditions of his people, a Leviathan winged with trade unionism and military conscription. Israel, a nation born of the religious obstinacy of a people, had a strange messiah to lead it. Ben-Gurion had more in common with the Seventh Avenue garment-workers than with the rabbis in Israel who were frustrating his legislation. The garment-workers had left much of their religion in Eastern Europe when they had said good-bye to that tormenting if devout old world. So had he, although his journey had been east rather than westward. But in coming to Israel, this irreligious socialist admitted that the Jew was stronger in him than the social-revolutionary. The religious Zionists were Jews only, but their spirit and his had just enough in common to unite in a single interest—the rebirth of the nation.

Neither Ben-Gurion nor Israel will know real peace until this conflict within the land is resolved. Ben-Gurion was not the one to be shaken by heckling from the sanctuary of the synagogue. And on the morrow of his New York triumph, before embarking on a tour of ten major cities, he took time off from official duties to visit a Fifth Avenue bookshop in browsing pursuit of his latest great passion, Oriental philosophy. Churchill's *Hinge of Fate* and Fung Yu-Lan's *History of Chinese Philosophy* were among his purchases. Ben-Gurion the eternal student was gaining the upper hand once more. It is a lovable characteristic, for he has never grown learned in the conventional sense. As a youth he was torn from his books to become a labourer, then to be a soldier, then to organise his fellow-workers, then to fight again, and now to wrestle with the formidable problems of his fledgling state. He loves his fellow-men and knows well how to bear with their foibles; but when he seeks complete relaxation, he finds it in a library.

During the ensuing two years buying bonds for Israel almost became a habit with Jews across the Atlantic, though not without some damage to the delicate web of corporate Jewry living there. While storms blew up among the various fund-raising machines, friendships cooled between men whose entire lives had been devoted to helping the *Yishuv*. The United Jewish Appeal broke off relations with the bond drive leadership, with neither side accepting mediation-moves by the Jewish Agency—the executive body of the Zionist movement acting with the high authority of the State of Israel in the Diaspora. The American Zionists themselves grumbled and muttered at being cold-shouldered, and a nominee of Hillel Silver was elected to their leadership as a warning to Ben-Gurion. But the bond drive did stave off imminent disaster. It allowed a vital breathing-space for the fatigued rulers of Israel during which they would think up new means, internal and external, of recharging their country's energies.

As for the mentality of the golden calf, it was at an end. The achievements of 1949 and 1950, magnificent in themselves, had been won at a cost of ransacking the country of all its slender resources, and of using up the stores of wealth collected through one channel or another from outside. In less than thirty months 460,000 Jews had been ingathered, compared with 470,000 in thirty years of British rule. Two hundred and forty new agricultural settlements had been established, involving the laying of roads and pipe-lines and resulting in a 65 per cent increase in agricultural production, and a 35 per cent rise in industrial output. There was at that time practically no unemployment. Life was austere, though not austere enough, and, as Ben-Gurion hinted, those with money or friends in the right places found ways of softening its rigours. But, given harder work and more productive labour, he foresaw a population of two million citizens within the coming four years, with all that that promised in development and security.

Even with such a credit balance to report, the Prime Minister erred in his lavish but unrealistic claims. His appeal to world Jewry, as indeed to his own people, was based on an intake of 200,000 annually during the next few years. He must have known, by 1951, that this was an extravagant guess. True enough, that year brought its influx, from Poland, from Rumania, from Iraq, in all about 15,000 each month. Nevertheless, he was now encountering difficulties from foreign governments forewarning a vast decrease in immigration. He rendered his case for funds needlessly vulnerable by his contention that money was now wanted, not to bolster up the present economy, but rather to cope with coming responsibilities. It was a good thing his businessmen supporters did not look at Israel in terms of a business proposition. If they had, they might have felt he was coming to them under false pretences, especially when within a year immigration slowed down to a trickle.

Here is the symptom of a disease which since 1950 has undermined good relations between the state of Israel and the Jewish people in other lands. For a full generation the appeal for funds for the national restoration had been based on sentiment and not on reason. In their enthusiasm Zionist emissaries abroad heaped glories upon the builders of the *Yishuv*, quite beyond their deserts. They exaggerated their achievements and played down their deficiencies. They described Jewish agricultural pioneering as something almost unknown elsewhere on this planet, especially exalting the collective farmers, whose obvious idealism required no embellishment. A man living in Palestine, they indicated, was a man shorn of the inhibitions and defects inbred into the *Galuth* Jew. A day's chores was a day of selfless heroism, the country's leaders were imbued with great technical prescience as well as a unique spirit of dedication. The Hebrew University, they said even before that institution had organised a proper curriculum of study, represented a renaissance of Hebraic culture to compare with the days of the Prophets. Their listeners enjoyed these stories, and paid for them gladly. The picture constituted a psychological defence against their tribal inferiority complex.

Now the Jewish world has come to realise that it is not witnessing the inauguration of a super-state. Visitors have been staggered by the truth, which is simply that Israel has extraordinary difficulties to surmount before reaching the level of efficiency and social harmony characteristic of the older nations of the world. It is a young country in a hurry, with pressing day-to-day tasks which do not merit space in the propaganda pamphlets. In its early years tourists who came to admire found they must contend with nervous and inexperienced civil servants and they saw the local population struggling against a graceless bureaucracy. Money subscribed had been swallowed in the maw of the huge trade-gap, and the factory or power-station they had intended to inspect had not yet left the blue-print stage. The Jews might have been more patient with Israel, had Israel made less inflated claims for itself.

Ben-Gurion eventually came close to restoring the harmony so necessary for the outcome of this experiment in Jewish self-determination, and mainly by qualities of intellectual resilience rarely shown by Zionist leaders abroad or by public figures in Israel. Nevertheless, he too stumbled into the widespread failing of exaggeration. The 600,000 immigrants for which in May, 1951, he insisted Israel must prepare, transpired by May, 1954, to number only 250,000. Although his calculation was erroneous, the flow of funds did not dry up as a consequence. He was in the favoured position of receiving his national income from taxpayers, the Jews abroad, to whom he was not constitutionally answerable. But one important moral of the past few years must be applied by his successors in office: it is that while Zionists may continue to regard with tolerance the aberrations that come from over-confidence in the possibilities of the Jewish state, a promise made to the Blausteins of world Jewry must be honoured.

2

Origins

THE CENTURIES WHICH separated feudalism from the Modern Age were a period of intensive intellectual activity for the peoples of Europe. In the fields of science, philosophy and the arts, they made discoveries which transformed civilisation. But this progress passed one European race completely by—the Jews. Held back in a dark age of their own, they reflected in their writings nothing of the influence of Shakespeare or Calderon, of the Encyclopaedists or Goethe. Down to the eighteenth century the Jews continued their obscure existence in a spiritual and physical ghetto. They were concentrated within the Russian Empire and Central Europe, under the control of an unenlightened clergy. Their bastions against progress were their own holy books, which after long years of mechanical study had become the object of superstition as much as of reverence.

Suddenly, at the dawn of the nineteenth century the Jews, who had seemed to suffer in their ignorance so contentedly, were caught up in the modern era. First, a group of their scribes broke free of their intellectual prison to preach rebellion against the Czars for holding Jewry within a confined geographical area (the Pale of Settlement) and rebellion against the rabbis for their obscurantism. They started a movement called *Haskala*, the Hebrew word meaning enlightenment. As a result Jewish emancipation found itself with three alternative outlets: physical escape from the Pale of Settlement which was taken by millions of the young and the agile; social revolt, with its claim for freedom of thought and action within the Russian Empire; and Zionism, in part related to the other two but looking back in history to Jewry's national origins and forward to the Messiah, to a time when Jewry would once more be a nation in

possession of a land of its own. This third course was the one adopted
by a family named Green, of the Polish town of Plonsk. Into this
family was born a child, David, destined to lead the tribe of Israel
in its struggle to resettle the land of Israel.

But we must first see what brought about the *Haskala*. In 1743,
three years after Frederick the Great's accession to the throne of
Prussia, a fourteen-year-old boy named Moses Mendelssohn left his
native ghetto of Dessau and tramped his way to Berlin. His intent
was to study the Talmud at the feet of the Master, Rabbi Frankel.
This, however, was before the boy's mind had been exposed to the
new winds which were blowing across Europe, but which had
not been felt within the impenetrable ghetto ramparts. For in
Berlin Moses not only read his Talmud, but taught himself German
and Mathematics and Latin as well—none of them subjects considered by the Jews of those days relevant to their pursuit of holiness
or the preservation of their racial purity. He won the friendship of
Lessing, and before long produced works of philosophy to rival
the authority of Kant. Unlike his predecessor Spinoza, Mendelssohn
neither renounced Judaism nor alienated its adherents. Instead he
reconciled his faith to the new age. He lived and died in Germany,
and, consequently, it was there that his teachings took deepest root,
especially as the German Jews were much less numerous than those
of Poland and Russia. Nevertheless his ideas penetrated to some
extent wherever Jewry was imprisoned by an obdurate religious
authoritarianism. The process he began in Germany was expedited
by the events of 1789 and all that followed from that tocsin year.

Slowly, the sense of change travelled eastwards. Difficult as it
was for the thousands of German Jews to shake off the fetters of
exclusive orthodoxy, the millions beyond the Vistula, swarming in
townlets, and eking out a precarious existence side by side with an
ignorant and downtrodden peasantry, found release infinitely harder
to win. Nevertheless, modern ideas did penetrate the crevices of
their medieval world and they eventually made contact, albeit
cautiously, with those who responded to new ideas. This was
Haskala. Though coloured a specifically East European hue and
limited in its aim, it was noble in its purpose. It strove to modernise
religious practices and social forms, and to extend the range of
Jewish intellectual experience.

The next stage was quickly reached—an overt challenge to the

long-accepted Jewish situation and its crabbed, timid, and un-
creative rules. A glance at the history-books will show the price the
Jews had had to pay for their survival as a recognisable racial entity
through centuries of persecution. In Poland, Rumania, and Austrian
Galicia they had no political rights except those that could be
purchased by bribes and subtle legal gymnastics. They were restricted to the most despised trades and in litigation denied the full
protection of the law. Sporadic outbursts in the form of raids upon
their property and molestation of their persons went unpunished—
indeed frequently these would be ordered from above and perpetra-
ted by the police. And always the Jews were the object of derision
and slander, for in fact they received no more than the respect
they merited. Against such stagnation a few men of the *Haskala*
alone cried out.

One of these pioneers of the eighteen-fifties was the grandfather
of the boy who was one day to be prime minister of Israel. This was
Zvi Arieh Green, a Jew with pretensions uncommon for those days.
He mastered Russian, and the language gave him access to worlds
beyond the Jewish quarters of Plonsk. He accumulated a large
library, and dabbled in subjects which the local clergy had proscribed as corrupting. A scholar, he gained an erratic livelihood
sometimes by teaching his brother Jews, sometimes in petty commerce. Arieh Green later drew inspiration from Tolstoy. He was
quick to comprehend the dignity of Tolstoy's rebellion against
Czarist society and to apply its lessons to the synagogue tyrants of
Plonsk. His grandson well remembers sitting on the patriarchal
knee and being regaled with stories, no doubt embellished in the
dimness of age, of the ancient brawls and tensions as the *Maskilim*, as
the followers of *Haskala* were called, infiltrated their views into the
houses of learning.

The Jewish reformation encountered the kind of hostility which
the logic of such historical movements would lead one to expect. Its
advocates met the most determined opposition, not from the
Gentiles but from their own high priests, the men who for 300
years had kept their people locked in fascinated contemplation of
the holy texts. *Chassidism,* a remarkable excrescence of Judaism,
permeated the atmosphere of Jewish life in Poland—particularly
in the provincial town of Plonsk, which it counted among its
strongholds. The *Chassidim* considered every revision of the forms

of Jewish worship, every protest against their God-given fate, to be a degeneration of the faith. They made their study of the Talmud (the inspired commentaries on the Bible) an extraordinary exercise in dialectics. They could goad themselves into a frenzy of exaltation at the mere sounding of its words; and the Hebrew language, too, was holy and reserved for communion with God. For the prosaic intercourse of man with man Yiddish was the permitted medium. They suspected, and correctly, that the displacement of a few rocks of religious orthodoxy would start a landslide, so they fought by fair means and foul to retain their iron grip over the masses. They were not beyond informing on their fellow Jews to the Czarist secret police, for the heretics were developing a sharpened social sense and protested against much besides the literal application of petrified religious doctrines.

Haskala diagnosed the ill. Now for the remedy; and this takes us to the next generation of the Greens of Plonsk, a family who play a part in each successive phase of our story. During the seventies and eighties of the last century a series of anti-Semitic excesses occurred in the Pale of Settlement, spurring the hitherto gentle protestants to a rebellion before which the *Chassidim,* though they never succumbed, had perforce to retire, at least momentarily. Many Jews moved westward, some into Germany, the majority overseas, especially to America and (more specifically) into the garment trade. In their pursuit of emancipation many were captivated by the teachings of Karl Marx, a man of their own race, and when they set up homes in new communities, their lives were dominated by the radical ideas which they had acquired either before they left home or in the course of their escape.

What of those who remained behind? To them came a new movement to replace *Haskala* and to absorb their restlessness and discontent. Pamphlets appeared theorising upon the root causes of Jewish servitude and advancing a cure, attractively religious, for its abolition. This offered the people regeneration through Zionism— nothing less than the restoration of the Jews to their homeland, which had been promised in prophecy and was now, with the help of God, attainable through the human will. It was less a developed movement than a formulated urge, as its name, *Hibbath Zion* (Love-of-Zion), betrayed. But its importance as the begetter of political action was crucial. It sprang to life simultaneously in all parts of the

Russian Empire, and even followed the emigrants to their new homes. Although societies of these Zionists were founded in Paris, London, New York, and Berlin, only in Eastern Europe was the movement to be expressed concretely in the personal transference of Jews to the Holy Land. With all this Hebrew was revived as a spoken language and made a prime condition of national revival. Avigdor Green, Zvi Arieh's son, was a leader of this risorgimento in Plonsk.

The town was a busy little industrial centre astride the railway-route linking Warsaw to the Baltic coast and carried on a flourishing trade with Germany, whose frontier, since the Congress of Vienna, had lain not more than 100 miles to the north. It took its name from a rivulet on its outskirts that flowed into the Wkra (Nida), itself a tributary to the Vistula. It was a distributing centre for grain and other country produce and boasted a fine market square enclosed by solidly-built eighteenth-century houses, some of grey brick, others timbered. Its Jews, who were no longer by the turn of the century consigned to a ghetto, formed almost one-half of its 12,000 population. They were strongly under the influence of their better-educated Russian brethren, and affected a more Europeanised culture than was usual with communities of this size. Russian-Jewish literature was avidly read by all who claimed to be enlightened and up to date in Plonsk, despite the warnings issued from the pulpits of all its four synagogues. To combat the Love-of-Zion sedition and thus preserve their supremacy the *Chassidim* threatened their opponents with social ostracism and enlisted the help of a kind of community espionage system. Little of this made much impression upon Avigdor Green, however, whose quiet mien concealed a personality not a little rebellious and supercilious. The family had prospered moderately since the days of his childhood in Zvi Arieh's home, and his prestige was high among both Jews and Gentiles. Avigdor was a lawyer of sorts, one of the unlicensed type common in Eastern Europe in those days. This gave him the right to undertake petty litigation on behalf of his clients, to write their official letters, and to represent them in minor property disputes.

His house was the local rallying-point for the followers of the new philosophy, a debating centre of its trends, and the place where they went to look at the Hebrew periodicals sent out by the Zionists of faraway Odessa, or for a talk about the problems of modernising Jewish education, or for a good meal. It was a house always bursting with noise, for in addition to the passing guest lodged for the night, there were constant committee meetings concerned with town politics, as well as the children—eleven of them altogether, though only six survived to grow up. Avigdor had a local reputation not only for wisdom and independence but also, it appears, for eccentricity. He discarded traditional Jewish attire—the caftan and fur hat—for frock-coat and trousers, and on his way to court could be seen sporting a shiny topper. Among other things carefully noted by inquisitive Plonsk was the fact that he numbered Gentiles among his clients and was a regular, though not excessive, smoker of cigarettes. He was very much the family man, took his conspiratorial role as Zionist leader most seriously, and entered with zest into every local controversy.

At the back of the Greens' two-story wooden house was a large yard, part of which served as a vegetable patch. During the long summer evenings Avigdor would have his meetings out there, and as a child David often watched the earnest discussions from his upstairs bedroom window. They would mostly be about planning ways and means to spread Jewish knowledge among the poor, and to explain the holy books to the illiterate, or perhaps about questions of charity and how best to extract a few roubles from those who were shy of contributing to the community purse. Sometimes reports would reach them of the intrepid young men and women from Russia and Rumania who even then were in Palestine and farming land provided by the fabulous Rothschild of Paris. For already there had arisen from the house of Jacob the first pioneers of Zionism, who were engaged—unbelievably—in tilling the sacred soil of Judea and Galilee.

Unpopular as Avigdor and his circle were with the rabbis, there was trouble from yet another quarter—the protagonists of emancipation through social action within the Russian Empire. The latter sneered at Zionism and suspected it of falling into the pattern of fake-messianism which had regularly fooled the Jews in every century since the Dispersion. *Bund*, the fiercely counter-Zionist movement of Jewish socialists, was still awaiting its founder, but already its forerunners pointed to the cracks in the Romanov edifice as betokening the possibility of a European revolution and the achievement of the brotherhood of man. "Don't be ensnared into placing your hopes in Palestine," they warned. "We must link our fate with the Polish workers here, in the land which grants us a livelihood, in the continent we have inhabited for centuries! Zionism is just another hoax conjured up by the rabbis, and the tools of the rabbis." This call never failed to confuse the masses, and in the new century it was loudly raised whenever the Zionist fortunes ebbed. In an age of spiritual humbug, when Zionism was still little more than a vague aspiration, *Bund* sounded an authentic note.

Undeterred, Avigdor Green carried the good work forward and he gained an important adherent to his cause from the very ranks of *Chassidism*. His friend Rabbi Simcha Isaac, a man of religion famous throughout Poland for his learning and piety, joined the Lovers-of-Zion and so increased the prestige and importance of their work that Plonsk attracted widespread attention as one of the most active centres of the movement. The propagation of Hebrew as a spoken language went on apace. The two friends travelled the countryside to collect funds. The subscription to Love-of-Zion was three roubles a year, and part of the funds was dispatched to the headquarters in Odessa. In 1884 a conference was convened in Kattowitz on the Silesian frontier and Simcha Isaac travelled the 200 miles from Plonsk as one of the town's delegates. On his return he informed the Zionist circle of the creation of special machinery to help the colonists already in Palestine and to encourage others to follow them.

Two years later Avigdor's wife Sheindal gave birth to the child whom the proud father named David. He was their sixth child, but only three of the others lived to become his playmates—two boys and a girl. Sheindal was a small, gentle woman and patiently acquiesced in the role of modest hostess that her husband's numerous public offices demanded of her. He in his turn applied all his teachings in the family circle. He insisted on the children's learning to speak Hebrew, and made them study long hours and even organised their games. David was an especial favourite of Rabbi Isaac, who was rich in glib Biblical similes to express his approval of Avigdor's conduct as paterfamilias. The bond between them was strengthened in later years, as we shall see.

The boy absorbed Zionism as he learned to talk and read. What struck his parents was his extraordinary power of concentration, his readiness to learn, and the long lapses into silence to which he was addicted. He too was small, with eyes that looked out piercingly from deep down in their sockets, and dark, crimpy hair. His father, keen above all on secular knowledge, suggested his learning history and geography to supplement the studies at the religious school. David's first memories were not of music or nursery laughter, but of Zionist debate and Hebrew talk. And from the age of six he learned to play chess, besides taking a hand in the amateur theatricals his father introduced to enliven an already bustling household. In the year of David's birth, and within the same Pale of Settlement, another boy, now hard on eleven, was being enrolled in the second-ary school of Pinsk. He came from a home atmosphere hardly dissimilar from the Greens, and the destinies of the two were to follow parallel courses for the next sixty years. This was Chaim Weizmann.

As a child David loved to hear his father tell of the stirrings in Jewry: the meetings that must be convened, the important visitors to be received, the young people who had to be won over. Children matured rapidly in that environment. Avigdor explained the various points of view within the Love-of-Zion movement, impressing upon his son the majesty of the great traditions they had inherited. The boy soon learnt the difference between those who stressed the religious aspects of Zionism and those who looked to it rather as the final bid for social justice. All three sons were united with their father in their impatience with the old rabbis. They swore never to rest till every Jew in Plonsk, man and boy, was of their number. Soon his brothers would go off in search of other diversions, but David's interest never lagged.

"We have a son who will one day be known the world over," observed Sheindal proudly. Avigdor nodded in absent-minded con-currence. The only prophets he trusted were those he knew from his Bible.

By now Love-of-Zion consisted of a wide network of cells throughout the Czarist Empire. It boasted no men of action, and its leaders, unaccustomed to precipitate changes in their people's fortune, were prepared to wait. Although the number of Jews emigrating to Palestine was minute compared with those who committed their hopes to the New World, they were not unduly distressed. In any event, the Turkish rulers of the Holy Land, in-formed of the new attention the Dependency was receiving among European Jews, grew alarmed and placed an embargo on further colonisation. At first the Lovers-of-Zion contemplated therefore a long process of educational work among themselves. The pamphlets circulated, the periodicals won more readers, conflicts with the *Chassidim* and the socialists waxed warmer. A gulf separated the East European Jews from their emancipated brethren of the West, and although Moses Montefiore of London had become a legend, and they knew of his, as well as of Rothschild's munificent endowments in Jerusalem and the recently-formed colonies, they had little cause to look for allies in that direction. They were aware also of the occasional Christian voices, such as those of the Earl of Shaftesbury, Colonel Condor, and George Eliot, that were raised in England to support the return of the Chosen People to the land of their forefathers; but they lacked the instinct to exploit these sympathies for political purposes. The effort, they were sure, must come from themselves.

Suddenly, Zionism took on a new and startling vitality. In 1896 a Viennese journalist, Theodor Herzl, with neither the training nor the piety to qualify him for Jewish leadership, published a booklet, entitled *The Jewish State*, in which he attacked the problem of anti-Semitism (whose force had deeply affected him when he was reporting the Dreyfus case as a newspaper correspondent), and advocated its solution by the mass transfer of the Jews to some part of the globe, not necessarily Palestine, where they could be granted complete sovereignty. Herzl's message circled the Jewish world. He was surprised to discover that his project was not an entirely original one, that men subscribing roughly to the same principle were already grouped in active organisations, and that in Eastern Europe Zionists had for years accepted his simple thesis and were busy decorating it with many and varied subtleties of their own.

Only after Herzl heard of the efforts of these people to colonise Palestine piecemeal on a minute scale whenever sufficient money could be collected to send a group there, did he see the significance of that country in the plans for a homeland for the revived nation. But he was not going to have his dream shattered or its realisation postponed by the petty fund-collectors and preceptors of the backward eastern ghettos. He envisaged high-level political negotiations with Turkey and the other Great Powers, and finance extending to many millions. He was a Jew acclimatised to the ways of the successful, he knew important people and he foresaw the implementation of Zionism in the transporting of whole communities with the acquiescence and under the protection of the world's statesmen. In 1897 he summoned a congress to discuss his proposals in Basle, and he addressed the cautious Zionists who flocked to hear him as though he were more the equal of monarchs than a suppliant of justice for the downtrodden. The delegates, coming as they mostly did from Russia and Poland, were puzzled and unhappy at Herzl's approach. They judged him high-handed and unrealistic and, accustomed to regarding their own Zionism as a near-conspiracy, they feared the consequences of his reckless public pronouncement about the restoration of the Jewish State.

He in his turn chided them for their inhibitions. Zionism was not a plot, he told them, to be kept from every minor functionary in the townlets of Russia. Herzl was no pragmatist, but had reached maturity as the roving correspondent and feuilletonist of an important newspaper, with no quarrel with fate until the full weight of Gentile injustice against his people struck him in the plight of the French Jew Dreyfus. The solution was as apparent to him as the problem; and what he projected entailed a political settlement as international, as universal, and as majestic as the Congress of Vienna.

The sweep of Herzl's vision, his prophetic personality and simple faith, these in the end prevailed. Zionism before him had lacked statesmanship and a unifying direction, and even the conservative Russians recognised that their movement now had a leader to voice the aspirations of Jewry. In Poland the devout saw in him a messenger from the All High. A picture of his handsome, full-bearded profile found a place by every hearth. Avigdor Green and Rabbi Simcha Isaac placed their trust in him absolutely and so of course did the children of Plonsk, who made of him an object of wonderment and legend.

The immediate consequences of the Basle deliberations, which settled on the formula that 'the aim of Zionism is to create for the Jewish people a home in Palestine secured by public law', was to give the work in Poland and Russia an edge of immediacy and audacity. Simcha Isaac especially, because of his religious authority, was effective among the young people of Plonsk, and he carried his campaign right into the territory of the clerical opposition. The Plonsk ecclesiasts were disciples of a venerable teacher, the

Rabbi Alter of Gur; and, after the fashion of their sect, they were known as the Gur *Chassidim*, notorious for their intractability and fanaticism. Simcha penetrated their houses of learning, grabbed the students by the sidelock and demanded whether they had not heard, had not been stirred by the great tidings of the raising up of Zion. And if the elders of the synagogue refused to hear of Herzl or his Basle congress, and contrived to repress the new movement as a profanation of the Lord's word, the young men were intrigued, and dared to defy them. They came to Avigdor's house to be told of the part they must play.

"You have but one duty," said the spirited rabbi. "Prepare with me to return to the land of our fathers, as is commanded by the Bible!" It was for talk such as this that he was one day intercepted during his holyday devotions and dragged from the prayer-house to be given a public beating in the streets. In the middle of these storms and this exaltation, young David Green was coming into his youth. The year Herzl arose to open a new era in the history of the people, the boy reached his first milestone too. At the birth of her eleventh child, his mother, 'Sheindal the righteous' as she was known throughout Plonsk, died. David was eleven years old, and henceforth the commanding voice of his father, urging upon the children the need to keep to their studies and leave their bedrooms tidy, was the dominant influence of his youth.

Prematurely deprived of motherly care, the six Green children drew closer to their father, who responded with love and wisdom. The family continued as before. They occupied the same house, and the meetings went on in the front room or the garden, as did Avigdor's professional work. Indeed, he now had a new aspiration which complicated his programme and involved him in more frequent visits to Warsaw, for he hoped, as the dawning century brought signs of the twilight of Czarist despotism, to be elected to the long-promised Duma of the Russias.

He had the great satisfaction of observing his teachings take firm root in his son David. The boy showed a deep interest in the newly-created Hebrew literature and offered pithy comment on all the communal happenings in the town, which his lively mind eagerly registered. He was fascinated by the news that reached them of Theodor Herzl's journeyings on behalf of Zionism. Herzl the Jew had actually discussed his plans with the German Emperor, in

35496

Constantinople! He had founded a Jewish bank, to be established in London, Queen Victoria's capital! As he talked over the great happenings with his father or his schoolmates, he yearned for a plan which the Jews could follow, once their beloved leader had persuaded the Sultan to grant them the right to resettle in Palestine, as everyone was sure he would.

David had two special friends and they both shared his fervent views. One of them was Shlomo Zemach, a boy of well-to-do family, quietly confident in manner and unconcerned by his parents' careful preparations for his future. The other, Shmuel Fuchs, was less of a scholar. He was a little older than the others and already showed signs of a young man's restless temperament. They loved taking long walks together, finishing up with a bathe in the river beyond the town. It occurred to them not to wait on events, but themselves to work among their fellows just like their elders. They were now in their early teens and this was a perplexing age in the sorry conditions of Jewish life in a small provincial town in sub-servient Poland. But why should they not form a society like the Love-of-Zion, organise the apprentices and the Talmud students, and persuade them to subscribe funds and learn modern Hebrew, and talk about Herzl?

They did so, and gave their group the name Ezra, after the Founder of the Second Temple. The leader from the West had urged the conversion of the communities as a pre-condition of suc-cessful Zionist activity. Youth movements were rare in those days, but this one prospered, gathering some thirty members within a year of its inauguration in 1900. The boys were mostly from fam-ilies of professional standing, sons of respected bourgeois citizens prominent in the synagogues, and there were plenty of youngsters serving their time with the cobblers and hat-makers, among whom they could work.

The loss of his mother at a tender age strengthened the fibres of independence in David, who, from being a frail child, had now become a sturdy, aggressive youth. There were still the long bouts of introspection, the taciturnity, the studiousness. He was considered morose. The sudden deprivation of maternal care was a greater influence on his subsequent character than many of the bitter ex-periences to be encountered through a life-time of hazards. The gentleness was gone, replaced by an acerbity and a determination to keep moving on and to grasp at opportunities, because there was no cheat like life.

Such qualities came into play in the taste of adolescent politics that membership of Ezra granted him. With Shlomo Zemach and Shmuel Fuchs he constituted its first committee, and in the allocation of duties it was left to him to do the public speaking, within the synagogue meeting-rooms as well as outside. Ezra became known even in Warsaw, not least because of the benevolence it was shown by Avigdor Green, who helped them with the expenses, as did the other Lovers-of-Zion. David found the work to his liking. There is not a surviving member of the group who does not refer with admiration to his instinct for the public platform, especially effective when flaying the youngsters hiding beneath the caftans of their Chassidic elders. He was well-schooled and even at that time could give the rabbis quote for quote. At fifteen he was already a grown man, though maturity in a Polish-Jewish milieu did not automatically carry tolerance with it.

Not a little of the schoolboy passion generated by the group had to be reserved to combat the devotees of that other revolution— socialism—who also found ready listeners among constricted Jewry. Ideologies in profusion floated before the newly-opened eyes of a million people caught up in revolutionary change; and into their view came *Bund*, to woo the masses with the slogans of materialism, patriotism, liberty and bread. The Bundists confronted the Zionists in sullen opposition, knowing they were each born of the same needs, and of the same instincts. Indeed, there was at that time no clear division between them. David Green, unlike his elder brother Abraham who regarded his Zionism as the fruition of a deep religious urge, could not conceal a latent sympathy with *Bund*. Who could reject utterly a movement that sought justice for the people? But for David the question was: What kind of justice? He therefore refused to put his trust in Poland, even if it were to become free and democratic. Had not Herzl, who knew the democratic world, made the position clear? Without a Jewish homeland there was no hope of destroying Jewish bondage.

Having once decided that Bundism was a menace, David gave its supporters no rest. He led his friends at organised debates and at informal rallies where opportunities for propaganda could be created. He pursued the enemy to Warsaw, where the lash of his young tongue became famous. Said Simcha Isaac joyfully: "Ten more like him and Israel will be redeemed."

If the rabbi was really of the opinion that the redemption of Israel could be achieved by a handful of virile propagandists, then he was due to be quickly disillusioned. At the Zionist Congress of 1902 Herzl could report little concrete return for his exertions, beyond some promising contacts with British statesmen, especially Joseph Chamberlain, and hazy negotiations to obtain a territorial concession to the Jews in East Africa or the Sinai peninsula. Young Weizmann was now a student in Berlin, and as a delegate he voiced the impatience of the rank and file. Despite Herzl's obsession that they needed nothing but a magic formula to grant them the key to Palestine, the road to the Sultan's heart seemed as long as ever, and his dispirited followers began to question the wisdom of leaving everything to one man and one method. Weizmann rallied a small group to demand the democratisation of the Congress machinery— a cry, incidentally, that never went unuttered through fifty years of Zionist politics.

Since 1897 the political movement had become a significant factor in the European scene; yet its leader, because of his inability to change within five years the legacy of five centuries, was being condemned as a failure. To those who were trapped within the volcano of Russian anti-Semitism that half-decade seemed an eternity. In town and village alike, Jews were feeling the whip-lash from von Plehve, the Czar's infamous Minister of the Interior. His reply to the rising clamour for parliamentary institutions was organised hooliganism, oppression and pogrom. In Plonsk, as elsewhere, Jews kept to their houses after dark and to their own quarters in the hours of daylight. Not long after the smiling Plehve had received Herzl and heard his request to engage in open Zionist activity on a large scale, anti-Semitism's grim climax took place in Kishinev, the centre of a large and flourishing Jewish population in the province of Bessarabia. The murderous agents of a degenerate government exercising the last rites of its sinister authority left men, women and children among the dead. Tolstoy assailed the police authorities for their criminal connivance at the slaughter; Bialik, national poet of the Hebrew revival, shamed his people into a recognition of their impotence; and while Herzl knocked politely on the chancellory doors, Jews stacked arms in their garrets, and the young men swore either revolution or escape. From the day of the Kishinev massacre Russia and anathema were identical terms to Jews from the Baltic to the Black Sea. And David Green, together with almost every young man yearning for the liberty of the free world, vowed that in the new Jerusalem there would be no oppression, no exploitation, no second-class citizens. Wedding his Zionism to a new order of living, he too embraced socialism. There was a movement ready to receive him, *Poale Zion* (the Workers of Zion). He joined and thus satisfied in membership of a single movement both the desire to find a Jewish homeland and also the longing for social justice.

In this climate the boys of Ezra became men, and manhood meant new responsibilities and ambitions. Another turning-point came, an event in Zionism then marked as a crisis but in reality its coming-of-age. Herzl and his friends had at last obtained for their ideal the serious consideration of the British Government, and they came confidently before the Sixth Congress at Basle with Joseph Chamberlain's invitation to establish a self-governing Jewish territory in Uganda. Chamberlain, perhaps the first British statesman to recognise the potentialities, in terms of strategy and wealth, of his country's overseas possessions, could also assess the value of the friendship of this people who were straying throughout the world. In Plonsk David Green and his friends hurriedly went in search of an atlas. They had not heard of the scramble for Africa, but, suddenly, the march of imperialism took their growing longing for a homeland in its stride.

They were settling accounts with their childhood; and in their minds Zionism meant a return to Zion (i.e. Palestine) and nowhere else. Nevertheless if Herzl's recommendations were endorsed in Basle, they would switch their preparations and their objective to a new point on the map. But they were not endorsed. Herzl had reckoned without the intensity of Jewry's long-retarded nationalism. Uganda was not Palestine. At the Congress the delegates from Russia, led by the Odessa Love-of-Zion leader, Menahem Ussishkin, invoked all that was holy in their history to throw the proposal out. Herzl was taken aback at this reaction to an offer which was the achievement of long and weary negotiation. Bitterly, he exclaimed to his friend Max Nordau: "These people have a rope round their necks, yet they refuse a chance to escape!" Congress split, and broke up in confusion. Few knew what to do next; all knew what must not be done.

Worn out by his exertions, disillusioned and conscience-stricken, Herzl fell ill. A lull drifted across the Jewish world and the dispirited Zionists returned home, to hope and to pray, their only sure resource in the leaderless intervals of their history.

David Green heard the news in Warsaw. He had outgrown the intellectual limitations of his native town, and had gone to the Polish capital and entered its student-life in order to educate himself for the future that he was planning. He took to the bigness of the city, its wide boulevards and historic ramparts, its fine cathedrals and palaces. He tramped the streets trying to discover the sources of the unity, the nationhood, of these 700,000 workers and shop-keepers and beggars. He came to understand the force of people in the mass and he was fascinated by the machinery of compli-cated civil services. Avigdor provided him with a small allowance, and this he supplemented by teaching Hebrew. Here there were Jews in plenty, some, like the future Zionist leader Isaac Gruenbaum, full of fire and impatience because the people were in the doldrums; others, packed away in narrow ghetto streets, and as they worked long hours with the needle or at the last, oblivious alike to the new concept of nationality and to the dignity to be won by a col-lective assertion of the workers' rights. It was a community of half-baked ideas and half-packed bags. *Bund* cried out to them to fight for socialism and a free Poland; Zionism beckoned to Palestine, but who was to take them there? Thousands were already trekking across Europe, to join relatives crowding the berths at Hamburg and Le Havre *en route* for the New World. Others shouted 'Wait and see!' in expectation of the millennium which was to follow the ragged elections for the first Duma. Consistent study therefore eluded David, and the matriculation he aimed for was hardly permitted to interfere with the pressing political activities into which he and the other young bloods of the University flung themselves. *Poale Zion*, his movement, believed that the struggle to earn an extra kopek, the recapture of the lost spirit of the Hebrew language, and the clandestine hoarding of rifles lest the pogromists strike again, were all one; and it offered this as a tangible policy to the gauche and ill-equipped multitudes of Jewry who were ready for the most part to discard the medieval caftan but unable as yet to manage the side-buttoned, working-man's shirt and a pair of western trousers. Certainly, there was little time for study. None knew this better than Avigdor Green. He had suspected the move to Warsaw from the start, and was waiting impassively for his son to get himself arrested by the Czar's secret police.

He had not long to wait. The youthful agitator was picked up in the streets of Warsaw one day and clapped into jail. There was nothing sinister in this: he was known as a noisy speech-maker among the students, and his hair was as unruly as his tongue, so the police singled David out as an example of the way a Jewish student in Warsaw should *not* behave. It was a mess that apparently only Papa could straighten out, and Avigdor, top-hatted and lawyer-like, arrived in response to an urgent summons. Long practice had made him adept at getting Jews out of minor scrapes, but in this particular case a coincidence shortened David's detention behind bars. Avigdor sought an interview with the police-adjutant, and presented his card. Scrutinising the provincial bourgeois with the neatly-trimmed beard, the adjutant said: "Funny, *my* name happens to be Victor Green." Within a couple of hours David was out of jail.

In strained silence father and son returned together to Plonsk, in those days an eight hours' journey from Warsaw. Neither could deceive the other. David knew his father was secretly proud of the role he occupied among the rising generation in the synagogue meeting-rooms, and among his fellow-students. And Avigdor was aware his son saw right through the mask of reproof he deemed it correct to wear. No one was better informed than David of his father's own conspiracies in Plonsk, the secret meetings, the stores of arms and illicit literature in the loft which turned their home into a humble fortress of the national movement. The one was no less determined than the other that, should the Jews have to face violence again, they would not meekly offer the other cheek.

On his arrival Ezra of course made a martyr of the young leader, and David modestly accepted the proffered glory. Then the talk was all of Herzl, his disappointment and physical breakdown. Would there be another leader like him, an adroit negotiator, a prophet? There seemed nobody. With Zemach and Fuchs, David hung around the local newspaper offices devouring the latest news before it had even reached the presses. Herzl had rallied again; now

a relapse. He had seen Nordau, his friend and adviser; he was taking
food. Perhaps there was hope. After all, Theodor Herzl was such a
young man, just forty-four, and already a power in the world.

But the worst happened. It was early summer in 1904, and the
three friends were together on holiday. Herzl was dead: all Jewry
was in mourning. It wept as a people and as a host of isolated little
communities. Its spirit was defeated. To the three youths it was the
end of an epoch. They decided that this was the time to escape
from Poland and the parish politics they now found so ludicrously
unreal. Palestine called to them, more clamorously than ever before;
and the call must be answered. They told Ezra of their decision,
and found many of the group to be of the same mind as they. David
then returned to Warsaw. Shmuel Fuchs quietly disappeared, and
when months later his friends received a letter, it was post-marked
New York, not Jerusalem. Zemach alone was able to make headway with his plan to emigrate to Palestine. It was difficult for him.
His family were rich, and possessive. They wanted him to enter a
profession, perhaps go to live in Paris, or Vienna. He spoke German
well.

One October evening, with 300 roubles taken from his father's
cash-box, Zemach secretly left Plonsk and set out for Odessa, the
first stage of his great adventure. He was a handsome, well-dressed
youth, snub-nosed and frank. It grieved him to go without his
parents' blessing. The schoolboy triumvirate of Plonsk was now
dispersed, and David was plunged into the gloom of isolation.
Letters from Shmuel Fuchs were nostalgic and pessimistic. Things
were not so good in New York, he had written. He hoped to become
a dentist, but at present had to be content with casual work as a
messenger-boy, or carrying bales of cloth to the east-side sweat-
shops. He eventually finished up in journalism.

Some important Zionists, among them Isaac Gruenbaum of
Warsaw, Menahem Ussishkin, head of Love-of-Zion, and Vladimir
Jabotinsky, one of the younger militants, were of the view that this
interim period should be utilised to improve the status of Jews
within the Empire. For the Duma was due to meet and they felt well-
formulated demands might gain a hearing before this parliament.
This was not David's belief. Eastern Europe, he was sure, offered
them no future. Furthermore, there was disquieting news of conflict
within the Jewish leadership. Max Nordau had gone angrily into the

wilderness, while no one seemed to take much notice of David Wolffsohn, the Cologne banker elected to fill Herzl's place as president of the Zionist Organisation. Yet were there not Jews in Palestine? Indeed, there were colonies and workers and vineyards and many thousands of Jews, and Shlomo Zemach.

It occurred to the young dreamer that all these people busily catching trains to attend conferences in Vienna and London and Basle somehow did not count for as much as one labourer in a Judean orange-grove. The one was living his Zionism, the others shaving it away with a fine dialectical plane. There *was* an answer to this dead-end in the movement. It was simply—Zionism!

Another year passed. It brought travel around Poland, more organisational work for the *Poale Zion*, fiercer struggles with *Bund*. David was now well-known as an orator of spirit, with the knack of switching easily from Russian to Yiddish or Hebrew. He never troubled to learn Polish, which he condemned as a 'provincial' language of little use to the Jew with ambitions of starting a new life elsewhere. He linked up with another youth, Isaac Tabenkin, a real fighter for the working-class in the Ukrainian towns and villages further east, and there developed an affinity between the two that lasted for a generation. Others joined them. The work was carried by their comrades into the northern cities, Riga and Vilna and Tallin on the Baltic, where the Jewish race was hardy and deeply attached to its ancestral religion and language.

David Green's generation was in active revolt. Faced by an intractable social situation, with Russia as the immovable rock obstructing their emancipation, they applied what appeared to them an irresistible force—an independent Jewish home, as in the days of Biblical glory, recast as a model socialist commonwealth, new and revolutionary and humanistic. It was an optimum of Jewish hope to counteract the minimum in Jewish actuality—and was thus bound to attract the inexperienced and the impractical. They knew almost nothing of Palestine conditions. It hardly occurred to them that the Sublime Porte might prove as unsympathetic as Czarism. This ignorance transpired in subsequent years to be a source of strength. Unconventional and intolerant, they refused to be involved in the cumbersome machinery set up by Herzl in alliance with the Love-of-Zion, and even as they grew in years and numbers they were tardy in coming to grips with the issues thrown up by the international

Congress. Instead they gave their bodies and souls to their , drove forward with their eyes in blinkers, unconcerned alike the scepticism, the apathy and the alarm of all—Jews, Arabs and British—who were to stand in their way.

Socialist Zionism found its leading exponent in Ber Borochov, a disillusioned Ukrainian radical who rose to lead the revolt before he was twenty-five. But more compelling than any words of Borochov was the call to action sounded by one already resident in Palestine, a man dismayed by the low state of Jewish colonisation there and impatient with the confusion in the ranks created by Herzl's death. He was a lanky intellectual, Joseph Vitkin, and in comparison with some of his fellows, seasoned in years—twenty-eight. "Let's not fool ourselves," he cried. "We have a Motherland, and all we lack is a people to cherish her. Come here and by the toil of your own hands purge the nation of its ills!" (Strangely enough, none of the Plonsk Zionists knew of Vitkin or were acquainted with his writings. Even the name meant nothing to David Green until ten years after Vitkin's death, which was in 1911).

The Jews came. Practical Zionism picked up its recruits from the towns and villages of the Pale of Settlement, young men and women who refused to be the camp-followers of the stout, respectable figures who waited long hours for a chance interview with Gentile statesmen. Rather they turned their ideal of Jewish renaissance inward, identifying the salvation of their people with the salvation of themselves. It meant changing their personalities, discarding the accepted city-existence with its discreet entry into a comfortable niche prescribed by the reigning capitalist economy of their home towns. They would go back to the land—The Land—and inherit a new majesty in the equality of labour. They glorified the soil, the spade, the trade union, the crust of bread and the wilderness that perforce they must transform. They abandoned secondary schools and rabbinical colleges and the ledgers of their fathers' businesses—the brothers Lavee of Plonsk, Berl Katznelson of Bobruisk, Isaac Ben-Zvi of Poltava, David Remez of Mohilev, Aaron Gordon, Joseph Baratz, men who were to be the founding fathers of a new age in Palestine. Altogether, from 1904 until the outbreak of the First World War, some 35,000 of them, glorying even today in the prestige of their epoch—the Second *Aliya* (immigration wave)—filtered their illegal way into the country.

We shall see what they did for Jewish colonisation as we follow David Green with his group to Jaffa port. David personified this immigration wave. With him we shall see how they lived in the early years, how they struggled with the barren earth, and how their toil was rewarded; how they learned to be farmers, and soldiers, and Asians; how they never forgot they were Jews, and fought to save their brethren, and grew in stature and from the ruled became the rulers. Then we shall know why it was David Green, and he alone, who had to be the first prime minister of the State of Israel.

Palestine

3
Arrival—and Departure

*David leaves for Palestine – Frustrations – Jaffa – Early days in Petach Tikvah –
Labour troubles – Political programmes – Galilee – Self-defence – Establishing
settlements – Isaac Ben-Zvi – David returns to Europe – Constantinople – Joseph
Trumpeldor – War – Arrest in Jerusalem – Expulsion – First visit to America –
Marriage – British Army*

SHLOMO ZEMACH HONOURED his promise to write fully of all
his experiences in Palestine. The arrival of a letter in Plonsk was
a great event, and whoever received it, whether it was his father or
David Green or someone else, made it his business to retail its contents to the whole community. Zemach had both good news and
bad to report, and for the first time he made them realise one great
Zionist complication: the Arabs. "It is very difficult for us Europeans
to compete on the labour market with the local Arab workers," he
said. "We exist almost entirely on bread and olives. Lots of our
people here can't speak Hebrew, or they won't. They prefer French.
We are fighting them. It is a great joy to live by the labour of one's
own hands."

After almost a year Zemach decided to come home on a visit. He
felt guilty at the circumstances of his separation from his parents,
and he wished for a reconciliation with them and to make them
understand his new mode of life. David awaited his return with
impatience, for he too had had fresh experiences during that year
and he fervently hoped that they would fit in with his friend's, and
so give consistency and logic to their separate activities. This did
not happen; Shlomo came back rather scornful of his friend's
dogmatism. He picked holes in the socialist approach to the
world's ills, and pointed out that Palestine required them to
assess completely afresh their belief in internationalism, an expression, he said, which Zionists dared use only with the greatest
reserve. They were nationalists, they were returning to Asia,
they wanted to live side-by-side with rural, individualistic Arabs;
and the simplicity which their back-to-the-land creed entailed,

disqualified them from marching together with the city-workers of the west.

When David proudly recounted some of the strikes in which he had been involved, both in Warsaw and Plonsk, Zemach was frankly supercilious. Why couldn't all this wait for Palestine? Zemach believed in workers' organisation, but he tried to tell David that the labourer's rights had one meaning in Europe and quite another in the deserts that had to be made fertile and Jewish. So the discussion turned over and over, in the crisp evenings of the spring of 1906. David described the great despondency which had come over them all, how their hopes had been dashed by the failure of the Russian revolution that year, and how his father had been disappointed at not being elected to the Duma. Nostalgically Zemach wandered through their old haunts: so different from Palestine where there were no great buildings and no fine bridges, but just rough colonies of shacks and brown mud dwellings stretching into the wilderness and baked by a remorseless sun.

All Plonsk looked on Zemach with awe. He was bronzed, toughened, exceedingly worldly. His stories were legion: of the Bedouin living in their low black tents, of the brutality of the Turkish soldiery, of the minarets of Jaffa, and of the vineyards of Judea and the great presses from which poured the ceremonial wine. David listened entranced. In spirit he was already far from Plonsk; and he was determined that when the time came for Zemach to go back, they would leave for Jaffa together. The break with Plonsk was to come quickly.

Avigdor was not surprised when he heard of his son's decision. He had been observing with no little misgiving his venture into politics, though his opposition never went beyond a few discreet words of warning. Yet he had not quite forsaken the furtive hope that the boy would one day grow away from all this work in the *Poale Zion*, and the scrapes it got him into with the synagogue leaders and the local Jewish employers, who were worthy citizens of Plonsk—and furthermore, his own clients. Zionism was all very well and he sincerely believed it to be the ultimate solution for their problems. But why should his son of all people have to go to Palestine, and so suddenly, even before his formal education was completed?

During their long conversations about David's future, Avigdor saw with sorrow that the seed he had planted in his child could not be discouraged now that the child had become a man. He turned for sympathy to his old friend, Rabbi Simcha Isaac. But from that quarter came another blow. "I'm packing up too," the grey-whiskered rabbi announced. "Isn't this what we have been praying for? David is right!" At fifty it was something of a decision. Avigdor was astonished to find that Simcha and his daughter Rachel, a girl of eighteen whose sole concern at that time should have been with the marriage-broker, were in league with David. But he acquiesced with good grace, and even gave David the money to pay for the journey. Quite a band of them were making ready to leave, and all Plonsk knew when the great day arrived, as with Zemach, seasoned traveller that he was, in charge of the arrangements, they set out.

Right up to the day of departure David was occupied with the workers and their rights, and his good work even boomeranged on the group's travel plans. He was leading a strike in a most important tailoring workshop—the one that was making a coat for Rachel Isaac for her journey. For once David had to relax his trade union principles lest they should all be held up.

Then the farewells. The sight of Jews making their way with their bundles to the little coaching-stations, *en route* for faraway places, was by no means extraordinary in the Poland of those days, but never before had there been so large a group treading the uncertain road to the Holy Land. It gave Plonsk a moment of fame in the Jewish world. People wept and sang anthems and took photographs—one of them showed David with his peaked cap loosely slung on the back of his head, in the centre of a cross-legged group of *Poale Zion* comrades in front of his father's house.

Once out of Warsaw and in the stranger country of the Ukraine—they were making for the Black Sea—David Green and his friend Zemach laid their plans. If their journey was to have any significance, they agreed, they must see themselves as the advance-party of a great wave of immigration. But instinct told them the Jews would not follow them to Palestine unless coaxed. They wondered how best to raise the banner of the 'conquest of labour' among the masses, and finally settled on a scheme to establish a periodical which could be sent out to the young people of Eastern Europe from the heartland itself. They remembered that Menahem Ussishkin was to be found in charge of the headquarters of Love-of-Zion in the Black Sea port of Odessa. Into his office poured the subscriptions of Zionists from all over Europe. He would be sympathetic. He would give them the money to start their paper.

Ussishkin received them with none of the warmth they had expected from one who had fought Herzl tooth and nail to ensure that Palestine should be the one country in which the Jewish National life was to be rebuilt. In fact he was abruptly sceptical. They saw him in September, 1906, and he seemed vaguely to disapprove of their whole enterprise—of going to Palestine under their own steam and before regular transportation had been organised. As for supporting another newspaper, he would not hear of it. In Odessa and elsewhere, he said, they had plenty of them. Let them send him whatever they wrote and he would see to its publication. It was the first of a long line of rebuffs the young pioneers were to receive from the old guard. And as they left his office their gloom was only slightly relieved by a warm greeting on the staircase from a rough Palestinian farmer from the village of Petach Tikvah, who had come to Odessa on business. By coincidence, Petach Tikvah was their own ultimate destination.

The closer he approached his objective, the greater grew the misgiving in David Green's heart. Was this Zionism? Were they to be met by cynicism and difficulties at every turn? He preferred to think Ussishkin carried the mark of the bourgeoisie, and feared the might of the Jewish working-class of which he, David Green, was a representative. He was learning to suspect the rhetoric of his elders. They would never plough a furrow, he decided, but use up their energies in catchphrases and sterile argument.

They put to sea in an old Russian cargo-boat with a crew who engaged in a variety of questionable traffickings along the Balkan coast. The journey from Plonsk to the Dardenelles took a fortnight, and he heartily wished it behind him. But there were more shocks ahead. Jaffa hove in sight, and Jaffa had broken the spirit of many a young hopeful in the cause of Zion.

The Jews in Palestine at the dawn of the twentieth century were of two kinds, united only by a common means of subsistence: charity. Some of them, about 50,000 in all, were descended from an ancient settlement of the Middle Ages. Devout, orientalised, and largely primitive, they lived on the alms despatched by their more prosperous co-religionists abroad, a subvention which grew or wavered according to their own ingenuity in seeking funds. They mostly lived in the four holy cities of Jerusalem, Tiberias, Hebron and Safed, were tolerated by the Turks and Arabs, and kept strictly to the houses of prayer as the one alternative to the monotonous contemplation of their dire poverty. Among them were some not born in the country, but drawn to it by their religion as a place of retreat in an atmosphere of complete piety. They were picturesque, obstinate and innocuous, and if they had an attitude to Zionism it was to regard it as a condition to be achieved in God's good time with the coming of the Messiah.

The others, 30,000 at the most, had emigrated for the same political and social reasons that had set the present group on its way from Plonsk. The first of them had come at the beginning of the Love-of-Zion movement, and for fifteen years after that there had been an insignificant but uninterrupted trickle of immigrants. These immigrants, who came before the political movement had turned the idea of a return to the Holy Land into an ideology, were a very different kind of colonist from the socialists who responded to the dramatic call to this 'conquest of physical labour'. Some of them brought money. Few, if any, dreamt of working the land themselves. They saw their place as gentlemen farmers and in the course of years settled down to a peaceable existence in a handful of villages created in strict replica of those they had left in Russia, Rumania and Poland. Their economy leaned on cheap Arab labour, and their problems, apart from that of where to marry off their daughters, were at first none too great.

Hard times soon overtook them. It was one thing to quit Europe and to come to Palestine fortified by a hope that one day the Jewish nation would rise again. It was another to grapple amateurishly with the rigours of husbandry in a sub-tropical climate, impeded by surly rulers whose language and laws were a mystery. Many were illegal entrants who came after the Turkish embargo on Jews and they had to bribe their way at every step. Yet despite enormous physical and psychological handicaps they managed to build Jewish centres in a dozen localities around Jaffa, on the Samarian shore-lands, and in an almost inaccessible and virgin area of Galilee. But their resources dwindled and before long they were threatened with

starvation. The hasty relief sent out by Love-of-Zion proved hopelessly inadequate.

Luckily, Baron Edmond de Rothschild, the Paris financier who
was then at the summit of his political influence, intervened and
practically adopted the villages. He devoted several millions of
pounds to the building of schools and hospitals, and to teaching the
settlers plantation-work and the rudiments of social administration.
He hired an army of overseers to go out to take charge of every
economic activity. They leased the lands the Baron had purchased
at almost nominal rents and bought the farmers' produce at high
prices. The manufacture of wines went on under their aegis at a
leisurely rate. As stewards of a great and high-minded benefactor
these overseers left much to be desired. Some were ineffectual
idlers, others domineering and arrogant. The weight of philanthropy
proved too much for the settlers, and not only their lofty ideals but
much of their self-respect disappeared as they fawned on their
masters in pursuit of privileges and easier living.

Such degeneration could be halted, and, eventually, it was, when
the Paris secretariat of the enterprises vested the administration of
the properties in the Jewish Colonisation Association, a foundation
started with the ample resources of another rich Baron, the Bavarian
Maurice de Hirsch. Some order was put into the diverse agricultural
projects during the eighteen-nineties and the farmers became reconciled to a form of dead-end colonialism in a Turkish province. They
spoke their ghetto-language of Eastern Europe, they placed their
children under the guidance of French or German-speaking peda-
gogues, and their whole life was directed by the remote paternalism
of western banker-intellectuals who vaguely identified their works
with the flowering of French civilisation.

As the only harbour of any size in Palestine, Jaffa was the sole
link which this strange Jewish existence had with the outside world:
it was its point of entry and its avenue of release. It contained, by the
time the boatload from Plonsk came to port, all the disillusioned
water-front hangers-on that two decades of mistakes in Jewish
settlement had produced. There was of course a bustling Arab
population practising legitimate commerce, but mingled with them
were shady characters after the pickings of every shipment. Two
dilapidated Turkish houses had been adapted by the Jews as hotels,
and other establishments quartered the office-workers of the Jewish

Colonisation Association. To complete the picture there were Levantine notables of every race and every degree of importance— and a Jewish bank.

This bank represented all that was truly concrete in the new Zionist movement's stake in the Holy Land. The Zionists had in 1901 established their own fund for the purchase of land. Though at first little more than a collecting-agency, its moral significance was considerable, and through the bank were channelled the meagre finances which could be mustered for the various projects that were waiting to be started. But everything was dwarfed by the flow of charity from Paris.

Despite the veto imposed from Constantinople, disembarking the newcomers presented few real difficulties. It was simply a question of paying a surety, not in the circumstances excessive, for each traveller; and for those without means collections were arranged at the two hotels, no doubt with the friendly co-operation of the bank. There were also the nuclei of political parties, and these acted as foster-parents for the new type of worker immigrants. Somehow they managed to divine who belonged to whom in every shipload, and each party looked after its own. By 1905 the few hundred Jewish workers living in and around Jaffa were separated into two socialist groups, with little for the uninitiated to choose between them. Small as they were, they were soon to have their rival labour exchanges, newspapers, cafés, and clubs. Party-membership became the way to swift adaptation in the country. Thus David Green had a branch of his *Poale Zion* already waiting to receive him when he made his way to the Hotel Chaim Baruch for his first meal in the Land of Israel. Shlomo Zemach went to the other group called Working Youth (*Hapoel Hatzair*), and so hinted to his friend that he scorned the idea of linking their destiny with any brand of Zionism whose roots spread outside Zion into the effete world in the West.

But the thoughts uppermost in David Green's mind as he clambered on to the jetty with his bundle were hardly of politics, or the workers and their rights. He felt that great emotional uplift which the Jew feels when he stands for the first time on the precious soil where his people have once been a nation, and which dominates its spiritual life. He was thinking, as all who preceded him and all who followed have surely thought, how this very act of landing was a privilege to be savoured and remembered and retold. In Palestine the world of Joshua and the glory of King David and the prophecy of Isaiah all became actual, and actual to a people who had wept for Zion beside the rivers of Babylon for two thousand years. He was no longer a youth from Poland coming to Palestine, he was the eternal wanderer returning home.

Therefore he could not bear to remain in Jaffa. After a swift glance to take in the town and the people he left at once for Petach Tikvah, the Jewish colony two hours' walking distance inland where he and Zemach intended to live and work. Of his first night there he later wrote: "It was sealed in my heart with the joy of victory. I did not sleep. I was among the rich smell of corn, I heard the braying of donkeys and the rustle of leaves in the orchards. Above were massed clusters of stars clear against the deep blue firmament. My heart overflowed with happiness, as if I had entered the realm of legend. My dream had become a reality!"

The dream was sustained for the next few days, while the two friends went around the dozen Jewish farms in search of employment. But the Petach Tikvah farmers shook their heads dubiously. They said they preferred employing the local Arabs, who were more used to the work and accepted it gratefully. David spoke to some Jewish farm-hands about their prospects. They were even more pessimistic, and openly acknowledged their defeat at the hands of their brethren. Eventually, he found employment, and when the others begged him to leave the country before he became destitute as they had, he hardly heard them.

As a Judean farm-hand he earned eight piastres a day, enough for a room to share with Zemach and a single meal. In the village he encountered other recent arrivals like himself. The short, intent young man made few friends, but he was respected for his quick skill in argument, his occasional bursts into song, and his unspoilt conviction that what they were doing was of historic importance to their people. At week-ends he tramped into Jaffa, to spend the Sabbath with his party-friends. Over bottles of strong local wine they exchanged reports of conditions in their respective colonies.

He learned that the employment situation varied from village to village. Petach Tikvah was a black spot, but at nearby Rishon le Zion and Rehovoth there were more opportunities for the immigrants to assert themselves. This was above all the case at the wine-presses controlled by the Rothschild agents, for ritual forbade the employment of any but Jews in its manufacture. Friday evening was the time when they used to hammer out ways and means of increasing the strength of the workers. But they had time also to eat and drink heavily, and to strive to accustom themselves to the local *arak* and then sleep off their fatigue in the courtyard. They lived in constant fear of malaria, a disease which felled many a young idealist and drove him back to Europe, or across the Atlantic.

To live rough was a matter of honour, as part of the apprentice-ship to peasantry. Yet the workers accurately assessed too the con-flict they felt must come between the bourgeois old settlers and themselves who represented a new pioneering age. The wine-presses were a constant centre of trouble. Much of the work was unskilled, and strikes alternated with lock-outs; and no wonder, for the farmers had a hand in the administration of the plant and an army of foremen were industriously engaged on precious little but keeping an eye on the labourers, many of whom were them-selves a clock-watching lot.

The first *Poale Zion* conference took place during the festival of Tabernacles, only one month after David's arrival in the country. About sixty members turned up, and throughout a day of intellectual stock-taking they grappled with matters of daily wages and political theory. They argued on whether they should use Yiddish, the language universally understood, or Hebrew, the language of national rebirth. They were perplexed youths confronting the unknown, armed only with their intellectuality. They felt they could vote themselves into the proletariat by strict adherence to democratic procedure. But in this they were disappointed. Then someone got up and told them they must never deviate from their pioneering mission to create a Hebrew-speaking working-class. This was already being hampered, he said, by the existence of two separate workers' parties, and he thought everything should be done to bring them together. When his proposal that only Hebrew be used was howled down, he shouted louder than they. It was David Green making his first public speech in his new life. It was remem-bered, but not accepted. It took years for the 'Hebraists' to persuade the 'Yiddishists' to forget the language of despised Europe, and longer still for the two parties to merge.

One evening David arrived in Jaffa to find consternation among the labourers. There was more trouble at the wine-presses, he was told. They had gone on token strike over a grievance regarding works' privileges, and the management had replied by closing the gates against them. What were they to do?

David was brief and to the point. It was no good venting grievances in odd one-day strikes, and in petty go-slow methods, he lectured them. They should formulate their complaints, and elect representatives to put them in an orderly way to the highest authority at the presses. They reacted by nominating him as one of the delegates to formulate their demands. They also chose Israel Shochet, a young Ukrainian also working in Petach Tikvah. The deputation was completely successful. It secured reinstatement for a few dismissed workers and improved conditions for the rest. David impressed by his sure flow of Hebrew, for the managers could only answer in Yiddish as none of the East-European immigrants spoke French. A victory won so easily by one so new gave David considerable prestige among the hundreds of Jewish labourers dotted over the hinterland of Jaffa. It established him as one of the figures of *Poale Zion* just as the party was on the point of embarking on a membership-drive and elaborating a political platform.

A few of another group of workers had come down for the conference after a long trek south from Galilee. David resolved to join them up north. They appeared more contented, had wholesome work in the cornfields or in the orange groves, and lived amicably with their employers. But they were separated from Judea by a long and difficult stretch of undeveloped territory dotted with unfriendly Arab villages and the whole area was honeycombed with lawless bands. He decided to go up as soon as possible. Around Jaffa he found an air of indolence and defeat.

But there was pressing work to be done first. The conference had revealed so much confused thinking that a committee of ten was nominated to work out a programme for the party. David was elected one of the ten. To hold such important discussions in Jaffa was out of the question. They were, after all, revolutionaries, and their ultimate objectives even at their vaguest were hardly likely to commend themselves to the Turkish military government, whose spies were reporting fully on the Zionist goings-on. So they chose Ramle, an all-Arab town half-way on the road to Jerusalem.

The meetings lasted three days, and David was chairman. They took place in an Arab *khan*, an inn safely tucked into a narrow, fetid lane, its thick walls sheltering them from the hot sun. Strengthened by innumerable cups of coffee they sat cross-legged on an earthen floor, with the following agenda before them: how to combat the tendency to schism among the various socialist groups; whether to found a newspaper in Yiddish or in Hebrew; how to attract more Jewish workers to Palestine; how to uphold the rights of Jewish labour in the Jewish villages.

Could a social-revolutionary campaign of action be worked out in the absence of a capitalist class and therefore of a class-struggle? Could it ignore the Arabs? So, apparently, David Green and his comrades believed. They made the Jewish farmer their enemy, and left the Arab worker an undefined factor to be considered at some later stage (none of the ten disputed the need one day to raise his living-standard lest their own conditions be undermined by the creation of a coolie class). Then they returned to Jaffa with an unrealistic, revised version of the Communist Manifesto, written in Yiddish, as the fruit of their deliberations. Yet their time was not wasted. For with it *Poale Zion* went right ahead with a sheet of proposals to rally all the unattached workers, while the rival party *Hapoel Hatzair* (Working Youth) remained as a disorganised if purer sectarian group without an effective political machine. This accentuated the difficulties of amalgamation, which eventually took place in 1930. But differences are discernible to this very day.

David got away from Petach Tikvah and moved to a newer village, Kfar Saba, where the workers were left much more to themselves. It was the same pick and shovel work, from early morning till night. "We are on a hill," he wrote to his father, "with mountains all around, and the air is clearer and healthier than at Petach Tikvah. The land is mostly planted with almond trees, and was bought from local Arabs a couple of years ago by the Petach Tikvah farmers. As yet there are no houses. Kfar Saba is under the jurisdiction of the Pasha of Nablus, and he will only allow foreigners to build on payment of a heavy bribe, and the farmers themselves prefer to stay in Petach Tikvah and just come up occasionally. But some young people have bought plots from the farmers and intend building soon. The price of land is increasing. We Jews get work here because the farmers can't spare foremen for the Arabs, who only work under supervision. We start at six in the morning, and as the sun rises high in the sky our sweat pours like a river."

After telling Avigdor of the *hamsin* and the malaria it brought as the hot wind whipped up the vapour from the moist valley, he goes on to speak bitterly of the disillusionment he encountered everywhere: "Every ship brings tourists to behold the beauty of this country, but there are no Jews among them. Our people think praying three times a day for Israel is enough. In Rome there are no Catholics and in Zion there are no Zionists. But" (referring to the workers' efforts to organise) "a Zionist movement is beginning to come to life here at last."

The news that Palestine was by no means a land of milk and honey distressed the elder Green, and he asked why those returning from the country painted it in such black colours. David was furious. "Let them smear the country with their evil reports if they like," he retorted. "These mummified Diaspora Jews wouldn't emerge from their bog even if they heard the streets here were paved with gold! But the new Jew is proud and full of fight. He won't turn back. I only feel sorry for those petty-minded people who have fled the battleground and then try and foist the blame on the bad conditions here. I know the country better than any of them. Haven't I told you all about our troubles, our hunger, our malaria? How I hate those slanderers!" And to show he meant what he wrote, he sent back ten roubles his father had enclosed with his last letter. The new pioneers would live by their own earnings, however humble.

He refrained from spending too much time in politics, though a strike, or the possibility of one, never failed to awaken his militancy. Instead he got down to acquainting himself fully with the ways of the soil, to learn all he could about the countryside and his Arab neighbours. He was no natural linguist, but through sheer pertinacity learned Arabic in his first year and became familiar with every village and wadi in Judea. 1906 and 1907 saw a larger, promising influx of young newcomers, from the Crimean and Ukrainian towns. One of these was the pensive Isaac Ben-Zvi, a polished young scholar who had had a hand in the training of self-defence units that had sprung up in reply to the wave of pogroms that followed the failure of the second Duma. Ben-Zvi had been in Palestine before, as a student, in 1904, and now immediately struck up an association with David Green which enriched both their lives for the next half-century.

Autumn, 1907, and another *Poale Zion* conference in Jaffa. A group of stone-cutters walked the sixteen-hour journey from Jerusalem to attend. David, Ben-Zvi and Israel Shochet were elected a three-man presidium. As he scanned the faces before him, David noted with dismay that not a few of the previous year's delegates had dropped out—early casualties in the desert war of Jewish metamorphosis. They debated the dangers of disillusioned ex-pioneers carrying their grumbles away with them. Perhaps their strategy was wrong, they thought. Was it wise to encourage workers to come when conditions were so unpromising? Perhaps they had better wait? They decided that education, to tell the facts of the situation to their friends in the Diaspora, would be one method of solution, and with this in mind they planned to start the newspaper David had considered with Zemach during their journey from Plonsk. It was, to David's disgust, to be in Yiddish. They would send it out to their friends, in Russia, Poland and America. Furthermore, Ben-Zvi and Shochet were nominated to attend the next Zionist Congress, and confront the entire Zionist movement with the charge that Jewish employers were prejudiced against Jewish workers in Palestine. They knew Congress would be tackling the problem of colonisation with a new earnestness, and they intended to be consulted over its plans.

The existing situation could not be tolerated. All progress was slow, and in face of the conservatism of the farmers a few of the hardier workers planned to wrest the initiative for themselves. Life was taking its inexorable course and some were now married, with families on the way. These workers wanted little farmsteads of their own. Yet they viewed every step with trepidation. Would this not lead to the corruption of their dedicated mission of 'conquest of labour', of non-exploitation, of a return to the pastoral life? Could they prevent themselves from going the way of the Petach Tikvah crowd? They were, in fact, afraid of prospering. It was all very young and somewhat precious. And with thoughts such as these heavily within him, David decided the time had now come for his move to Galilee.

On the outskirts of Jaffa and just beyond the Judean colonies lay a twenty-mile stretch of desert, occupied by Bedouin and isolated

Arab villages, extracting a scanty livelihood from patches of watered ground. To the east the land sloped gracefully upward, and during the winter rains the hills exploded into startling daubs of mauve and green and yellow, with sudden waterfalls twisting their white way down before disappearing into the plains. Those Judean hills concealed all that was vital and independent and romantic in Moslem Palestine. From the mountain fastness of Nablus the *effendi*, gloriously attired in flowing robes of black and white, rode out on his camel to keep guard on his possessions, and to cast a wary eye to the lowlands, to make the long rough ride to Jerusalem, or to strike east to the rich valleys of the Jordan. Mule-trains with their cargoes of grain and oil followed the winding paths, the tracks soft and sure and unchanged over centuries. Over the whole the Sublime Porte cast its almost imperceptible administrative imprint, and nobleman and *fellah* looked with equanimity upon the rolling contours of their land as it burgeoned into September life. Only westward did they see their peace disturbed, by the stumbling, short-coated European, in his close-necked *rubashka*, his brain feverish with the statistics of some improbable future population.

The Jew journeying northwards from Jaffa must cross the desert strip in one day, and get his rest at Zichron Yaacov or Hadera, gateway to Galilee. At dusk he could trust neither hill nor plain. Then through a break in the highlands between the Carmel range and the Judean escarpment he must steal another day's travel to Mount Tabor, opening on to Galilee with Nazareth to his left and Lake Tiberias glistening before him. Another two hours brought him together with his people again, concentrated in a small pocket of settlement defiantly encamped on the dry, unfriendly earth where once walked Jesus the Nazarene. Today, this settlement was a plunge into the unknown.

Shlomo Zemach and Israel Shochet had already made the long tramp and were at Sejera, David's goal, late in 1907. The colony consisted of a dozen brick hutments shared by the farmers and their hands; and the land, leased for intensive cultivation by the Colonisation Association, was broken up into allotments of some fifteen acres each. Sejera was one of a group of four or five villages which were an outpost of great significance to the Zionist pioneers, and refreshingly free of the brakes upon initiative exerted by the wine-presses of the south, where David had latterly worked. The work was with the plough, and this gave him enormous satisfaction. He was overjoyed at being able to live and work again with Zemach. Two years of struggle against hunger and malaria had left them both with lined, thinner faces. David's hair was already streaked with grey, though he was but twenty-one.

Sejera was on the point of a momentous decision. There was trouble with the Arabs. The native population of the Judean littoral had barely stirred at the arrival of the new colonists and even drew some advantage from the prospects of extra work around Jaffa. Not so in Galilee however. The local Arabs saw here something quite different, a foothold made deep in their country by men who would not on principle employ Arabs and who were settling in with all the obduracy of a peasantry. The Jews worked feverishly hard, and their oil-lamps burned deep into the night while they planned, no doubt, to increase their holdings. Their neighbours tried to deter the settlers by a campaign of pilfering and arson. Near Sejera lived the Zubach tribe, which many years before had split into robber bands that terrorised the entire neighbourhood. And at the adjacent village of Kafr Kama were Circassians, a people of wild and uncontrollable passions. Circassians were hired by the Jewish farmers to guard their flocks and cornfields day and night and the whole area was impregnated with sullenness and mutual hostility.

The Jewish workers then struck upon an important principle; and David Green, soon after his arrival in Sejera, became its most assiduous propagandist. They decided that if this area was to be permanently theirs they had to guard it themselves. 'Jewish self-defence', first practised in Sejera and the neighbouring settlements, and then cast into a maxim, developed throughout the country and became one of the fundamentals of the labour doctrine in Palestine. The farmers grew alarmed at what they considered to be unwarranted arrogance. The Jews had no cause for complaint and the bearing of arms was not a Jewish skill, they said. Jewish self-defence would lead to resentment and recrimination and if the Arabs cared to do so they could ride into their villages and massacre them all in a day.

The two friends from Plonsk shared a room. But they quarrelled over this decision about Jewish defence, which was to change the character of Zionism. For the *Poale Zion* in Jaffa were also thinking

along the same lines, and at a meeting in Ben-Zvi's room a secret
society was sworn into existence, named after Bar Giora, the last
Jewish defender of Jerusalem in A.D. 70, to train a corps of whole-
time Jewish watchmen for service in every point of settlement.
Zemach was against the whole idea. He prophesied, not inaccur-
ately, that this would lead to a feud between Arab and Jew which
would grow to terrible proportions in the course of years. They
were not hostile to the Arabs, he maintained. They were not hostile
to anybody. They were in Palestine to return to the simple life in
their historic land. The Arabs could be made to accept them if they
were given evidence of the Jews' friendship and desire for peace.

A wide gulf separated David and Zemach. David too wanted to
win their neighbours' friendship; but he also intended that Palestine
should become the centre of Jewry's national rebirth. How could
this be achieved behind hired bayonets? He welcomed the initiative
taken by Ben-Zvi and the Jaffa group, and looked forward to the
arrival of the armed watchmen in Galilee. Meanwhile, they would
do the job themselves. They would labour by day, and guard by
night.

A consignment of rifles and pistols was unloaded discreetly at
Haifa, then a tiny harbour. These weapons were sent up by mule-
train and quickly distributed among the Galilean workers, who
were placed under the general supervision of the permanent corps.
This permanent corps kept the air of mystery alive, and formed
themselves into a kind of officer caste. The mystery grew when
those in the know, including David, discovered that the leading
spirit of the whole organisation was a woman. She was Manya
Vilbushevitz, the Paris-educated daughter of a well-to-do Russian,
who was later to marry Israel Shochet. She was known to have been
the architect of a daring, though abortive, plot a few years earlier
to assassinate the Russian Minister Plehve, the instigator of pogroms
against the Ukrainian Jews.

The Circassians, summarily deprived of employment by the
Jews' determination to arrange for their own protection, were not
unnaturally incensed by the turn of events. One night a Jewish
sentry was killed while challenging a stranger in the fields. A blood
feud began after an interchange of shots between Arabs and Jews
on the open road to Haifa. One day David went out to rescue a
comrade who had been involved in an affray, and brought him back

dead. After this neither he nor his friends left the village without hiding a pistol under their coats.

Shlomo Zemach took no part in all this and he told David, soon after the trouble began, that he was going away. He was a member of *Hapoel Hatzair* and from it he received instructions to move on, and try to open up the village of Rosh Pina, still further north, to Jewish labour. Soon he joined a party of travellers on their way to the rock-side city of Safed, some fifteen miles away. At this point the paths of the two friends from Plonsk parted. For two years Zemach worked in various villages as a kind of free-lance Jewish pioneer. Then he went to France to study agricultural science, and did not come back to Palestine till after the end of the First World War, ten years later. David remained faithful to the radical wing of Zionism, which seized the initiative in the practical work of national regeneration.

He now looks back on his days in Sejera as among the happiest and most significant of his life. He later wrote of the settlement and its inhabitants. "They were colourful times. We were only a handful of people and came from all corners of the globe, speaking a medley of tongues. The labourers occupied five hutments. There were Jews from Kurdistan, broad-shouldered and tall, as uncouth as their gentile countrymen; spare-looking Yemenis, with an extraordinary knowledge of Hebrew and Jewish traditions; youngsters from Russia, raised by the *Haskala* and formed by the atmosphere of revolution; natives of Palestine who had left their prayer-houses in Safed and Tiberias to grasp the plough; some Russian converts to Judaism from the shores of the Caspian. We spoke Hebrew, Arabic, Aramaic (the Kurds used this ancient scriptural tongue), Yiddish, Russian, French, and Spanish."

The group were invited by Dr. Arthur Ruppin, head of the recently-established Jaffa office of the Zionist Organisation, to farm some lands at Kinneret, on the shores of Lake Tiberias, belonging to the Jewish National Fund, as the financial agency established in 1901 was termed. It was to be pioneer labour in virgin country, and would represent for the workers an important breakaway from employment in the subsidised farms of the Colonisation Association. They assembled to discuss the proposal, at a meeting over which David presided. Some members of *Hapoel Hatzair* had previously taken possession of the area and had found it appallingly disease-ridden.

After long discussion the proposal was turned down. David told Ruppin of the decision and gave as their reasons that the land was ill-prepared for cultivation, and that they considered the manager selected to supervise their work to be lacking in Zionist 'intensity' and therefore unsuited to dedicated Jewish pioneering. Ruppin came up from Jaffa to meet the workers. He admitted the justice of their attitude and offered instead an adjacent area, which was in a very different condition. It had just been purchased, and bore the name Um-Juni.

This offer was accepted. A dozen of them took over the property and began to work it for a daily wage and a share in the profits. Gradually, they were given full deeds of leasehold, and they shared whatever was produced and marketed. They gave the new colony the name Daganya. It became the first collective settlement in Palestine (the Hebrew language already had a name for it—*kibbutz*), and the forerunner of a long chain of communal villages which were soon to give the agricultural economy of Jewish Palestine its distinctive character.

David could not himself go to Um-Juni. He received an urgent summons from Ben-Zvi to come to Jerusalem, where a fresh educational task had to be undertaken. The third conference of *Poale Zion* had taken place while he was in Sejera, and had decided to establish a Hebrew monthly for the movement, as the Yiddish paper had failed after three issues. Ben-Zvi and a newly-arrived young girl, Rachel Yanait, were selected to edit the journal, which was to be called *Unity* (*Achdut*), and they wanted David Green to work with them. He was reluctant. The soil was just beginning to unfold its mysteries, and he had no great wish to desert it now that he had learnt so much about farming. Besides, several new colonies were being projected for Galilee and he felt most secure in close touch with the workers. Still, where else could they turn for someone with sufficient knowledge of Hebrew and experience of the movement to assist them?

He decided to wait till they were quite ready, and in the meantime journeyed from settlement to settlement in order to get to know intimately all aspects of the worker's life in Galilee. It troubled him to watch the multiplication of narrow intellectual cliques. Psychologically, the workers were poor 'mixers', and, for social revolutionaries who were going back to the land, and had moved from one continent to another, they were unexpectedly conservative. They clung to prejudices born before their migration, and there was a tendency for loyalties belonging rightfully to the Diaspora, usually grouped around some leading personality, to persist in the new village. David noted the symptom, and determined to work for its eradication when he began writing in *Unity*.

In other fields the Zionist movement was gathering confidence, and it now embarked upon a period of consolidation. Urged on by Ussishkin and Ruppin, the Jewish National Fund grew more adventurous in its land-buying policy and started developing the sand-dunes north of Jaffa, despite heavy opposition on the part of the Turks. A suburb, at first only one long street, was begun, and at the end of the row of houses the Herzlia Gymnasium, a high-school named after their first leader, was built with funds provided by a Bradford businessman. They called the suburb Tel-Aviv. It became the first all-Jewish city in the world. Among the students enrolled at the school were some youths affiliated to *Poale Zion*. David Green looked to the boys to give the party a much-needed academic leavening. They would be useful in other ways too, for their parents had come in a previous immigration wave to his, and possessed Turkish nationality. Three students in particular were not to disappoint him, Moshe Shertok, Eliahu Golomb and Dov Hos.

A period of comparatively uneventful, yard-by-yard Jewish reconstruction was only possible if the situation remained static. But in 1908 a violent change took place in a part of the world which closely concerned Zionism. Revolution shook Ottoman Turkey. The Young Turks seized power and declared they would end the corruption and oppression of Sultan Abdul Hamid's régime. *Poale Zion* thought this was the moment to press for their freedom, to organise the workers openly, to demand easier land-purchase, and to clarify the legal status of the Jews. They took on trust the promise of the Young Turks' Movement of Union and Progress that it would befriend the many minorities within the Ottoman Empire, and the founding of a *Poale Zion* newspaper therefore became urgent. Although in Galilee the Jews were not immediately affected, there was an appreciable increase of Arab aggressiveness in Jaffa. The Arabs on their part had grievances against the Turks in plenty, and, led by a radical spearhead in Beyrouth, they began to formulate demands of their own.

David Green had one personal matter to tidy up before he could publicise his existence in print. If the revolution went according to its early auguries, Jewish illegal immigrants such as himself would be able to declare themselves openly and obtain citizenship. But it would mean, in the first instance, revealing his Russian nationality; and according to the laws of that other empire, he would automatically be posted as a deserter, for he was due to perform his military service in the Czar's army.

He decided to go back home at once, and get the chore done with lest reprisals befell his father. So late in 1908 he left Palestine, to reappear again in the streets of Plonsk. He had barely time to recount his experiences to Avigdor before he was summoned before a medical tribunal. Miracle of miracles, he was exempted for bad eyesight! He planned to return to Palestine. Then another letter came, countermanding the reprieve, and ordering him to report to the nearest army depot.

David was a Russian soldier for exactly one week. It was but a formality of enlistment, to absolve his father from all further responsibility. He left camp one night, boarded a train, and in a few hours was over the border in Hungary. Two months later Avigdor Green received a letter: "Here I am back in our dear land, on the shore of Lake Tiberias, and free from the yoke of the Czar. I am just on the point of making a tour of the new Galilean colonies, for in a few days I am due in Judea to commence new work. I am visiting all the new villages in this region." Of one of them he wrote: "Eight months ago I was here and the place was covered with thorns, it was stony and desolate. Now I find European houses and fields newly-ploughed by the latest methods. Hebrew workers have made it part of our life. People should remember that a new village in Palestine counts far more than all the *shekalim** purchased, all the meetings, all the congresses. Settlement on the land is the only Zionism I know. All the rest is a waste of time." It was the old ardour, burning more fiercely than ever.

The Turkish revolutionary movement hardly fulfilled its early promise of tolerance and progress. But *Poale Zion*, remote from the realities in Constantinople, remained blissfully unaware of the true character of the new régime. In 1910 the Jewish workers moved

---

* The *Shekel* was a document signifying membership of the Zionist organisation, which had to be purchased annually.

their party headquarters from Jaffa to Jerusalem, to put in their claim for recognition. David Green became a full-time party official, combining organisational duties with editorial work on *Unity*, which was established in a little shop in the Zichron Moshe district not far from the centre of the growing 'new' city. Jerusalem is not a place that reveals its full charm at first sight. It takes time for one to fall under the spell of the ancient alleyways and the oriental silhouette of the fine stonework against the wide blue sky. David learned to love its splendours, after the gimcrack façade of the sea-port. The party paid him the equivalent of ten shillings per week, more than Ben-Zvi and Rachel Yanait, who were only on a part-time basis. The first article to come from his pen was laboriously written in the obscure, complicated sentences of one unaccustomed to literary work and he devoted it to a statement of the aims and policy of the paper. It was signed 'Ben-Gurion', the first time that he used the name which he had chosen for its authentic Biblical ring. It signified that the emigrant from Poland had indeed become a man of Palestine.

He and Ben-Zvi felt that Zionism, in the way they understood the term, could best be fostered by the complete identification of the Jewish workers with the new progressive forces in Constantinople; and while Ben-Gurion wrote and lectured specifically on party programmes, Ben-Zvi was the expert on the minority situation within the Empire, on the half-million Jews spread over the Near East, and on the part they must play side by side with the Arab and Balkan peoples in their demand for local autonomy. Rachel was not yet proficient in Hebrew and she wrote articles for David to translate. The paper, first a monthly and later expanded to a weekly, could not hope for a large circulation, as many of the workers obstinately clung to Yiddish. But they sent it to the other important party-centres in Eastern and Central Europe and America, and this brought its editors recognition as the *illuminati* of the proletarian revival in the Holy Land. Others joined the paper's staff: Jacob Zerubabel, an old Poltava comrade of Ben-Zvi's and a young man whose political leanings were to take him later to the extreme left of the labour movement; and Joseph Brenner, one of the few men of real literary talent then in Palestine. He brought experience to the job and he had, indeed, edited a Hebrew magazine in London, where he had worked for a Whitechapel printer. Three hundred and fifty copies of *Unity* came off the presses with each issue, one hundred of them for distribution abroad.

Every article signed 'Ben-Gurion' was a harangue—on the essence of workers' power, on the components of practical Zionism, on how *Poale Zion* could take command of Jewry's political destiny. He abounded in confidence, contending that the 100,000 Jews living in the country could become a potent force if only they forgot their differences, spoke the same language, and relied on each other for labour to run their own economy and for police to protect it.

But what of the Jews' present need, more immigration? He and Ben-Zvi made up their minds that this depended solely on the recognition of their position as one of the bastions of the Empire. They had to prove to Constantinople that the régime they sought to create would contribute to the general well-being, and indeed that a prosperous and free Jewish community would benefit Turkey as a whole. But their good intentions were hampered by their ignorance of Turkish law and institutions. As it happened, the Zionist Organisation itself was increasing its activities in Constantinople, and was planning to send Vladmir Jabotinsky, its most gifted publicist, to take charge of the propaganda there. The two editors of *Unity* felt that this move suffered from the disadvantage that it came from outside. They wanted to go further. By presenting themselves in the capital as the Porte's faithful subjects, they could make themselves experts in its law and, perhaps, one day sit in a Turkish parliament as the representatives of the Jewish masses in Palestine. With their rights thus assured, immigrants would pour in.

Poale Zion headquarters ratified their plan, and gave them leave to enrol as law students at the University of Constantinople. Rachel Yanait, with Brenner and Zerubabel, would carry on the newspaper, which now had a literary page in which Hebrew readers could read Wilde, de Maupassant, and Tolstoy in Brenner's translations. Ben-Gurion left first, making his way to the Turkish capital via Salonika, which had a large Jewish community and where he could familiarise himself with the Turkish language. In a letter to his father, David sought to justify what, in view of the Zionist glorification of manual labour, seemed a retreat from hallowed principles and a return to the middle-class urban way of life and study.

"I shall have to make up my mind whether to become a farm-labourer or a lawyer," he wrote. "I have a feeling for both occupations, and could, I think, practise one just as easily as the other. All I am concerned with is, which choice should I make for the ultimate good of the Land of Israel? Whatever I do will be from devotion to my aim, which is also my greatest happinesss, of working for my people." Avigdor left his son in no doubt as to his satisfaction with the change. He sent David thirty roubles a month, for as long as he kept to his studies. The money was this time gratefully accepted.

Other party members, who had the same intention of forming an Ottoman-Jewish intelligentsia, joined them in Turkey. Shochet, no laggard in the testing of new ideas, was among the first. Moshe Shertok, who had now finished at the Herzlia Gymnasium, followed. They were an active nucleus of young Palestinians, and felt superior to the Zionist politicians they encountered in the capital. One day, after years as an itinerant socialist organiser in the illegal Jewish movements of White Russia, a certain David Remez came to join them. A generation later this group of student radicals were at the head of their party, to take charge of the Jewish consolidation in Palestine, and to form a shadow cabinet of the state in the making.

Closer acquaintance with the grave malady of the 'Sick Man of Europe' was a startling experience for them. Constantinople seethed with pressure-groups and political intrigue, and all looked to Turkey as to an aged uncle who they hoped would not forget them in his will. Ben-Gurion had no sooner left the city of Salonika than it was captured by the Greeks; there was the Bulgarian revolt; Italy pocketed Libya and the Dodecanese. David commenced a study on the relationships between the central authority and the outlying *vilayets*, and on the causes of weakness on the Ottoman perimeter. For it would be important to know how the Syrian provinces would stand in the event of a general collapse. The results of his researches were embodied in a slim book *Vilayet Legislation in the Ottoman Empire*, published in Hebrew, the first notable contribution to the subject in that language.

With a corrupt and volatile aristocracy on the one side and a miserable and disease-ridden proletariat on the other, the students of Constantinople could not but be distracted from their courses to plunge into the fetid politics of the decomposing empire. Yet the group around Ben-Gurion (he became secretary of the Jewish Students Union) were blind to all the signs, so clear to European observers, that the régime would not endure. Instead they lived in happy fascination with what they considered their impending 'ennoblement' into the Turkish intelligentsia. The Young Turks switched abruptly from a policy of decentralisation to one of stricter Ottomanisation, but Ben-Gurion and his friends would still not disillusion themselves. They tried to join the army, when a call went out for volunteers for the Balkan front. They were refused, not because they were Jews but because they were students. It was all very frustrating. They offered their services to the official Zionist representatives stationed in the capital, but they were rejected on account of their youth no less than their politics.

Only those interested in the development of the workers' movement knew of Ben-Gurion and came to see him, on their way from Russia to Palestine. Some arrived with high reputations, Russified Jews who were known as expert soldiers, 'gentlemen' almost, and even ignorant of Yiddish. One day Joseph Trumpeldor, a tall, handsome man whose exploits as a lieutenant in the Russian army during the Russo-Japanese war gave him the reputation among Zionists of a Jewish Suvarov, turned up in Constantinople. He had heard of Ben-Gurion through a friend living in Palestine with Brenner. They talked about the defence movement and exchanged stories of Menahem Ussishkin's obstinacy, for Trumpeldor too had had no luck when he had approached the Odessa headquarters for help.

David showed him the sights of Constantinople. When they came to enter St. Sophia the guide asked his companion to take off his boots. Strangely, Trumpeldor refused, and became rather huffy. It was only later that David realised that he had only one arm, and could not remove his boots without assistance. The incident made a strong impression upon him, so unaccustomed was he to the sight of a Jew maimed in war. But it gave him further food for thought. Ben-Gurion realised that in the event of a general war Jews everywhere would be loyal to their own countries, and would be compelled to fight each other. Even in Russia, with her record of anti-Semitism, influential Zionists would not oppose the government. What would happen to the little community in Palestine if the

1 (*Above*)

In the courtyard of the Green family home in Plonsk, members of Poale Zion bid David farewell on his departure for Palestine, 1906. He is in the centre of the front row ; his father is at the window on the right

2 (*Right*)

Student days in Constantinople, 1914. Ben-Gurion is on the far right with Israel Shochet next to him. Ben-Zvi second from left

4. The trade union organiser, 1924

3. The British Army private, 1918

Jewish world outside, with its irreconcilable loyalties, divided against itself?

The horizon darkened. The Balkan War dragged on, and then came August 1914. Ben-Gurion and Ben-Zvi decided it was time to return to Palestine for a short stay to see what effect the war was having there. Leaving all their possessions in Constantinople, they embarked on a Russian ship. It was fired on by a German gun-boat in the East Mediterranean. The captain had to change his course and they found themselves in Port Said instead of Jaffa. To their consternation they saw large numbers of Jews in flight from Palestine. What was happening to their people?

At length in Jerusalem, they discovered the reason for this exodus: famine. Food ships from the west were not arriving. Those whose sole support was charity found themselves without funds. Worst of all was the position of those immigrants like themselves, who had for years allowed the question of their nationality to fall into obscurity. The Turks were on the point of entering the war on the side of the Central Powers, and sought to establish the status of every resident, in order to decide whether he should be called up, interned, or expelled. Trumpeldor, a reserve officer of the Russian Army, left his plough at Daganya and set off for Egypt. Shertok was commissioned in the Turkish Forces. Everybody who was neither Russian nor Turkish was transported north of Jaffa, away from the front line that looked like developing across the Sinai desert.

Rumour swept the country that Chaim Weizmann, now risen to great prominence in the Zionist movement and living in Manchester, had succeeded in impressing official circles with the almost complete identification of Zionist and British aims in the Middle East, in the event of a Turkish collapse. This meant that the Zionist movement was now to all intents an ally of Russia, an idea which did not commend itself to Ben-Gurion. He went back to work on *Unity* and urged in its columns the enlistment of foreign Jews in a battalion of the Turkish Army for the defence of Palestine. As it was, most of the old religious inhabitants of Jerusalem were Turkish subjects, as were some of the old farmer class, and they were consequently liable for enlistment like Shertok. But the newcomers did not know where they stood.

The *Poale Zion* leaders saw the progress of years lost overnight. Many of the young people, upon whom they looked to bring about

6

a revival of the nation in the laboriously-planted colonies, fled. Thousands of Jews, in an attempt to escape from what was now less a home than a tiny no man's land between the warring sides, sought a safe refuge far away in America.

The governor of Syria, Jamal Pasha, brought a Turkish expert on Zionism to Jerusalem to keep watch on the Jews. He had Ben-Gurion and Ben-Zvi trailed, and made a close examination of *Unity* (in hot water anyway for complaining loudly at the brutality with which the governor had cleared Tel-Aviv, split up families, and driven some of the men into a Damascus jail). The editors went on blithely writing of new social-revolutionary forces at work in the Porte, and offered their allegiance, solidarity and fraternity to the peoples of the Empire in their hour of crisis.

Jamal was a courteous and tolerant soldier, unwilling to disturb what he judged was the pious tranquillity of the Jewish population. But his adviser on Zionism, Hassan Bey, warned him that the Jews were far from harmless. They were secretly amassing arms in their settlements, he said, and through an international organisation were in league with the enemy. After the failure of his armies to capture Suez, Jamal Pasha decided the time had come to act. And he authorised Hassan Bey to take what steps were necessary for the security of the country.

The latter did his work all too well. He swooped upon every *Poale Zion* member of the self-defence movement, among them Shochet and his wife Manya Vilbushevitz. Ben-Gurion and Ben-Zvi were clapped into an Old City jail. The offices of *Unity* were raided, and the captured files gave a comprehensive picture of what was going on in Jewish Palestine. Within a few days Ben-Gurion was brought before Hassan Bey for interrogation. The following remarkable conversation ensued:

"When did you join the Zionists?"

"I was a Zionist in Russia, before coming to this country."

"Some time ago you attended a Zionist Congress in Vienna. Who elected you a delegate?"

"My friends in America."

"But it says here"—pointing to some papers before him—"that you were elected in Constantinople."

"No, it says I came from Constantinople. I was elected in America."

"Oh," said the interrogator, coldly scrutinising the short, untidy figure before him, "was there no one else they could find in the whole of America?"

"Apparently not."

"Where is the letter confirming your election?"

"It took place so long ago, I have not kept it. It may be among my belongings in Constantinople." Hassan Bey became impatient. He felt he was not getting very far. He asked angrily:

"By what organisation were you elected?"

"The *Poale Zion*."

"Are you sure you were not elected in Constantinople?"

"How could I be? No such organisation exists there."

"Who are the leaders of this movement in Jerusalem?"

"I."

"And who else?"

"My friend, Ben-Zvi."

"And who else?"

"I know him, and I know myself." Now the other grew abusive.

"You are just a lot of dogs. First you come here from Russia, without permission, then you set up your own organisations, with selfish aims that can only damage this country." David stood his ground.

"Sir, everything I have said is true. And please do not insult me" —this with all the dignity he could muster—"I am not a dog."

The Turk got on to another tack. "What do you know of the *Hashomer* party?" he asked. (*Hashomer* was the Hebrew name for the secret defence organisation begun by *Poale Zion* and led by the Shochets.)

"There is no such party in Palestine."

"Do you know the *Hashomer* organisation which is connected with the *Poale Zion*?"

"*Poale Zion* is not connected with such an organisation."

"Then who founded this organisation? Do you know them?" Hassan Bey shrieked.

"No!" Hassan Bey turned in defeat to his secretary, busy making a transcript. "Take him back to jail," he commanded, "and bring the other one in."

The examination of Ben-Zvi produced no better result, and a few days later the two were informed that they would be expelled

for having founded a conspiratorial society whose aim was to encourage the disaffection of Turkish citizens in order to found a Jewish
state. It was no more than they expected. They had already made up
their minds to go to America and start a pioneer immigration
movement there. But first, in a direct appeal to Jamal Pasha himself,
they made a last attempt to convince the Turks that their activities
in no way conflicted with their loyalty to Turkey:

"The ties binding us to this beloved country," they declared in
a statement, "are not merely the ties of a land dear to us but also the
ties to the Ottoman Empire, which has given our people shelter
for hundreds of years. We went to Constantinople to learn the
Turkish language, and by enrolling in the legal faculty of the
Ottoman University, sought to link our future with Turkey, its
laws and customs. You may judge our attitude to Turkish interests
by examining the articles we wrote in our paper. Yet in spite of all
this we are charged with opposition to Turkey and membership
of a secret organisation. We are particularly aggrieved by the
humiliation of the expulsion order, for this means you regard us as
foreigners. We believe we have the right to be treated as Ottoman
citizens. If you feel we have committed a crime, punish us as such.
We shall accept your sentence."

The prison was conducted with some laxity, more as a lodging-
house with fixed hours than a jail. Ben-Gurion contrived to attend
meetings of the *Poale Zion*, and made arrangements with a fellow
Sejera worker, Yavnieli, and with Golomb and Dov Hos (who had
meanwhile left the Herzlia Gymnasium), to carry on his and Ben-
Zvi's work. Zerubabel, as a collaborator on *Unity*, they knew
would have to follow them in exile. They also kept in touch with
Tabenkin and other key party-men in the north.

One day Ben-Zvi had a chance encounter with Jamal Pasha. "I
have torn up your letter," said the general. "You will have to go.
We cannot have people of your opinions in the country."

They were sent to a transit-centre on the outskirts of Jaffa where
expellees were interned until they could make their arrangements to
leave. This proved difficult, as the two friends had no travel
documents. Eventually they reached Alexandria, only to be arrested
again, this time by the British, as enemy aliens! It took them three
weeks, and the intercession of the American consul, to disentangle
themselves and persuade the captain of a Greek trans-Atlantic liner

to take them aboard. Rachel Yanait, who was later to marry
Ben-Zvi, had accompanied them until the point where they took
ship, with tarbushes on their heads, hardly a penny in their
pockets, and apprehension in their hearts. Who could say when
they would see their beloved land again?

America, land of opportunity and release! It did not seem so to
Ben-Gurion, when he arrived on Ellis Island in the summer of 1915,
there to await with his friend their comrades of *Poale Zion*. It was
the first of many visits to a nation whose energies he would learn to
admire, and whose generosity he was later to invoke. Never before
had he seen such numbers of Jews enjoying such freedom. Yet he
found it a limited freedom. It failed to shake his conviction that
complete freedom lay only in Palestine, to be achieved only when
his people had restored their corporate existence on its historical soil.

Zionism, Ben-Gurion discovered, was now vastly different from
the movement he had known during his occasional journeys to
Europe before the outbreak of war. And the New York community
was unbelievably large, confident, and noisy. They collected what
seemed to him fabulous sums of money, and gave it away wildly
wherever they thought Jews were adversely affected by the war.
The various groups were undecided whether they should be political organisations, or relief agencies, or campaigners for a new
philosophy of Jewish life. In all this hubbub *Poale Zion* was a despised
and uninfluential Yiddish group. Judge Louis Brandeis was the
acknowledged leader of Zionism, but he was by no means a man of
the people, less so than ever since he had been elected to the Supreme
Court.

As a body the Zionist movement was still an uncommitted neutral,
like America itself. Some Palestinians in the country, among them
the mysterious British agent Aaron Aronsen, were quietly working
for the British cause, as they had in Palestine. But *Poale Zion* had no
leaders of substance, and kept to the East Side, politely debating with
Bundists, anarchists, and every kind of Jewish crank.

The two newcomers approached this scene with a crisp simplicity.
They laid before the party the situation in Palestine and the bleak
struggle they were having to establish even the most rudimentary
Jewish economy. They spoke impatiently of the ghetto-like atmosphere that had been brought to the New World by the wanderers

from the Old, and they were heard with deference. Here were Jews:
there was Palestine. The people had to learn about their land. One
day the war would be over, and the Jews would have to return
to it.

Working as a team, Ben-Gurion and Ben-Zvi wrote, lectured and
attended conferences. One or other of them visited communities as
far away as the Middle West and Canada. They went principally
in search of young men and women who would undertake basic
agricultural training and learn Hebrew. They wanted settlers for the
new communal villages, not social workers organising whist-drives.
Poale Zion in Jerusalem had issued them a directive and they carried
it out to the letter. Soon Zerubabel and another old comrade, A.
Hashin, joined them. The four were unrivalled for their knowledge
and experience of Palestine conditions, though others, such as the
veteran socialist Nachman Syrkin, had more political sense and
sophistication; or like *Poale Zion*'s leading theorist, Ber Borochov,
felt more intensely the need for solidarity with the international
working class. They argued bitterly with the 'bourgeois' Zionist
groups, especially over proposals for a united Jewish front in America
and its possible representation at an eventual peace conference.

German propagandists were spreading all kinds of promises
among the Jews of America. In 1916 it was by no means certain
that Britain would be the first to make an official statement of
policy in support of Zionist aspirations, and Ben-Gurion had as yet
no reason to regret his espousal of Turkey as the most likely champion of Jewish rights. He had learnt in Egypt from Trumpeldor
and Jabotinsky of the proposals to form Jewish units to fight for the
Allied cause, but he was not at all convinced that this was in the
interests of the 70,000 Jews who existed by courtesy of Jamal Pasha.
He hated the thought of Jews fighting a war on the same side as
their traditional enemy, Russia. The Zionists of America showed
their influence by sending a mercy-ship, the *Vulcan*, with supplies
to Palestine. It was a timely act of relief, and proved the value to
his people of America's neutrality.

The four Palestinian socialists collaborated on a book, *Yiskor (In
Memoriam)*, in which they described the growth of the pioneer
movement, and especially of its illegal defence arm. Dedicated to
those comrades who fell while guarding the colonies, it contained
a chapter by Ben-Gurion on his own experiences as a labourer. The

book was written in Yiddish, and had an immediate success. Much to Ben-Zvi's and Zerubabel's annoyance, a revised edition was brought out while they were away from New York campaigning in the West. It took Ben-Zvi a long time to forgive his friend for leaving his name off the elaborately-designed cover, but the quarrel was soon smoothed over and they got together on another work, *The Book of the Land of Israel*. This book took them a year to write and grew into an encyclopaedic reference-volume on the history, geography, and ethnography of the Holy Land.

The Jewish prospect in Palestine, and indeed the world political situation, changed drastically between the book's commencement and its completion. Kerensky's revolution occurred in March, 1917, and Jews everywhere welcomed it as marking the end of centuries of Russian persecution. Borochov came to Ben-Gurion and told him excitedly that he was going back to Russia, to throw in his lot with the liberals. At thirty-six, Borochov still put his faith in the innate virtues of the proletariat, and was confident that justice, to him another word for reason, could not be stayed in its inexorable march to victory. Britain was being hard put to it to keep her armies going and her people fed, with nearly a million tons of her shipping dragged to the sea-bed each month by enemy submarines. Then, suddenly, America came into the war and there was no further doubt that Turkey, and all who supported her, would finish up on the wrong side.

Ben-Gurion had to do some quick thinking. He and Ben-Zvi realised that this was the time to make a specific Jewish contribution to the Allied campaign in the Near East. Tardily, they came round to the view that Trumpeldor and Jabotinsky had been right, and that Chaim Weizmann's instinct had not erred when he had placed his trust in Britain. They switched their activities to enlistment of Jews for the British army (America had not declared war against Turkey) and allied themselves with the Palestinian agents of Britain whom they had previously opposed. Jabotinsky was then in London. They sought to contact him, but when they failed undertook the work alone. At last Ben-Gurion's old yearning to wear the uniform of a nation whose voice mattered in Palestine was satisfied.

The year 1917 had begun unpromisingly, but now his confidence was boundless and other joys were still to come. In November the Jewish world was given that famous document to which it has clung ever since as the great political benediction of its aspirations—the Balfour Declaration. It brought Weizmann to the pinnacle of his influence and kept him there for a generation. It confirmed the English Zionists in the political and diplomatic leadership of the Zionist movement and won for Great Britain a place of affection among the Jews which was sometimes to fade but never to disappear through every subsequent crisis.

At this time David Ben-Gurion was a strapping, determined young man of thirty-one, joyfully celebrating from Canal Street to Times Square with his friends as if all that separated them from possession of Palestine were a few crumbling regiments of half-starved and demoralised Turkish militia. Neither he nor any other Jews in America had any conception of the complications that the promise raised with the Arabs.

Ben-Gurion was no longer the awkward, unsociable youth he had been. While still in New York he proposed to a young lady he had met at the East Side meetings, and asked her to share his life in the new Jewish country that could now be created without hindrance. Paula Munweis was a medical student who had been compelled to take up nursing by the sudden death of her father, an immigrant from Minsk. She worked in the Jewish hospital opposite Ben-Gurion's lodgings on East Broadway, and was little attracted by the idea of Zionism. Yet a man who could think of nothing else won her. To the recent immigrants life in America was the golden gate to social justice—at least it seemed so to those who, like Paula, read the articles of Abe Cahan, the leading Jewish journalist, and heard the speeches of Samuel Gompers, the Jewish trade union organiser. Nevertheless she fell in with Ben-Gurion's unrelenting sense of mission. Their marriage was a simple ceremony at City Hall; their honeymoon an uncertain lull between austere party work and impending enlistment. If the Balfour Declaration was for Ben-Gurion a memorable wedding present, there was tragedy to mar the day: Borochov died suddenly in Russia. So that youthful fire was now extinguished for all time! He and Ben-Zvi dedicated their book, now ready for the press, to the memory of the one man they would acknowledge as their leader. Then they left New York for Boston, took the oath of loyalty to King George V, and were soon in camp in Windsor, Nova Scotia. By July, 1918, David was on his way to England.

4

The Strands of Power

The Judeans – The Zionist Commission – The British in Palestine – Attempts at labour unity – Histadruth formed – Ben-Gurion and Paula – Riots in Jaffa – The Arab Question – Vladimir Jabotinsky – Zionist Congress – Unemployment and economic crisis – Berl Katznelson and the struggle for political action – Shaw Commission – Mapai founded – Electioneering in East Europe – Arlosoroff's murder – The Zionist Executive

BY THE TIME Ben-Gurion's detachment arrived in Egypt as part of the 39th Battalion, Royal Fusiliers, General Allenby had already entered Jerusalem and was pressing north and east. The Jewish soldiers were therefore kicking their heels in the anti-climax that follows victory. One of the ruling factors in military organisation is that troops which are fighting in the hope of securing some political or ideological advantage are seldom as effective as enlisted men who expect no greater reward than their day's pay. The 'Judeans' were no exception. They sometimes proved more trouble than they were worth, were suspicious of their officers, disobedient and impatient. "We did not enlist to be kept hanging around in Egypt," they complained, "to spend endless hours at drill or to shift stores from one end of Tel-el-Kebir to the other and then shift them back again!" Such volubility was embarrassing. Their cockney sergeants could not understand them: instead of passing their evenings in the wholesome, boisterous atmosphere of Naafi bars, these soldiers devoted their hours of relaxation to earnest philosophical debate.

Ben-Gurion was promoted to the rank of corporal. He took this promotion rather more seriously than might others better acquainted with the ways of the English, and even this step he felt merited his most earnest consideration in relation to his life's work. The stripes did not exclude him from associating with his comrades, of whom 200 were Palestinians who had been in exile in America and 150 more were drawn from the pioneer groups he and Ben-Zvi had founded as potential reinforcements for the workers' movement.

As Allenby advanced, further volunteers came forward from the conquered areas, or from the Jewish prisoners among the captured Turks. The *Poale Zion* kept its organisation alive right through the war and had prepared its attitude towards their liberators. They would, if given the opportunity, enlist in the British forces, and so strengthen the weight of Zionist claims by having as large a body of Jews as possible on the winning side.

Three important figures had emerged during Ben-Gurion's absence in America—Berl Katznelson, Eliahu Golomb, and Dov Hos. It was their job to persuade their followers to adopt this policy. Hos became sergeant-major of one of the companies of the locally-enlisted 40th Battalion. Golomb had made himself an expert in problems of defence and was playing a key role in settlement-security. Katznelson, not fully tied up with *Poale Zion*, was strictly a socialist intellectual absorbed in the creed of Jewish labour. Isaac Tabenkin was another man who rose in left-wing circles. He did not join up, but remained in the background as a civilian leader of the Jewish underprivileged. The other workers' party, *Hapoel Hatzair*, had steered clear of enlistment, and it was important for a watchful eye to be kept on its activities. Most of its members were pacifists, and regarded the war as a struggle in which they had no reason to be involved.

Ben-Gurion was no sooner off the boat at Alexandria than he had an attack of dysentery, which forced him to go into hospital in Cairo. His first visitor was Ben-Zvi, bringing Rachel Yanait, who with characteristic determination had, as a welfare worker, found her way to the tent-lines of the Judeans and to the side of her fiancé. David had happy news for them. Paula had given birth to a daughter, Geula, and was preparing to join him as soon as it was possible to travel. Ben-Zvi brought tidings of the old friends left behind in Palestine who were now recruits in the new battalion. There were first-hand accounts of the *Yishuv's* experiences during the fighting. It was a story of hunger and disease, with an Arab population no longer apathetic to political developments. Clashes in the neighbourhood of Jaffa had been frequent, but the Jews had achieved temporary unity in the interests of welfare and self-defence.

What of the new rulers of the country, the British? David learned that first impressions were not promising. The military authorities

were unbriefed in the Balfour Declaration and its implications, and
had rejected a claim put forward by the Palestinian regiments to
be sent home for occupation duties there. Apart from this, the
situation was hopeful, for the Zionists could do their work backed
up by an internationally-accepted document, while a Zionist Commission, led by Dr. Weizmann, was on the point of arriving in the
country to look after the needs of the Jewish population. That Commission regarded itself, and was considered by the *Yishuv*, as the
nucleus of a civil administration free to expand what was already
being called the 'National Home' until Palestine became, in Weizmann's phrase 'as Jewish as England is English.' This notion was
encouraged by the pomp with which Weizmann had been sent
forth from England on his mission: he had even been given an
audience with King George V. The very existence of such a mission
increased Ben-Gurion's and Ben-Zvi's sense of frustration, and they
made up their minds to attach themselves to it as the representatives
of Palestine's workers. But the military had other ideas. They looked
upon the strange civilians from London, armed with their imposing
credentials and busily hopping from place to place, as an unwarranted interference with their own unhurried arrangements. They were
resentful of the Commission's plans and did not hesitate to say so.

So by the time Ben-Gurion recovered from his illness, had
been transferred to the 40th Battalion and given leave to visit
Jerusalem, the Zionist Commission had lost both its chief
personality (Weizmann had returned to Europe to prepare for the
Peace Conference) and its aura of a quasi-Jewish administration. Its
functions were delegated to purely local groups. It left a legacy
among the Palestinians of disillusionment with the political influence
and trustworthiness of Zionist leaders who worked in close contact
with the British. In fact, its only moment of glory had been the laying of the foundation-stone of a Hebrew University on Mount
Scopus.

Back in Jerusalem, Ben-Gurion was shocked at the havoc which
war had caused among his people. The old farmers had held their
own, and were back in the vineyards, but some settlements had been
overrun and destroyed, including Kfar Saba, with whose foundations he had been connected; the Orthodox of the four holy cities sat
cowed and perplexed, awaiting the charity that would warm them
back to the life of piety again; not more than 60,000 Jews all-told

remained in the country. The rest were either lost for ever by
emigration and resettlement in other countries, or had succumbed
to imprisonment or privation and were dead, while a few were in
the various armies awaiting demobilisation. As he saw it, Palestine
was theirs for the taking, or very soon would be, with no Jews at
hand to take possession of their patrimony.

His brief leave expired, Ben-Gurion went back to his regiment.
This was the moment for *Poale Zion* to act, he urged his friends.
More easily said than done, they felt. They were out of the country,
they were in uniform, they had to deal with a new master. Study
at the University of Constantinople or years on New York's
East Side were not the best introductions to the ways of the British.
Impatiently, he brushed their hesitations aside. They would not be
in the army for ever, he told them, and in any case, the people who
mattered were here, in these very battalions, strung along the delta
of the Nile. If they united all the workers' forces now they could
take the initiative in the restoration of their country. Nothing was
more important, especially as with the return to peace there was
hope of new blood flowing into their small community. The pioneers
were on the march again, and they had to be welded into an
organised working-class when they arrived, or they too would drift
away.

Ben-Gurion was a forceful personality, and only spoke up when
he had thought his ideas out completely. Soon many of the others,
Golomb, Katznelson, Hos, were all thinking like him, and a new
round of fervid debate began in the army tents, to be continued in
Jerusalem and the colonies after demobilisation. The years had dealt
differently with Ben-Zvi, whose standing was now higher than that
of any other *Poale Zion* leader. Much admired by the other elements
in Palestine for his wise and erudite personality, the gangling youth
had turned into a gentle, reflective man more tolerant of the inadequacies—or such they seemed to Ben-Gurion—of the Zionist
leaders in London. The party chose him to represent them in wider
national affairs, and in fact he was soon to be marked out for an
executive position in a provisional council of the *Yishuv*. But he was
not talented in politics and hardly tried to influence the party's
policy. After 1918 political decisions were increasingly made by
Ben-Gurion, with whom working-class unity now became an
obsession. His immediate ambition was for a united Labour Party

which would direct the formation of a Trades Union movement, stimulate the programme of agricultural settlement and shape the socialist character of the country.

Ben-Gurion did not doubt that in procuring for herself the Mandate over Palestine, Britain was motivated more by imperialist self-interest than by a desire to encourage Jewish aspirations. Like so many Europeans of those days, he was bound to react with distrust to almost any move from Whitehall. Nevertheless, he was encouraged by the British Labour Party's support of the Balfour Declaration and believed that whatever Britain's ultimate designs, the opportunity must be exploited to the full. Katznelson, who was regarded by the executive of the *Poale Zion* as the spokesman of the unaffiliated workers, disliked Ben-Gurion's strong emphasis on class-interest, and advised moderation when basing a programme specifically on workers' needs. In his view they must strike a combination of class and national interest. His advice was taken, and provided a healthy restraint on the *Poale Zion* plans of that period.

He was ready to concede that the workers were the principal consideration in the fuller development of the nation and did not, of course, dispute the importance of continuing the pre-war doctrine of Jewish labour in Jewish enterprises. But he stood up to Ben-Gurion about the need for *Poale Zion* to eradicate some of the Diaspora traits among its members, the most important of which was the persistent survival of Yiddish. Ben-Gurion was able to satisfy him on this. Speaking from the heart, he pointed out that many of their 'Yiddishists' had left the country, and were unlikely to return; that those who would stick to Palestine as an ideal and as a way of life were those elements in *Poale Zion* which had come already before the war and were strongly attached to Hebrew as a spoken language. On these terms Berl Katznelson undertook to bring a large number of agricultural workers into a Labour Party formed on a broader basis.

The greatest difficulty was to win over *Hapoel Hatzair*, still obstinately hugging its individuality under Joseph Sprinzak and Joseph Aharonowitz. The thin ideological film separating this group from Ben-Gurion's party had thickened considerably during the past few years. *Hapoel Hatzair* had its own methods of looking after newcomers to the country, and continued using its own labour exchanges to place workers in the settlements, as well as running its own canteens in Haifa and Jaffa, both of which activities competed with the *Poale Zion* organisation.

Sprinzak received the proposal for amalgamation coolly. In the first place, he said, he did not consider *Hapoel Hatzair* a political party at all, but a rallying point for those subscribing to the Jewish return to the soil. He was no supporter of internecine Jewish strife in Palestine, did not like *Poale Zion*'s allegiance to a world confederation of Jewish socialists centred in the Diaspora, and had no doubt that political work was best left to Zionist diplomats like Weizmann, who had established a relationship of confidence with the British and other governments.

If Ben-Gurion and Katznelson were ready to elaborate a general labour organisation concerned with welfare, he would be interested. If by union they meant the introduction of class-warfare, and the complete socialisation of the Jewish national home, he was not interested.

This, in fact, was what Ben-Gurion intended, and so the united movement had to be formed without *Hapoel Hatzair*. The foundation conference took place in February, 1919, at Petach Tikvah, and the new party was given the name *Achdut Avoda* (Unity of Labour). This name had a splendid ring—but the unity behind it was not very profound, as later discussions in conference revealed. The building operatives of Tel-Aviv and the railway-workers of Jerusalem heaved a sigh of relief each time their comrades from the settlements went back to their farms and practised their socialism in the seclusion of the countryside, like big happy families of communistic monks.

Sprinzak and Aharonowitz retained the loyalties of fully a third of the workers, of which there were hardly more than 3,000 in the entire country. Then Trumpeldor came back with more novitiates for the collective life rescued from a Russia in the grip of revolution and civil war. His Zion Mule Corps, which had seen action under Sir Ian Hamilton in Gallipoli, was disbanded in 1916, the military considering it to have outlived its usefulness. The disgruntled Trumpeldor returned to Petrograd with a vague plan for raising a Jewish army to enter Palestine from the north, a scheme which involved a 120,000-strong legion and had secured Kerensky's blessing. But when the Russian situation changed radically and the

'White' generals Petlura and Kornilov launched their atrocities against the Jews, the young men he had interested in his ideas found other work to do in local self-defence units. Nevertheless, between 1917–19 he managed to set groups of pioneers on the move to Palestine, and, finally, arrived himself with one of them.

This was the beginning of a new wave of immigration, not very large, but superior to previous immigrations in that it was organised in advance, was specifically trained to enter the collectives and was strongly indoctrinated with Zionist purpose. The blood-transfusion came just in time.

Trumpeldor was disgusted by the discord he found among the workers and their leaders. He had grave news of Eastern Europe. The entire Jewish world east of the Elbe was, he said, in the process of distintegration. Being mainly from the middle-classes, their people had lost their wealth and were adrift in areas torn by administrative anarchy. Life was intolerable for them in Poland, while defeated Germany and Austria were in the throes of an emotional and economic crisis. So he came forward with another effort at unification, and then stalked off in high dudgeon to push a plough at the uppermost tip of Galilee, on the very border still to be demarcated by Britain and France. This time Sprinzak was better disposed towards negotiation, and talks began among all sections of the workers with the establishment of a common labour confederation as their aim.

Ben-Gurion was of the opinion, as were all those who had worked with him in the mobilisation of volunteers, that the Zionist leaders in London had missed a very important opportunity. The two battalions of Judeans (he was less concerned with the 38th Battalion, which resented being lumped in with those who had not enlisted in England) should have been sent to Palestine and left intact as part of the occupying force in the country. This would have placed the Jewish population in a most advantageous position, prevented bloodshed and given the world outside a ready-made token of Jewish national existence. This was not done. They were demobilised and dispersed. The political men in the regiments put the blame for this set-back on the weakness of Weizmann and his colleagues, though they might well have taken some of it on themselves. Instinct frequently got the better of duty. On one occasion they mutinied, and on another, during the short period they were stationed in

Palestine, their Commander, Colonel Margolin, was severely repri-
manded and posted away for exceeding his duties. Ben-Gurion
was soon to have the opportunity of confronting Weizmann face to
face with his grievances.

At long last Paula reached Jerusalem, with the child which Ben-
Gurion had not yet seen; but no sooner had she settled down in her
new country than he took them both away with him to London.
This was in 1920, and a big Zionist conference was due to be held
in the Albert Hall in July, requiring the participation of the Palestinian workers. Ben-Gurion was chosen to represent them. Undaunted
by the array of august personalities on the platform, he flung charge
upon charge in the air. His tale was mostly a record of the impatience
of the Palestinians to go ahead with big plans for development, and
the contrasting inertia of the Zionist movement in general. Since the
formation of the Zionist Commission, Ben-Gurion complained,
outsiders had placed a barrier between the people and the rulers in
Palestine: "In the old days we settlers had direct access to Jamal
Pasha. Now we have to do everything through intermediaries."

This was rather overstating the case, but when he saw the caution
with which Weizmann handled the issue of Jewish objectives in
Palestine, his misgivings increased. Weizmann did not see the problem in terms of struggle. He advocated slowness. Others were against
speeding up immigration because no funds were available to settle
newcomers. Where Ben-Gurion felt that the Jewish position must
be strengthened in the shortest possible time, the Zionists in London
considered that if events were left to take their course they would
operate in the Jews' favour.

Ben-Gurion and Paula occupied a small flat in Maida Vale. Their
second child, a son, was born while they were there, and one day
as Ben-Gurion was nursing the two infants visitors arrived. They
were Moshe Shertok bringing David Hacohen, son of a well-known
Hebrew writer, with him. These two had been friends at the Herzlia
Gymnasium, and were now studying at the London School of
Economics. They talked of growing agitation among the Arabs.
Trumpeldor was dead—killed on a frontier outpost during an
exchange of shots which arose from the mistaken belief held by
some Arabs that he was a French officer holding the post so as to
secure its inclusion within the Lebanon. The incident arose from a
misunderstanding: nevertheless, Trumpeldor, in death as in life,

5. Jewish leaders in conference with Neville Chamberlain and other Ministers at St. James's Palace, 1939. Ben-Gurion in the foreground, on the right of Chaim Weizmann

6. Reading the Declaration of Statehood, Tel Aviv, 1948

7. Presiding at the first Cabinet meeting after the General Election of 1949

endowed the Jewish self-defence movement with the stuff from which legends are born. He became the symbol of Jewish labour pioneering on the frontiers of civilisation, for a new civilisation, and his death sharpened the urge to unite labour and give it the teeth of a secret army.

Soon afterwards Hacohen received a message from Golomb to meet him in Vienna. On arrival there he found *Poale Zion*'s military expert with another party member, Levi Eshkol, packing rifles in a suburban warehouse. He was told to help: the three were caught redhanded. Golomb and Eshkol were set free, but Hacohen, whom the police wrongly took to be the ringleader, was clapped into jail for a month. This episode serves to illustrate the lengths to which the Jews were prepared to go to arm themselves after the death of Trumpeldor.

The Ben-Gurion family also crossed the Channel and a period of exhausting travel for Paula and her children began. Her husband found work to be done in a dozen cities all the way to Plonsk, where he wanted to rest for a while and give Avigdor the opportunity of making the acquaintance of his daughter-in-law and of Geula and Amos, his new grandchildren. They lingered first in Paris, then in Vienna, where an international *Poale Zion* conference was taking place. Ben-Gurion was elected to the three-man executive of a world confederation of Zionist socialists. Then eastwards again, with long speeches and discussions to keep him in touch with the people who knew him best, and whom he understood so well. This was the territory which he knew must be won if the Jewish masses were ever to dominate the movement.

In modest hotels along the journey, Paula had plenty of opportunity to ponder on the disadvantages of the life she had chosen as the wife of a Jewish politician. She recalled the poky room he had found for her in Jerusalem, appallingly uncomfortable after the New York apartment. She thought of the manners and standards which she found so primitive, while the interminable conferences, the restlessness of the Arabs, the resentment towards the British, had all given a neurotic tinge to their daily lives. And in London too, the as yet little-known labour leader lived humbly and isolated with his family, with the additional strain for Paula of pregnancy in a strange city. But here at last was the Plonsk of her husband's childhood and she was happy again. Avigdor had meanwhile **remarried** and the Green family circle was large and hospitable. David was more relaxed there than at any time since their marriage.

This idyllic peace was not to last. News came from Jaffa of a serious outbreak of disorders. Apparently, some communists had found cause to demonstrate against the newly-established Jewish labour confederation (of which, incidentally, they were members) and in the confusion Arabs had rioted and attacked. A hundred Jews and Arabs were killed, among them Chaim Brenner, the wistful, poetic colleague of Ben-Gurion's journalistic days before the war on *Unity*, and Zvi Schatz, Brenner's closest friend, who had been responsible for sending Trumpeldor to Ben-Gurion in Constantinople. Sir Herbert Samuel, the High Commissioner, whom the Jews had welcomed the year before as the new Messiah leading the scattered people back to their ancient land under the Union Jack, went, to their consternation, to extremes of conciliation to appease the Arabs. Immigrants were arriving at the rate of a thousand a month, but for some months Sir Herbert stopped the flow completely. A proven Arab agitator, the fanatically anti-Jewish Haj Amin el Husseini, had been in exile, but he was now summoned back to a position of alarming power and authority as Mufti of Jerusalem; the Balfour Declaration applied to all of Palestine, but the High Commissioner advised his government to exclude the part which was east of the Jordan from Jewish colonisation. To his wife's dismay, Ben-Gurion left his family in Plonsk and returned to Jerusalem.

The situation was troubled everywhere. Politically, the Jews were losing ground and their domestic condition had slumped to rock bottom. Thanks to Tabenkin, the new pioneers were being successfully absorbed in agricultural settlements. But they were an almost insignificant minority among the newcomers, most of whom were packing into the new city of Tel-Aviv, where overcrowding was barely relieved by housing now being hurriedly thrown up without plan or sense of permanence. Unemployment made recruits for extremist groups, both of the left and the right, there and in Haifa.

The new confederation of workers united *Hapoel Hatzair, Achdut Avoda*, and any other groups who cared to join. It proved to be the one dynamic organisation in the country, with 110 seats out of the 200 on the Jewish representative assembly which had been inaugurated in October, 1920. The *Histadruth*, as the confederation was briefly called, was feared by Jewish employers, while its communist members were an obstructive nuisance. Strikes and strike-breaking became almost daily occurrences.

Ben-Gurion was nominated chief secretary of the *Histadruth*, and later became general secretary. This enabled him to devote all his time to strengthening its organisation, and he strove to direct the workers' energies into constructive Zionist channels. Menahem Ussishkin, formerly of Odessa, was head of the Palestine Executive —the successor to the Zionist Commission—and Ben-Gurion harried him into putting money into the creation of more and more settlements, and into drainage projects on new stretches of marshland which had been purchased in the Vale of Jezreel—a purchase originally vetoed by the London leaders. He felt they were bogged down not by the marshes, but by the practical inadequacies of the movement and the subtle alliance of Arab antipathy and British stonewalling.

Somehow, the lumbering apparatus of Zionism was driven forward. Weizmann called for a great mobilisation of Jewish finance to inaugurate the development of the country in earnest, but the response was so poor that he could only urge the local planners to go slow. Four years after the Balfour Declaration Weizmann and his advisers found themselves tied down by incessant haggling with Samuel and an Administration (whose higher ranks included a number of prominent English Jews) that refused to become an agent of Zionist colonisation.

It was Ben-Gurion's good fortune that his days were spent neither with the British nor with the Jewish leaders. His province as general secretary was with the new immigrants who at the end of 1923 numbered 35,000. They had to be organised, settled, and educated to their part in the nation's revival. During the next few years he toured the country, talking to the workers on the job, impressing upon them the theme of labour solidarity—this could not be taken for granted for a day in Palestine—and the high significance of things achieved by the work of Jewish hands. Just about one-third of the newcomers fitted into the proletarian sector of the growing Jewish economy. The rest came with small sums of money, and in the general uncontrolled development they started workshops or small-holdings after the fashion of immigrants in every country of the world. They used whatever cheap labour was available.

The General Confederation of Jewish Labour was not, as elsewhere, solely a grouping of trade unions. One could join individually, or through the various trades and the affiliated welfare or political organisations. It had a sense of historical mission, and under Ben-Gurion this combination of might and right became almost impregnable. Only the communist members raised the problem of Arab workers to prick the conscience of the confederation, but in 1923, much to Ben-Gurion's annoyance—for he considered the strength of the organisation more important than the politics of any individual—the communists were expelled for issuing a poster calling upon the Arabs to resist Jewish development of an area near Afule. The Arabs were given every encouragement to improve their own conditions by the confederation—but outside the sphere of Jewish economy.

Wages were deplorably low, especially in government road-making and rail development work, and the massses of unmarried young men (whose families were mostly in Europe) were a mobile and often unstable element. Ben-Gurion's job was to avoid strikes, though more often than not he was compelled to instigate them. The career he was making for himself as the champion of the unskilled labourer brought him into opposition with any Jew who was an employer, who was opposed to trade unionism in Palestine or who, thinking God was exclusively on his side, assumed he had divine backing for any line of conduct which suited him. In speeches to the workers Ben-Gurion would take the opportunity to describe each newly-built mile of road as a stepping-stone to the new Jewish society; in interviews with visiting Zionist dignitaries he would point out that the road was being constructed by sweated labour, and that the building of Zion was being achieved on an empty stomach.

In those early days before each trip out of Jerusalem he would go to David Zakkai, who combined the offices of cultural secretary with treasurer for the *Histadruth*, and ask for an advance of pay or a few piastres for the night's lodging. Zakkai would carefully note the amounts in a tiny pocket-diary. Ben-Gurion urged him to keep a full record of their activities. "This is history," he said. "All these petty-cash slips and labour schedules will be illuminating additions to the archives of the movement."

He remained practically unknown to the British or to Colonel Kisch, the aristocratic English Jew sent by Weizmann to represent the Zionist Organisation in Palestine. He left to Ben-Zvi the task of interpreting the Labour Movement to the Mandatory officials, a task performed conscientiously but without brilliance by a man who loved people for their own sakes, not for the opinions they were said to hold. Sprinzak fought the workers' battles with Kisch and with those holding the purse-strings of Zionism while Remez and Tabenkin looked after the absorption of new people for the collectives. Katznelson went to work to give Labour its own daily newspaper, and when this first appeared in 1925, became its editor. The *Histadruth's* political expert was a newcomer to Palestine, the twenty-five years old Chaim Arlosoroff, a member of Sprinzak's *Hapoel Hatzair*, moderate in outlook and a profound admirer of British institutions. He kept Ramsay MacDonald and other Labour leaders in London well-supplied with pamphlets about socialist-Jewish objectives in Palestine. The British liked Arlosoroff: he seemed more civilised than the roughly-dressed, assertive union officials of local vintage.

The team took not only their work, but themselves, most seriously, and bore the common defects of insularity. Tabenkin, rapidly consolidating his position as the high priest of the collective idea, displayed some resentment at the influence of *Hapoel Hatzair* in the *Histadruth* coalition. Arlosoroff, the only member of its top council to have been educated at a Western university, was more worldly than the others, and had the young man's thrill of doing an important job that kept him in the public eye of the nation in embryo.

In the early twenties this labour confederation was numerically small. Its total membership was insignificant compared with the whole Jewish population of Palestine—8,000 out of 100,000—and minute when measured against the world Zionist affiliation of three-quarters of a million. Yet it was born to power. Why? Simply because the men controlling it made Palestine the fulcrum of their thinking, were concentrated within the country and dealt not with abstractions but with matters that concerned their daily lives and the security of their families. It was a compact, easily manœuvrable force, while the dispersion of the rest of the Zionist movement, and its very nature as a loose international system of affiliations, prevented its making the impact upon events that its size and means warranted. Other Jewish groups within Palestine (the so-called

General Zionists of the right and the Religious Zionist party) were
interlocked with sister-bodies in the Diaspora and depended much
more upon the biennial Congress to formulate policy. The very
establishment of the *Histadruth* defined the difference between the
Palestinian and the Jew. In the course of years that difference was not
to grow less.

Thus the man occupying the central organisational role in the
Histadruth controlled the massive political energy contributed by
clerks, labourers, doctors, stevedores, school-teachers, farm-workers
—all of whom found a place in it. For these people the errors
and triumphs of Zionism were reflected in terms of more or less
bread, more or less freedom to run their own lives, more or less
danger of death at the hands of the Arab sniper. Ben-Gurion knew
his strength; and when he used it to fortify the partisan position of
the worker, he honestly believed he was strengthening the national
position of the Jew. He had the knack of clothing his objectives in
phraseology that endowed labour in Palestine with a poetry, and
his sense of mission percolated through to the humblest newcomer.
This is how he once addressed the Jerusalem navvies: "Our organisation is composed of a spiritual essence and an historical will.
Therefore it is a union of the builders of a kingdom; not a kingdom
of despotism and oppression, but of work and equality. We are
training ourselves to be pioneers who will settle not in this colony
or in that village, so much as into a united community, a workers'
society."

To him each new blade of grass thrusting through the arid plain
was a portent, and he wanted the whole world to know of it. In
1923 he took some exhibits to an international agricultural fair held
in Moscow, and proudly held aloft the flag, fast becoming a great
rarity in the Soviet Union, of Jewish nationalism. He spoke
to Russian trade union leaders of the new socialist society the
Histadruth was building. They were polite but mildly incredulous—
Palestine would never belong to anybody but imperialist Britain,
they said.

Meanwhile, the Zionist organisation was not making an accurate
estimate of its revenue and was fast overspending itself. Arab land-
lords dangled their land invitingly before the Jews, but held out
till the Jews would pay inflated prices. Not only was settlement
costly, but the only people prepared to ruin their health on

soil-drainage operations in malarious swamps belonged to squads of mobile workers enlisted on a basis similar to the shadow self-defence units. They formed a pioneer corps drawn largely from the Galilean colonies; they knew their own strength and under the leadership of Tabenkin had their own spokesmen in the *Histadruth* councils, which they made a habit of treating with some irreverence.

Already strong and ubiquitous, the *Histadruth* now ventured into a new field of activity: it founded its own contracting organisation, controlled by David Remez with David Hacohen, newly-arrived from London with his economics degree, to assist him. Under the name of Solel Boneh, this combine competed with private building companies with the result that employers found they had to cope with the *Histadruth* on the managerial, as well as the union, level. They were confronted with *Histadruth* agents wherever they turned. Its members grew food in their own settlements, had the produce collectively marketed by their own wholesale undertakings, deposited their profits in their own banks, went to their own doctors, started their own schools. In fact, the *Histadruth*'s need for the bourgeois Zionist movement was for one thing only—money to balance its budget.

After its second national conference in 1923, the *Histadruth* thought it was time to take up the question of the Arabs in earnest, and did so by bringing a message of workers' solidarity to them. Then private enterprise revolted. It was not that the Zionist leadership disputed its responsibility towards the Arab population—quite the contrary. But it believed that conciliation of the races should not be a partisan affair and could not be served by stirring up agitation among the lowly *fellah*. It was a task for gentlemen, sitting around a table, and in support of this view they quoted the agreement made between Weizmann and the Emir Feisal in 1918, and the frequent meetings in Amman between Kisch and Feisal's brother Abdullah.

Ben-Gurion was behind the move to teach the Arabs the rudiments of trade unionism. But he was moving too quickly. Employers now deliberately went out of their way to put Arabs on their pay-roll, and the *Histadruth*'s prompt reaction was to order their members out on strike. This produced precisely that racial conflict which all wanted to avoid. Sprinzak, the *Histadruth*'s spokesman on the Zionist Executive, was in the uncomfortable position of having to defend an organisation which had grown accustomed to receiving applause throughout the Jewish world rather than criticism. Sprinzak was reasonable and ready to compromise. Ben-Gurion was not. He failed to see why objections should be advanced against the activities of those who *were* building roads, *were* draining marshes, *were* absorbing newcomers on the land. All the parties determined to take their grievances to the next Congress, which was to be held in Vienna in August, 1925, and which now loomed ahead as a major battle-ground.

A parliament which meets once every two years furnishes few opportunities for enlightening, factual debate. This was always the shortcoming of the Zionist Congress, and especially so in periods of great strain and despondency. Speeches were rarely more than a long catalogue of complaints, often highly partisan and obscurantist. At that Congress it was difficult to believe that these 300 delegates, representing 600,000 Jewish voters, were united on even the most basic of Zionist propositions. Jabotinsky, the *enfant terrible*, chastised the leadership for its pusillanimity and ineptitude. He refused to accept a situation of gradual growth and he threatened to go outside the machinery of the organisation to transform the Jews in Palestine into a majority. He would not hear of the broadening of Zionist leadership to embrace non-Zionist philanthropists and other personalities with whose help alone the organisation could hope for solvency, and he demonstrated his utter inability to subordinate his views to those of the majority.

Then speaker after speaker got up to condemn the waste, the duplication, the greed of the workers' sector of the National Home's economy. When Ben-Gurion rose to reply he made the speech of an angry man, intemperate, irrelevant, and personal. Dressed as it were for the proletarian part in open-necked rough shirt, he stood at the tribune and stared aggressively at 200 Zionists who lived in every country of the world but Palestine. Other members of the *Histadruth* had spoken, but they were not there to give trouble. Arlosoroff was Weizmann's 'favourite son' and Sprinzak dealt dispassionately with the less contentious subjects of colonisation and unemployment-relief. Ben-Gurion talked five years of frustration out of his system. He began with Sir Herbert Samuel's stewardship: "We regarded him with reverence when he came. How did he help us? What did he give us, but Haj Amin el Husseini as Mufti of Jerusalem, and the

Churchill White Paper?* Samuel reported a discovery back to his government," Ben-Gurion went on ironically, "a discovery that the Jews alone are building their National Home. Is that why we had a High Commissioner, to state the obvious? Palestine does not exist in a vacuum, remember. *We* cannot alter the political and economic frame in which the country is locked. We were entitled to some assistance from the Mandatory, but instead of smoothing over our difficulties it made them infinitely worse."

Every denigrating reference to the workers he threw back into its author's teeth: "Let me inform you gentlemen that Zionism has no content if you do not constantly bear in mind the building of a Jewish state. And such a state is only possible on the basis of a maximum number of *workers*"—he hissed the word meaningfully—"and if you cannot comprehend that, woe to your Zionism!"

Of Weizmann (who was not present during his speech): "He has meekly accepted all the restrictions imposed upon us." He attacked the leadership in general, for its lack of political insight: "Recently, a Labour government was in office in England. You made no note of this most significant event. One day such a government will be in power, not merely in office. They, the British workers, understand the workers' movement in Palestine"—how wrong he was destined to be!—"and the workers' movement is growing in the East. We must find a way to the heart of the Arab people, and not through any empty words and platitudes you might utter!"

The speech was of course received with hostility, and subjected to repeated interruptions. He was frequently called to order by the chairman. What was the man talking about? delegates testily asked each other, with his Jewish state, his awakening of the East. Did he not know of their woeful shortage of funds, of the plans which had been dropped for lack of suitable technicians? Was he not aware that some colonies, after prodigalities of equipment had literally sunk into the marshlands round the bay of Haifa, were now being dissolved?

In this atmosphere of bickering and doubt the Congress dispersed.

* The exclusion of Transjordan from Jewish colonisation was advised by Samuel to Winston Churchill, then Colonial Secretary, who embodied the proposal in his 1922 White Paper.

Ben-Gurion, with Ben-Zvi and Arlosoroff, went to London to strengthen the links with the workers from whom they hoped so much. In their absence the situation went from bad to worse. Solel Boneh was pressing the Executive to give it a monopoly of all Jewish 'national' work—an impudent attempt to pull itself out of its growing insolvency. Disorders occurred, not between Arabs and Jews, but among the Jews themselves, and always because workers went on strike, or because employers insisted on carrying on business despite the strikers. Whoever worked on government contracts had to be satisfied with wages of less than £5 per month, whether he was a Jewish or Arab Palestinian or whether he came from Egypt or the Hauran, as was sometimes the case.

Yet none of these troubles deterred the flow of newcomers. In fact, during the years 1924–26 there was a steep rise in immigration, which increased the Jewish population by no less than 60,000. For, in 1924, America closed her doors to immigrants, or all but closed them, and Palestine became the major outlet for the Jews struggling to leave Poland, where the recent collapse of the currency had added considerably to the rigours of their existence. It was unfortunate that just when the slender strength of the *Yishuv* would have found the best of human material difficult to absorb, few of the newcomers were prepared for the conditions they had to face as they disembarked at Jaffa. Mostly they came without any money, at a time when Zionism was urgently seeking it from any source. Of those in possession of capital, no small proportion were fleeced by unscrupulous speculators during the journey south-east. Ben-Gurion went over to Poland in 1925 to try to put some order into the movement of escape. He found ominous symptoms of political extremism among the Polish Jews, and he saw the danger of their coming into the country just as the *Histadruth* was beginning to lose its grip. And in the middle of all these troubles the Zionist steam-roller of immigration, education, housing, draining, afforestation, threatened to come to a dead halt, while the treasurers scraped the barrel and threw up their empty hands in despair.

In Ben-Gurion's opinion the *Histadruth* must now eradicate its one vital weakness if it was to retain its supremacy in the country and canalise the flow of new men and women to basic industries. It must become a more compact political force. The subdivision of the confederation into the parties of *Achdut Avoda* and *Hapoel Hatzair* must be abolished once and for all. This was a reasonable proposal. The country was in the process of such rapid transformation that the policies formulated in previous decades were hopelessly out of date. It had once been accepted that an immigrant worker was instinctively on the side of socialism, multi-form as the creed was. Now the worker could just as easily be a follower of Jabotinsky, anti-trade unionist, with an open mind as to how he earned his bread, or what language he spoke. Some were strictly Orthodox Jews, of the Mizrachi party—and their record did not augur well for the future supremacy of Jewish labour.

Since the return of his wife and children from their stay in Plonsk, the Ben-Gurions lived in a small house in Tel-Aviv's Pinsker Street, and the moment he got back there from London, he began to plan the complete fusion of all political factions within the *Histadruth*. To pull off such a move he required the support of one man above all others—Berl Katznelson, editor of the *Histadruth*'s daily, *Davar*. The two worked together in complete harmony.

The situation was as follows: while the two major left-wing parties could operate as one in the fields of trade unionism and social welfare, they were cancelling each other out politically. Their rival manifestos confused newcomers, who thus became easy prey to the extreme politicians of the urban right-wing. Unless the workers acted in unison the *Histadruth* would experience difficulty in countering their inducements or the appeal made to the nation by Moshe Smilanski, veteran leader of the farmers, who advocated an attractive scheme of bringing a quota of Arab workers into every factory and farm unit, to assuage their neighbours' animosity. In the eyes of Ben-Gurion and Katznelson this could only have the effect of grafting an Achilles heel on to the Jewish body politic. In the sphere of reconstruction Labour's prestige was high, but its political role was disputed and disparaged. Unless there was complete fusion the weakness would infect the fabric of the *Histadruth*, and they would have to retreat before the advance of a capitalist economy.

As though to prove their thesis, which Katznelson laid down in a series of articles, a malaise began to attack Zionism at its roots from Dan to Beersheba. In the absence of capital to keep up the pace of development, almost all building ceased in Tel-Aviv and Haifa, so that thousands became unemployed. Solel Boneh, which had so proudly laid its claim to responsibility for all public works, crashed, and shamefacedly ended its existence in bankruptcy. (Though it was resurrected a few years later.) A typhoid epidemic added to the Jews' troubles. In the settlements, many of which were still little more than isolated tented encampments, the children were going hungry. Large numbers decided to put Zionism, socialism, the Hebrew language, the Arabs, behind them, to end the nightmare and find homes elsewhere. Palestine was an easier place from which to emigrate than Poland. To an audience in Tel-Aviv of 5,000, that included 2,000 unemployed, Weizmann confessed that immigration had to be slowed down and that a policy of retrenchment must be firmly begun.

Under such conditions, Katznelson wrote, their labour confederation could not hope to survive the conflicts and rivalries within it. Delving into the ideologies which separated them, he found that *Achdut Avoda* differed so slightly from *Hapoel Hatzair* as to make their continued estrangement ludicrous. This truth was however only apparent to complete outsiders or to those like Katznelson, who set unity above all else. For most of those involved, the differences were intensely personal, not restricted to the debating chamber, but carried over into their daily existences. They conditioned the individual's general attitude to life. *Achdut Avoda*'s energies lay in the *kibbutzim,* in 'pure' socialism as an international concept, in the thrusting of the collective idea into all facets of the economy. *Hapoel Hatzair* members were so terrified of the importation of Diaspora characteristics that, they maintained, until the Jewish people were metamorphosed by their own manual labour Zionism could not attain full realisation. Therefore, they would not even allow their farms to be defiled by excessive mechanisation, and in their doctrine of the simple life of the East they were as incorruptible as Robespierre.

Arlosoroff was furious at Katznelson's articles. For his part Sprinzak considered that dragging the *Histadruth*'s internal difficulties into specifically political debates was a ruse to force him and Arlosoroff into opposition to the wider Zionist leadership. Both distrusted Ben-Gurion and feared the looming, aggressive figure behind him of Isaac Tabenkin, with a chain of *kibbutzim* under his thumb, which could hold the *Histadruth* to ransom. Sprinzak, as principal labour officer on the Zionist Executive, was working on a comprehensive scheme of public works to absorb the unemployed, a scheme to which Lord Plumer, Samuel's successor as High Commissioner, was prepared to contribute government resources. Sprinzak had no wish to prejudice the *Histadruth* position further just as he was patiently coaxing it back to popularity.

But once the word unity was flung as their panacea to the workers queueing at the Zionist offices for their five-shillings-a-week dole, the decision was out of Sprinzak's and Arlosoroff's hands. The two parties translated their passionate respect for democracy into literal terms and each conducted a referendum on the issue. In both cases a majority voted for fusion. In Palestine many things worked fast, but not political negotiation. It was decided to leave discussion of the subject until December, 1926. But in that month 40 per cent of all Jewish workers were idle, and the matter was put off to await an improvement in the economic situation. This however obstinately refused to materialise, and in July the following year the union leaders decided they could no longer postpone meeting the local representatives.

This *Histadruth* conference lasted for no less than seventeen days, and worked itself up to a great emotional climax. Other items on the agenda (one of which, the establishment of a Palestine Workers' League, envisaging an organisation for the Arabs similar to the *Histadruth*, and which revealed a certain anxiety about impending racial strife) were despatched with relative speed. Not so the question of union. Katznelson hammered out his differences with Sprinzak and Aharonowitz. Shlomo Zemach, now back in the country and one of its foremost agriculturists, also took part as a senior comrade of *Hapoel Hatzair*. One evening Ben-Gurion left the conference-table complaining of a headache, and went home to bed. At five the next morning Pinsker Street suddenly filled with noise. Joseph Sprinzak, at the head of a trooping procession, was making for Ben-Gurion's house. He went in, awakened Ben-Gurion, told him they had argued all night and were settled on a formula. The other, deeply moved, got up and arm-in-arm the two leaders appeared on the balcony to acknowledge the cheering crowd below. (In those days Tel-Aviv lived its own intimate suburban life, doors were kept unlocked and everyone knew everyone else. Therefore no police interfered, no sleepy neighbours protested.) Down below they could see Arlosoroff dancing a *hora* with other, more staid, delegates. They were united, in spirit at least. The complete dissolution of the separate existences of the two parties was to take another three years.

Those three intervening years cannot be brushed aside in a sentence. Students of the Palestine problem see them as the preliminary drum-beat in a war which was fought to its bitter conclusion exactly twenty years later. They were the years which separated British, Jews and Arabs in Palestine into three distinct elements, and the triangle could have hardened into an eternal stalemate had not one element later abdicated from the conflict to leave the other two to fight for the prize.

In that period Ben-Gurion's thinking was steered into a new direction—towards the path of Jewish independence; and where previously this idea was no more than a useful emotional fillip for mass-meetings and pious resolutions in committee, it now became his goal, rarely expressed but never forgotten. Hitherto only Jabotinsky—and he was repudiated by most Zionists participating at the Congress—was prepared to use the concept of an *Endziel*, but he had debased it by bandying it about. Jabotinsky talked a fascinating line in impracticabilities at Jews and Italians, even at Englishmen, in fact to whomever would listen to him—not in Palestine, because the authorities banished him from the country—but in Warsaw, Geneva, Rome, New York, Johannesburg. No Jew in full possession of the facts believed such talk could produce anything but mischief when but 160,000 of them lived in a country whose entire population was a million, and when more Jews were going out than were coming in (as was the case in 1927).

Now another Jew dreamed of statehood—and planned for it. In those three years which separated two epochs Ben-Gurion came to the conclusion that the Arab *effendi* were bent upon the destruction of the Jewish experiment, and that the British no longer played the role of catalyst to Zionism but had become simply an encumbrance. The Jews must reinforce their ownership over what they had created with economic and political achievements too powerful to be denied.

In 1927 the bankrupt state of Zionism's exchequer compelled Congress provisionally to scrap the representation of political parties on the Palestine Executive of the movement. They were replaced in Jerusalem by three non-party officers, Kisch, Weizmann's other self whose back-breaking job was to represent Zionist interests to the Mandatory and smooth out inter-party conflicts; Henrietta Szold, a modern American Florence Nightingale, in charge of welfare and education; and Harry Sacher, an English lawyer in practice in Jerusalem. The triumvirate took over the small Jaffa Road offices, from which the scheming partisans were swept clean. They found the teachers on strike for non-receipt of pay, an overdraft of £300,000 in the bank, squatters on Jewish National Fund land and the Mufti inscrutably observing the mess from behind the Old City walls. Sacher's simple remedy for bringing the *Yishuv* back to solvency was to jut out his long chin at every request for money and make the monosyllabic reply, "Ain." (There isn't any.) This merely exasperated Ben-Gurion, who had no feeling for the hard rules of finance. He expected settlement to go on as before, road-building and colonisation being for him a Zionist task that went beyond the semi-serious occupation of ledger-balancing. The colonies were still hampered by primitive communications, while even throughout whole areas of Tel-Aviv a walk meant wading foot-deep in sand.

Then Lord Plumer, a firm hand at restraining Arab extremism, returned home. He was succeeded by Sir John Chancellor, a just and impartial administrator. But 1928 and 1929 were not days for impartiality. If at any time Britain should have offered some evidence that she was in fact the League of Nations trustee in Palestine, whose mission was to 'facilitate a national home' in that country, as stated in the Declaration embodied in the Peace Treaties, this was the moment. The Mufti of Jerusalem's patience in withholding a concerted onslaught upon the Jews until they reached supreme vulnerability was now amply rewarded. For in 1928 the correct ingredients of politics, religion, and prejudice all contributed to an incident at the Western Wall (the so-called 'Wailing Wall' in the Old City of Jerusalem) and produced a situation that was volcanic.

Tension had mounted as the Arab leader, whose office was that of a high Moslem cleric, warned his people that the Jews proposed taking possession of the Mosque of Omar to rebuild the Temple there. It was a fantastic lie, refuted many times by the Jews, but it did its work. Noisy demonstrations and counter-demonstrations were organised, and the Jews' misgivings grew at the refusal of the police to increase security measures. By July, 1929, it was apparent to everyone in the country, except the stolidly impartial British, that a storm was about to break. Kisch and his two colleagues had another Congress to attend, and Ben-Zvi was left to look after matters in their absence. Information reached him that murder-squads were on the point of entering the Jewish quarters of the city. Ben-Zvi sent an urgent message to Kisch, who thereupon rushed to London to seek high-level intervention by the Colonial Office and so alert the local authorities and provide arms for the Jews. No heed was taken of the warning.

On August 23rd gangs of young Arabs entered Jerusalem and, with knives and clubs, indulged for two hours in killing and pillaging to their hearts' content before the police fired and dispersed them. The pogrom was simultaneously re-enacted in Hebron, and a month after spread to Haifa and Safed. One hundred and forty Jews died in all, many more were injured. Only then were troops brought in and this time Arab blood was spilled. The Jews who died belonged mostly to the old Orthodox sector of the community which had lived for centuries in peaceful neighbourliness with Arabs in the holy cities.

A Commission of Enquiry led by Sir Walter Shaw established the unprovoked nature of the attacks, and reported that neither the Mufti nor other Arab leaders had made any effort to restrain their people. But the Commission volunteered a further opinion, and it was this which was given most prominence in the British Press and the weightiest consideration by the government. It found that the deep-seated reason for the disorders lay in the Arabs' disappointment in their political and national aspirations, and their fear for their economic future. This was the first move in what now emerged as Britain's plan to halt Zionism at this point of its development.

Move number two was the officially endorsed opinion of Sir John Hope Simpson that there was no room for further agricultural development in the country, since Jewish colonisation so far had resulted in the dispossession of large numbers of Arabs. Ramsay MacDonald's government then issued a statement of policy (the Passfield White Paper) in which it accepted Sir John's advice and announced its intention of temporarily suspending immigration of workers without capital, while land-purchase for further Zionist development would not be permitted during the continuance of the crisis. This was move number three.

The policy of the Labour government (Ben-Gurion had said 'the

British workers will understand what we are doing'!) may have been well-intentioned. To the Jews, to the Permanent Mandates Commission in Geneva, and to many British figures, including Stanley Baldwin, Austen Chamberlain, Lord Hailsham, Winston Churchill and the Archbishop of Canterbury, it appeared as a lamentable yielding to force. Chaim Weizmann resigned from the presidency of the Zionist Organisation and General Smuts wired his perturbation from Cape Town in protest. "The Balfour Declaration," he said, "represents a debt of honour which must be discharged in full and in all circumstances."

Ben-Gurion took the extreme view. He decided that Britain would, if she could, freeze the Jews into the status of a permanently-small minority and find an excuse (probably after the next Arab outburst) to block any further immigration. If this was how the British Labour Party treated Zionism's proud socialist experiment, what could the Jews expect from the Tories? He therefore eased up on his trade union work and became a politician. With Remez, Katznelson and Tabenkin, he went to *Hapoel Hatzair* and laid before its leaders the official public unification of the two parties into one large, dominating Labour Party. No one was now in the mood for procrastination, and at a great conference in Tel-Aviv, with Remez presiding, the marriage was legalised. They called the new association *Mapai*.★

Unobserved by Harry Sacher and Kisch, Ben-Gurion was carefully putting his principle of national strength through working-class unity and power into operation. He worked out a plan with his colleagues Sprinzak and Kaplansky (now relieved, to their regret, of day-to-day work on the Zionist Executive) for the equitable distribution of the employment available. This meant travelling the country, persuading workers to accept two days' work each week rather than a few having it all, leaving the rest totally unemployed. To the workers' credit they accepted the proposal, until the general situation improved. Golomb and Tabenkin took upon themselves the brushing-up of military training in the settlements, and distributed arms among the defence squads in anticipation of further trouble.

Attempts to organise the Arabs, through the medium of the Palestine Workers' League, were not proving too successful, though

★ In full, *Mifleget Poalei Eretz Israel*—the Workers Party of Israel.

8

in Haifa the local Jewish labour leader, Abba Hushi, who had a special talent for dealing with the Arabs, was able to exert his personal influence upon them and relations were harmonious. Ben-Gurion now devoted a great deal of thought to the Jewish-Arab problem. Could they live together? Could the Arab's standard of living be raised to equal that of the Jew? And if so, would they have to surrender their principle of exclusive Jewish labour, now so strongly under fire? Perhaps a bargain could be struck between the two peoples, on the basis of live and let live in separately-defined areas? He sketched out a scheme to Berl Katznelson for autonomous islands of Jewish and Arab settlement, all united under a cantonised federation. Katznelson did not like it. Like so many Palestinians, he felt it was to the Jews' tactical advantage not to press for definitions, but to postpone being trapped into a formulation of their maximum aims. The strength of the phrase 'Jewish National Home in Palestine' was that it could cover everything or nothing. But Ben-Gurion hesitated to discard his vague plan. They would not be under the domination of foreign masters for ever.

The outcry against the Passfield White Paper forced MacDonald's hand. He agreed to a debate in the House of Commons. Dov Hos, Golomb's brother-in-law, was at that time in London, where he had some good friends in the trade union movement. He went to one of these, a West Countryman controlling a powerful group of workers within the Labour Party.

Hos talked to him of events in Palestine. "Your government is impeding our work," he said. "It has not been seriously restraining Arab extremism and now it wants to prevent us Jews from bringing people in and buying more land." The subject was new to the trade union leader and he wanted to learn more. Dov Hos told him.

"Well," he said, when the Palestinian had finished, "my union has a dozen members in the House. If MacDonald doesn't do something about it I'll tell the boys to vote against him on this." The union was the Transport and General Workers, the man Ernest Bevin. It all helped to produce, in 1931, in a celebrated letter to Weizmann, a partial retraction by MacDonald of the Passfield policy. Labour had spoken to labour, and for once they had understood each other.

Time cured the financial crisis. A number of prominent non-Zionist Jews, mostly American and British, found a way of co-operating in the work of colonising Palestine through the creation of a so-called Jewish Agency, adumbrated years before in the wording of the Mandate but hitherto frustrated through the inability of the Americans to accept certain of Weizmann's ideas. The little Palestine Executive disbanded and local men took over on the old party basis. Arlosoroff succeeded Kisch as political secretary, with Shertok (another of Golomb's brothers-in-law) to help him. Jabotinsky formed a strong party to fight the enlarged Jewish Agency, *Mapai*, the *Histadruth* and the exclusion of Transjordan from the National Home policy. A new period began, and strangers to their movement now raised an influential voice in the councils of Zionism.

Ben-Gurion had not opposed intervention of this new element, for it commanded fresh sources of wealth which would be translated into more villages, more industries, more people. Nevertheless, he did not let the occasion go by without a hint: "It is the worker in the Land of Israel who will be responsible for Zionist enterprise, and he is therefore the guide and leader of the movement. Zionism will be achieved when the workers, and all their economic and agricultural settlement undertakings, are accepted in this principal role. We shall not surrender one unfulfilled Zionist idea. But despite the events of the past two years, we shall be party to no policy of revenge or counter-disturbance. We are returning to our land to rebuild our future with our own strength; it will not be done at the expense of our Arab neighbours."

Mapai became the political piston-rod of the workers' economic machine. With its bank, sick-fund, school-system, transport co-operative, collective farms, semi-collective villages, labour exchanges and theatre, *Histadruth* spread its tentacles across the country, from the Jordan to the Mediterranean. Its headquarters were in Tel-Aviv's Allenby Road, in a blunt, grey block named in memory of Joseph Brenner. The nest of offices was a land-mark in the sprawling city. The upper stories were occupied by the politicians and the managerial staff of this new brand of syndicalism. In the basement, labour teams, operating in small mobile groups each with its own foreman, came to be assigned their day's work. In the early thirties prosperity conferred respectability upon those above-stairs, but down below snobbery of another sort prevailed. "We are the real workers," they insisted, "with no time for idle talk." Instead they shouted and swore in the Slav profanities of their youth, living hard on the edge of a boom city that was haphazard yet intimate, law-abiding though quarrelsome, and dazzling white in its unseasoned stucco.

The strands of power in the hands of the forty-four year old general secretary were many. He was laconic in committee, verbose and a craftsman of impressive rhetoric on the platform. Like Citrine in England, Ben-Gurion made his the key office of the movement, and only the guardianship over his privacy exercised by his wife Paula kept him robust when the health of others flagged under the double strain of nervous tension and a sub-tropical climate. In his leisure he read widely and indiscriminately, though his favourite subject of study was the nature of Palestine in Biblical times and its wars and conquerors. While Sprinzak and Remez and Arlosoroff concentrated on selective tasks which secluded them from contact with the masses, Ben-Gurion was as often below stairs in Brenner House as he was on the top floor. He was better known to the Arabs than to the Mandatory officials. He was rarely called upon to school himself to the social restraints of cocktail-parties at Government House, or, indeed, to handle business in association with the respectable English gentlemen responsible for Zionist policy in London.

The country was too young, and its gregarious tendencies too strong, for all differences within the left-wing to be dissolved by the formation of *Mapai*. The communal villages made life easier for themselves by grouping into loose associations, and as the settlements throve (at considerable cost to the overall Zionist exchequer) they became more selective in their choice of recruits. Of the three settlement groups that emerged, by far the strongest was that led by Tabenkin and his commune of Ein Harod, a proud village which had sprung out of the old marshes of the Vale of Jezreel. Ein Harod was the keystone of *Kibbutz Hameuchad* (United Kibbutz). Its members acted as a body and during the thirties it was only natural that the *Histadruth* should concede to them the central role in the organisation of a defence network, already known by its name of *Haganah*. Under Tabenkin they shunned the corruption of the towns and looked with distaste upon the luke-warm socialism of the labour aristocracy ruling from the top floor of Brenner House.

Belonging to a commune required genuine pioneer mettle, but in return there was the exaltation of participation in a new pattern of society. Agricultural workers unable to measure up to the test grew lonely and dispirited. They drifted to the towns to live among the unskilled, underpaid workers crowding the bachelor hostels of Tel-Aviv and Haifa. The farmers were handicapped by a shortage of labour, but whenever they sought to employ Arabs to save their plantations from ruin, the massed power of the *Histadruth* was turned on them. Jabotinsky's followers alone undertook to break the vicious circle, and brought into existence a tacit alliance between the right-wing General Zionists and the political extremists and activism of what later became the *Irgun Zvai Leumi*.

Ben-Gurion was fascinated by Jabotinsky. There was much to unite the two men—a common streak of mysticism, a common disillusionment with Britain. Ben-Gurion respected the sense of discipline inherent in the Revisionists, misdirected as he considered them to be. Most important, Jabotinsky drew a strong following from the East-European masses, the people whom the Labour leader considered as his own source of strength.

Jabotinsky was a poet, a politician who also made foreign literature available in Hebrew. Ben-Gurion thought of him as the Zionist Trotsky, but with greater opportunities for menacing the central structure than existed in the communist world. Jewish corporate life aspires to be so passionately democratic that mere opposition within an organisation becomes an intolerable frustration. It is an old pastime to express one's dislike of one's rabbi by going off and building another synagogue. In 1931 Jabotinsky seemed on the point of doing just this, and with Weizmann's position weakened, his synagogue might, after another show of force from the Mufti, be the only one.

At that time Ben-Gurion had no ambition to lead the world Zionist machine; but he now feared for socialism in Palestine should Jabotinsky and his right-wing gain the upper hand. Weizmann, for all his shortcomings, was politically neutral, an ally of the *Histadruth* whose part in endowing the growing economy with a healthy Jewish base he would always defend. It was largely due to him that a lunatic feud did not break out—not between Arabs and Jews, or British and Jews, but between Palestinians and Zionists. As Jabotinsky's devotees grew, Ben-Gurion determined to make a bid for the poet's friendship and try to bring his following into the *Histadruth*. If there was one thing the Labour movement detested above all else it was the Revisionists, with their townee-orientation and their tendency to plan for the political master-stroke, which they confidently expected would give them ownership of Palestine the easy way. Unlike his colleagues, the taciturn Ben-Gurion was uncommitted. He was not prepared to abandon Jabotinsky as a lost soul when he could speak so passionately about the continuance of immigration.

Supporters of Dr. Weizmann had hailed the MacDonald Letter as nullifying the work of the Shaw Commission and the Passfield White Paper. In fact that communication incorporated important qualifications which indicated that the spirit prompting the Balfour Declaration fourteen years earlier was now dead. Weizmann had a way of charming British politicians by his prophetic bearing and scientific accomplishments into saying flattering things about Zionism; but a cooler examination of such statements would often reveal their hidden sting. Weizmann lived in London, not in Palestine, and the tempo of London Zionism was, at its best, far slower than the other. Simultaneously with his decision to woo Jabotinsky, Ben-Gurion concluded that the world leader (for though he had resigned from the organisation's presidency Weizmann was still effectively at the helm) was about to buy peace with Britain and perhaps toleration from the Arabs at the cost of foregoing the ultimate aspirations of the Jews of Palestine to attain a majority. This would of course be a repudiation of the logic of the movement, which had started as an effort to abolish the Jewish minority condition, not transfer it from one place to another.

Congress was due to be held again in Prague in 1933. It was time, the *Histadruth* general secretary told himself, to enter the larger arena, clear the old guard out and defeat the Revisionists before making a deal with them.

They were days of relentless factionalism in the Jewish world. Jabotinsky, having eight languages at his easy command, excited audiences of rich and poor with roseate pictures of the majesty of independence, and made their blood tingle with its urgency. His magic was that of the warrior-bard, exiled from the land he loved, suffering yet compassionate, gentle, and yet so dangerous that the powerful British government dared not let him reside in Palestine— he was the misunderstood, Byronic symbol of national regeneration. How well he weaved the spell! Then there was Chaim Weizmann, friend of statesmen, luncheon-guest of kings, vain, aloof, mysterious: let the heavens fall but he would speak his moderation, for his words were the words of a man in whose person the Jewish national idea had been so elevated as to receive veneration from friends and instil fear in enemies as a new manifestation of God's will, with a deep force almost beyond the understanding of mortals. Finally came the unschooled popular leader, difficult to know, awkward, earthy. He talked of Zionism in terms of Jewish craftsmen and Jewish policemen, roadworkers that were Jewish, children to whom any tongue but Hebrew was alien, the struggle against exploitation, the shame of hunger. It was the last year of freedom for a Europe at the crossroads, prey to wild political opportunists, and coveted by every diminutive Napoleon. When Ben-Gurion was sent by the *Histadruth* and *Mapai* to launch that electoral campaign, he had his last look at the world of his childhood.

It was the old battle-ground: Warsaw, Riga, Memel, Lodz, then west to Vienna, Berlin, Prague. To secure an absolute majority at the Congress he needed many more socialist delegates to add to the certain majority of left-wingers that would be returned by the Palestine electorate. He had to win those votes from Jabotinsky's party, which was making alarming headway in Poland. A storm-centre by any standard, the region was already within earshot of the Munich beer cellar.

Mass meetings took place in assembly halls, in the streets of the ghettoes; meetings to honour the memory of Herzl and Borochov, to voice defiance of Britain. He had study-sessions at Zionist training-farms, jamborees with the young, another look at Plonsk (though by now all his immediate family, including Avigdor, had followed him to Palestine). Every speech was taken up with warnings against the consequences of Revisionism, whose young supporters strutted in military formation along the suburbs of the ghetto towns, and whose associates heaved like battering-rams against the wall of organised labour in Palestine.

"I accuse Jabotinsky," he told a Lithuanian gathering, "because his methods will give us neither security nor statehood. He tries grandiose negotiation with heads of states. We do not believe diplomacy will help us, we believe in our own strength, and our own sacrifice, and ceaseless toil. Only thus can we defeat the dangers." He feared the appeal of Revisionism among a youth deprived of entry into the universities and the liberal professions, and barred from escape to the western world. "Zionism is not founded on enmity. Revisionism trains the young to an intolerant chauvinism saturated with racial hatred. It discredits and destroys the moral value of Zionism, spreading the impression in the world that we are the enemies of the Arab nation."

The Jewish masses took their suffrage earnestly. Ben-Gurion's message was of the emancipated Jew, newly-reared in the free life, and it seemed that he talked to them from outside the prison-walls, beckoning them to liberty. In the midst of it all Adolf Hitler came to power. Now not merely were the prison doors locked, but the cells were on fire. Hitler's arrival in power ended the legalistic debate on the contradictory interpretations of the Balfour Declaration. The Jews had to be saved. It would hurt the Arabs, it would unsettle Britain's attitude of 'we have done our best'. Their brethren in Palestine would take them if other countries would not. The existence of Hitler justified the use of any means to rescue the trapped people while there was still time, with or without immigration permits. From that moment the entire Jewish population of the world connived at breaking the man-made London laws governing Palestine.

Three-quarters of a million anxious people in almost every European country except the Soviet Union queued at the ballot boxes with their votes. Ben-Gurion went home. The word on everyone's lips was Hitler. The whole world then discovered the existence of a Jewish problem. Germany's Jews were an assimilated, proud community quite alien to Zionism except for some leading technicians mostly specialising in law or colonisation. Even now it was only with reluctance that they looked towards Jerusalem, and remained uninspired by the complex of ideologies carried over from east of the Vistula. Many of them nursed the pathetic hope that perhaps the dark clouds would pass. The Palestinians, who spoke and thought in terms of catastrophe, told them: "We shall do our best to get you out while we can." Chaim Arlosoroff was despatched to Berlin, to ascertain whether the Nazi policy of expulsion and the Zionist willingness to receive could not be fruitful of some grim alliance. If Germany would facilitate departure of her Jews Arlosoroff had no doubt Britain would open her heart and the gates of Palestine. It was a difficult and tense mission, but Arlosoroff knew Germany well. The Arabs watched and waited.

What he might have achieved will remain for ever a matter of conjecture. Arlosoroff returned to Tel-Aviv after the preliminary conversations and reported first to his colleagues, then to the British. One June evening he was walking along the beach with his wife. A man approached, asking for a light. As he fumbled for a match, a shot rang out. The next moment the young political secretary's wife stood there alone. Arlosoroff lay dead, killed at point-blank range.

The murder gave rise to the fiercest controversy in Zionism's history. There had rarely been a murder in the all-Jewish city before then, never a political assassination. Guilt centred around a certain Abraham Stavsky, a young Revisionist. He was convicted by a first court, though subsequently released on the grounds of insufficient evidence. The entire socialist movement, most British officials acquainted with the case, and many others had no doubt that Stavsky had been selected by the Revisionists as their agent to remove a powerful personality, only thirty-four years old, the nominee of Weizmann and a friend of High Commissioner Wauchope. They said Arlosoroff met his violent end because his sole 'crime' was —moderation.

The episode shed some light on the subcutaneous workings of Palestinian Jewish politics. Ben-Gurion was convinced of Stavsky's guilt, and said so soon after the murder occurred. The Revisionists made this hurried condemnation their justification for launching counter-charges against Ben-Gurion and his immediate confidants. The dead man's differences with Katznelson were shown up in sharp relief, and a vision of Katznelson as a public inquisitor, with Dov Hos and Golomb as the gangsters of the *Histadruth* executing his judgments, was conjured up.

Until then the atmosphere in which the Palestinians played out their politics was noisy but comparatively harmless. Wordy duels, a generous exchange of insults, these were the stock commodities of party strategists who never changed, merely grew older and angrier. Yet it was all rather parochial, and venom would melt in the quiet of a warm Sabbath eve when Judaism demanded politeness of all men. Violence to the point of killing was a shattering innovation. The air was rank as the lawyers exposed to an astounded people the sordid background of murder: Arlosoroff's amorous adventures; the accused and his associates plotting in musty one-room dives; suggestions of corruption in high places—it all shocked the ordinary Jew's conception of Zionism, that collective endeavour of the people towards a modern fulfilment of Biblical prophecy.

Stavsky was released, and forgotten. Arlosoroff was canonised by Labour, and Ben-Gurion led the annual pilgrimage to his grave. Then fifteen years later to the day, in the very same setting, actors representing the same forces relived the tragedy of 1933 against the background of the Arab-Jewish war, and Arlosoroff's ghost was there to witness Ben-Gurion, Prime Minister and executioner, send Stavsky to a watery grave.

An unwonted sobriety marked the proceedings of Congress as it assembled late in August, 1933. The count of votes gave the socialists almost half the 320 seats. Ben-Gurion's campaign had done its work, and the dominant role in Congress was played by the four *Mapai-Histadruth* leaders—Ben-Gurion, Katznelson, Shertok (it was already agreed he should succeed Arlosoroff to the political portfolio) and Eliezer Kaplan, of the former *Hapoel Hatzair* faction.

In the final reckoning Labour would have had a majority on the international Zionist Executive, but shrank from such responsibility. It would entail bargaining at the highest level with Britain, and their men were unsure of their capacity to compromise over immigration (always a matter of hard-fought compromise) and still keep their power with the Palestinian workers. Katznelson was the most unwilling of all. Ben-Gurion refused to take office without him. This left the two 'juniors', Shertok and Kaplan. They, on the other hand, were equally adamant about serving with the others or not at all. So Ben-Gurion was pressed on to the Executive with them, while Katznelson jubilantly rushed around announcing to all and sundry of the socialist bloc, "I got out of it, thank goodness!" Berl Locker, another socialist, served as the representative of left-wing Zionism in the Diaspora.

The jockeying for position on the Executive was a prolonged game of political hide-and-seek, and contrasted oddly with the serious issues involved. It contained those pretending they had no wish to serve, and excluded others nursing their wounded pride. Jabotinsky took his supporters into the wilderness; while the religious groups, at the bottom of the poll, were the most difficult of all to satisfy. Weizmann was responsible for the solitary act of statesmanship at the Congress. He took over the creation of a new department for the rescue of German Jewry. As for Ben-Gurion, he determined to work with the others for two years only, until the next Congress; and to devote his office to talking all parties round to the creation of a healthy, comprehensive coalition.

The time was ripe for Ben-Gurion to make his deal with Jabotinsky the warrior-bard. Ben-Gurion had no doubt that if Jabotinsky asked them, his followers in Palestine would sabotage the work of construction, march against the Arabs, even commit murder. He left Prague and made straight for London, where Jabotinsky was then living. It was a gamble, but he was ready to bargain away hallowed principles for a truce with Revisionism.

5
The Shadows Lengthen

Peace with Jabotinsky – Histadruth rejects agreement – Immigrants from Germany – Arab national awakening – Chairmanship of Jewish Agency – Talks with Arab leaders – Rebellion in Palestine – Peel Report – Zionists' divided reactions – Conflict with Britain – Partition scheme abandoned – White Paper

PARIS, THAT CITY of unemployed revolutionaries, was in the thirties the headquarters of the Revisionist wing of Zionism. This wing already considered itself the *Résistance* of Jewry, but in reality its membership in Western Europe was of such uncertain dimensions that for reinforcements it had to content itself with whatever Polish-Jewish students the Latin Quarter might harbour. Nevertheless, Revisionism had emissaries in Eastern Europe organising illegal immigration. Its supporters boycotted the official money-collecting machinery represented by organisations such as the Jewish National Fund, and at the same time refused to recognise the half-yearly schedules governing immigration.

The Revisionists gave unquestioned allegiance to Vladimir Jabotinsky, a one-time radical whose convictions had been dashed by the Russian Revolution. For them, he was Mussolini and Pilsudski combined; for others he continued in the strict Herzlian tradition of Jewish leadership, sure of the goal but approaching it by the wrong path. From time to time he issued written instructions in numbered circulars styled as military orders-of-the-day which were carried out to the letter by his following. The Order by which his people ignored the rules of immigration and brought Jews to Palestine (usually at high cost to the individual) was known as Circular 60.

The negotiations initiated by Ben-Gurion in London began through an intermediary, Pinchas Rutenberg, a Russian *émigré* who had been associated with Kerensky in 1917 and was known to Ben-Gurion since the war-time New York days. Later, he was to carry out an important electrification scheme in Palestine. Ben-Gurion had a sneaking affection for Jabotinsky, and after their first meeting sent him a letter couched in the most flattering terms. It was read with blushing pride by the Revisionist leader to his central committee gathered together in Paris.

Jabotinsky's ignorance of the internal situation in Palestine put him at a disadvantage in the talks. So he sent to Tel-Aviv for a consignment of *Histadruth* and *Mapai* publications, and one day Ben-Gurion found him poring closely over some socialist newspapers.

"Well," asked Ben-Gurion lightly, "have we found a new recruit?"

"Yes, if only you would change the name of your party from *Mapai* to *Mabai*," was the answer.★

Their discussions revealed a basic community of interests. Both agreed that the bringing in of the maximum number of Jews to Palestine within the minimum of time was paramount, despite British and Arab opposition. But Jabotinsky felt the Jewish leadership was too easily overawed by British politicians. "We have never threatened them," he said. "The British inevitably bow to strength." He had every belief that he alone was capable of standing up to the British, and showed no concern at his unpopularity among the Palestinian workers. It was the Jewish power dispersed in a dozen world capitals, not the weakness concentrated within the remote boundaries of Britain's orphan colony, that mattered.

By October, 1934, the two men reached agreement. To eliminate the fratricidal violence on the labour front they drew up a five-point 'treaty' embodying important concessions by both sides. It ensured an equitable distribution of work, the association of the Revisionists with the *Histadruth*, and the cessation of strike-breaking activities. The *Histadruth* undertook to conclude a series of collective pacts with employers and to introduce a system of compulsory arbitration. No strike would take place if 25 per cent of the workers opposed it. This gave the much smaller body of Revisionist workers the power to veto strike action. In return they would tear up 'Circular 60', accept their quota of immigration permits, and end the boycott of Zionist funds.

Ben-Gurion planned to return home to persuade his comrades on

★ The play on words referred to the difference between *Mifleget Poalei Eretz Israel* and *Mifleget Bonei Eretz Israel*—not Palestine Workers Party but Palestine Builders Party.

the *Histadruth* executive to accept the agreement—no easy task, as
he knew. But before he could get away from London details of his
pact with Jabotinsky leaked out, and a news agency retailed its
contents to the Palestine Press. It shocked almost the entire *Histadruth* membership. Even Ben-Gurion's closest associates judged it an
ill-timed, high-handed action in which they had got the worst of
the bargain.

It speaks a great deal for Ben-Gurion's authority in the socialist
movement and in the country that he was nearly able to convert this
hostile reception of his move into an endorsement of it. Only a
totally unexpected alliance of the right-wing group in *Mapai* with
the extreme left defeated him. Sprinzak and his old *Hapoel Hatzair*
backing had lost in Arlosoroff one of their very own, murdered, in
their view, by a Revisionist. Tabenkin and all who followed him in
the Jezreel and Jordan valley settlements aggressively repudiated the
right of any member of the party to vote its socialist conscience away,
and they said so in terms that left Ben-Gurion in no doubt of their
displeasure at his personal conduct. Yet he refused to give in without
a fight, and would not accept the humiliation of a retraction of the
agreement until the entire membership of the party had spoken. A
special conference was convened at Hadera (a half-way house, not
without its symbolism, between the northern communes and Tel-
Aviv) to thrash the subject out in all its implications. He found that
Tabenkin would, if need be, destroy the recently-won unity in
Labour before accepting the proposals; and the right-wingers
might well go along with him.

The conference was persuaded to conduct a party referendum.
By a considerable majority this rejected the agreement. "You have
sinned against the *Histadruth*," Ben-Gurion said angrily. But to the
average worker struggling with his conscience, the dead Arlosoroff
counted for more than the living Ben-Gurion. Nevertheless, large
numbers, hating the 'strike clause' though they did, voted for the
pact.

Informing Jabotinsky that the whole thing was off, Ben-Gurion
explained uncomfortably that "the opposition was largely psychological." He emphasised the anxiety of *Mapai* to put an end to
clashes between the workers, and in fact there was a short and
blissful period of tranquillity in the large towns. Doubtless both men
had been guilty of a grievous error of psychology. The workers

were shrewd enough to repudiate a contract, disguised as a move to create workers' solidarity, which was in essence a political bargain with an embarrassing rebel.

Jilted, Jabotinsky was now confirmed in his view that Zionist nationalism and socialism were incompatible. His high hopes of returning to official Zionist councils without losing face were thwarted. Now he set about creating his own completely separate Zionist organisation. On his side Ben-Gurion had sown deep the seeds of suspicion against himself, with Tabenkin convinced that he was for ever plotting some dark design behind their backs.

In a more normal political situation Ben-Gurion would have had to face the implications of the referendum. He would have been compelled to resign his office in the *Histadruth*, and therefore his seat on the Jewish Agency Executive: men have been known to end their careers on the outcome of such an issue. Strangely enough, Ben-Gurion was stronger after the vote than before. He returned to Congress again in 1935 and to an Executive which, for the first time, was able to bury personal differences and create a broad coalition; though the Revisionists, having committed political *hara-kiri*, were hardly heard of again except in the ghoulish form of terrorism in Palestine. Far from being out of the international Jewish picture, as he himself had claimed as his desire two years earlier, Ben-Gurion was now chairman of the Executive. This made him the practical leader of the movement, the first and only Palestinian Jew to be given charge of the pace and direction of Zionist affairs.

Weizmann's presence assured the continuity of Zionism's relationship with Britain, at least in appearance. At the Lucerne Congress of September, 1935, Weizmann warned them not to discard their association with London lightly. "We do not have too many friends," he said in his presidential statement, "and the British government is the only one that has enabled us to develop Palestine." But below the surface a new set of forces was at work. A new Palestine was growing, a new world situation was coming into its own. The unquestioned hegemony of Britain in the Near East ceased to be accepted by other European powers; and the Arab world, like a great and unpredictable monster of the prehistoric age, having slept for five centuries, now showed evidence of life as it shook itself into wakefulness.

The immigration of Jews in the year 1933 proved, to their own satisfaction at least, that the Zionists were justified in regarding Palestine as the one country able to solve the problem of Jewry's unwantedness. Over 30,000 of them came, among them men and women not disgorged from the choking Polish ghettoes, but gifted scientists and technicians, frequently with their own means, and bringing also the industrial processes which had earned them European reputations. The next year there were 42,000, and the land of sleepy villages, isolated farm communes, and long un-inhabited tracts of desert resounded with a new activity and a wild confidence. By 1935 the large-scale German evacuation was really under way. In that year 62,000 Jews came to Palestine. At this rate the Jewish community would be converted into a majority within ten years. The stream carried with it artists, musi-cians, intellectuals of the highest rank, shipbuilders, bank-managers, many of them ready to discard city life and, in an orgy of atonement, to take up spades and pneumatic drills and fill the gaps between the Jewish homesteads and what they looked upon as the Arab world of yesterday—but which was in fact a world making its own plans to meet tomorrow.

The Arabs knew they were nearing the moment of decision. Well might the Mandate speak of safeguarding their rights, but soon they would be transformed into the minority race, and then their rights would not be in the safe-keeping of Britain, or of the League of Nations, but of the Jews. Fifteen years before, when the first pioneers humbly walked into Jaffa with little capital but their dreams, the Arabs were an inarticulate and long-ignored particle of world society, traditionally represented, if that is the word, by the rival family groups of Husseini (to which the Mufti belonged) and Nashashibi.

In 1931, a Moslem congress, consisting of delegates from all parts of the Arab world, was staged in Jerusalem; and the Mufti put him-self forward as the guardian of Islam's interests at the most advanced point of European infiltration. The following year the first Palestine Arab political party, *Istiklal* (Independence), was formed, proclaim-ing a struggle for the national freedom of their people. Clearly, at a time of great Zionist economic and political thrust, the Palestine Arab was learning to speak and act in national terms. As a result of ten years of conscientious British educational improvements and of co-existence with the Jews from whom they were quick to learn, and because of the inevitability of progress anyway, something approaching a public opinion was being created and consistent lines of political conduct were being formulated. What further unsettled them was the knowledge that over the border their lesser-educated brothers in Syria, the Lebanon and Egypt were successfully pressing their reluctant European masters into conceding them self-governing institutions. Further south a calculated piece of international robbery was coldly being enacted as Mussolini's legions closed in on Addis Ababa. The Arabs discovered that they were living in an angry world. Hitherto they had been despised and ignored. Perhaps deservedly so. Now it was time to strike back.

The consequences of the situation escaped neither General Wauchope, the High Commissioner, nor the Jewish Agency, which by now had achieved a comprehensive intelligence service throughout the Arab world. At the 1935 Zionist Congress Ben-Gurion was advancing the need, and proclaiming the right, to bring a million Jews into the country. In his mind he was already emptying the entire European continent of his people. The Arabs clamoured in their newspapers and in the mosque for the complete stoppage of the 'foreign invasion' and for immediate self-government. Wauchope was not in any case a strong administrator, and he succumbed to flattery from both Jews and Arabs. He was driven hopelessly into a corner by their irreconcilable ambitions. He spoke politely with the Arabs, knowing that behind his back they were preparing to take the law into their own hands to keep the Jews out; he conducted an airy debate with the Zionists on the economics of population absorption, on whether it was a static or a dynamic factor, but of course it was an open secret that whatever he said they would continue to smuggle in their people, with or without permission.

Sir Arthur Wauchope proposed the establishment of a Legislative Council, a stop-gap measure towards self-government, in the hope of avoiding the impending collision. Of all the leading actors in this struggle only one—Chaim Weizmann—had a kind word to say for the proposal. He had a genuine admiration for the High Commissioner and although the composition of the Council would have given the Arabs the louder voice, he felt that the continuance of immigration as a responsibility of the British government would ensure the safeguarding of Jewish interests, while at the same time

9

close day-to-day collaboration of Jew and Arab might teach them mutual toleration.

Ben-Gurion would not be forced into any implied admission that the Jews would accept minority status. He insisted upon a categoric rejection of the scheme, and he won the day. For he wanted the field clear while he worked at another of his master-strokes: he was engaged in direct talks with the Arabs, and believed he could reach agreement with them before the brewing revolt burst into the open.

The *Histadruth* was carrying on as best it could with its policy of conditional co-operation with the Arabs in the economic and trade union spheres. But the information reaching the Jewish Agency from its sources in the Arab journalistic world, from men such as Abba Hushi and David Hacohen in Haifa, from Ben-Zvi in Jerusalem, and from those pre-war settlers still held in affectionate esteem by their Arab neighbours, made Ben-Gurion pessimistic of the results. Real understanding, he saw, could only be based upon political co-operation. He needed to secure a hearing from the people with personal influence with the Mufti of Jerusalem. And bearing in mind that the one characteristic shared by Jews and Arabs was resentment against Britain, he began discussions with Musa Alami, once Attorney-General of Palestine, a man of European education, high integrity and social conscience.

Alami was connected by family ties with the Mufti, and it was with the latter's cognizance that he met Ben-Gurion on a number of occasions in Jerusalem. As a mark of his own goodwill, Ben-Gurion brought to the meetings the head of the Hebrew University, Dr. Judah Magnes. Ben-Gurion heartily despised Magnes, because around him at the University he had collected a group prepared to co-operate with the Arabs on the basis of neither side insisting upon national autonomy—a hypothesis rejected by all other Zionists as an unrealisable dream and a trick to force them to surrender in advance their right to control immigration. There was one condition attaching to the participation of Magnes in the talks: he was not to speak at all. In fact he sat as silent as the Sphinx during all the negotiations conducted by Ben-Gurion with the Arabs.

As a substantial landowner, Musa Alami was impressed by the achievement of the Jewish National Fund in its soil-reclamation schemes. The one gleam of hope in the discussions was his recognition of the benefits bestowed on the country as a whole by the importation of Jewish capital and skill.

Ben-Gurion told him at the outset that agreement must be on the basis of an independent Jewish state—nothing less. He conceded the importance of winning Arab consent for the creation of such a state, and by a Jewish state he meant full citizenship and opportunities for every Arab in the country, with all that this held out for the native population as twentieth-century technology was brought to the service of fertilising Palestine's arid spaces.

Musa Alami agreed to take the plan back to the Mufti. His strongest objection to it was that it involved dealing with a people who did not regard the population of Palestine in static terms. It was not an agreement with 400,000 Jews, it was an agreement with millions of Jews in the outer world, all of whom were, according to the Zionist doctrine, potential citizens of Palestine. Nevertheless, he appeared anxious to work around to some compromise, and returned to Ben-Gurion's home again and again, even in 1936 when the atmosphere was thick with hostility and Arabs suspected of dealing with the Jews were marked down for murder by their own people. He advised Ben-Gurion to go to Geneva and contact there a nationalist Palestine-Syrian committee. Ben-Gurion did so, and was scornfully told by its head, Adil Arslan: "You want us to agree to your becoming a majority? Even the British won't give you that!" So he departed empty-handed. Musa Alami begged him not to give up hope of reaching accord, but when the Arab committee in Geneva, contrary to a pledge of secrecy, published an account of their meeting with the Jews in their paper *La Nation Arabe*, he was too ashamed to meet Ben-Gurion again.

There were other schemes, and more talks. Ben-Gurion had an idea for a federation of Near-Eastern states in which Palestine, with a Jewish majority, would be part of a predominantly Arab unit of considerable extent and importance. The plan certainly was not without its attraction for several highly-placed Arabs in the nationalist movement, and had the tacit approval of the High Commissioner, General Wauchope. The Arabs shared a widespread but inflated conception of Jewish power and influence, and a few of them considered the offer of political and economic help from a Jewish government in Palestine in the creation of Arab unity over this great area as one not to be despised.

The scheme was seriously considered by three commanding personalities in the Arab world when Ben-Gurion laid it before them. They were George Antonius, a prominent Christian Arab, Auni bey Abdul Hadi, leader of the *Istiklal* party, and Riadh es Solh, a founder of the Syrian nationalist bloc, who subsequently became Prime Minister of the Lebanon. The latter met his death years later at the hand of an assassin in Amman, while he was on his way to formulate a plan with King Abdullah for peace with an independent Israel.

All three finally withheld whole-hearted support from the federation scheme. Because of its location, would not a Jewish Palestine form a wedge within the contemplated system of Arab states, and deprive them of their natural linch-pin? Would they not all be submerged economically by the Jewish element in the federation? Were not the Jews in close and indissoluble alliance with Britain, that powerful obstacle to their national development?

Yet even these were not insurmountable objections. Had their condition been desperate they might have overcome their misgivings. But on the contrary, with the darkening European situation, their hopes were on the rise again. The political dust raised by Hitler as his army marched into the Rhine provinces, France's internal difficulties and Mussolini's mounting truculence told them of the new era of force at hand, with the European Powers at loggerheads and the League of Nations a shattered ideal. They ceased to believe in the inevitability of Western control over their destiny. And, in a world which events taught them had come to respect violence alone, all those with whom Ben-Gurion spoke joined, willingingly or unwillingly, with the Mufti of Jerusalem. They pledged themselves to revolt, disaffection and boycott until they won, as Syrians and Egyptians and Iraqis were winning, their rights as an independent nation in Islam.

The rebellion began on a modest scale—a general strike, a few well-placed murders, passive resistance. In the Jewish colonies rifles were brought out for overhaul, and the unofficial defence forces made their preparations. Despite the arrival of military reinforcements from Egypt and Malta, July, 1936, witnessed a crippling scourge of sabotage. A division was sent from Britain. The toll of dead and wounded were counted first in hundreds, and then in thousands. Stanley Baldwin announced the despatch of a Royal

Commission of Enquiry to investigate on the spot. Only in November was it deemed safe to send its members out.

We need not concern ourselves here with a detailed examination of the enquiries of that Commission, led by Lord Peel, except to observe that they produced a cool and balanced appraisal of a problem surely among the thorniest to perplex the statesman's mind. Its summary of the Jewish case constitutes a noble document, enhanced by the humanity of its authors and the vivid style of its draftsman, Sir Reginald Coupland, while the evidence of Chaim Weizmann must be classed among the great pieces in the literature of Zionism. The Commission was held in suspicion by the Arabs, and at first the Mufti refused to testify. Yet despite the grave difficulties hampering its work, the Royal Commission penetrated deep into the Oriental mind to draw out and distil for the world's judgment—and perhaps for the first time—the tangle of emotional, psychological and political objections the Arabs held against the Jewish plan for Palestine, and translated it into a reasonable and formidable statement of their case.

While both parties sought to prove that the conflict between them was being exacerbated by Britain's vacillation, or heartlessness, or refusal to step in at one particular moment or to restrain passions at another, or to honour whatever pledges the heat of the World War had forced upon her, Lord Peel and his colleagues accurately diagnosed the problem as being rooted in the utterly incompatible aims of the two competing nationalisms, each faithfully convinced that time was working against it. The Report of the Commissioners stated (p. 371):

"An irrepressible conflict has arisen between two national communities within the narrow bounds of one small country. About 1,000,000 Arabs are in strife, open or latent, with some 400,000 Jews. There is no common ground between them. The Arab community is predominantly Asiatic in character, the Jewish community predominantly European. They differ in religion and in language. Their cultural and social life, their ways of thought and conduct, are as incompatible as their national aspirations. These last are the greatest bar to peace. Arabs and Jews might possibly learn to live and work together in Palestine if they would make a genuine effort to reconcile and combine their national ideals and so build up in time a joint or dual nationality. But this they cannot do. The War and its

sequel have inspired all Arabs with the hope of reviving in a free
and united Arab world the traditions of the Arab golden age. The
Jews similarly are inspired by their historic past. They mean to show
what the Jewish nation can achieve when restored to the land of its
birth. National assimilation between Arabs and Jews is thus ruled
out. In the Arab picture the Jews could only occupy the place they
occupied in Arab Egypt or Arab Spain. The Arabs would be as
much outside the Jewish picture as the Canaanites in the old land
of Israel. The National Home, as we have said before, cannot be half-
national. In these circumstances to maintain that Palestinian citizenship has any moral meaning is a mischievous pretence. Neither Arab
nor Jew has any sense of service to a single State."

In these circumstances, the Commission found that the Palestine
Mandate, entrusted by the principal Allied Powers to Britain at the
San Remo Conference of April, 1920, was in principle unworkable. It
therefore recommended the abandonment of the policy of the Jewish
National Home as laid down in the Balfour Declaration and the
restriction of immigration to not more than 12,000 Jews annually
pending the early partition of Palestine into two independent states.
Though there were important qualifications, the Jews were awarded
sovereignty over almost the whole of Galilee and the narrow
shorelands down to a point twenty miles south of Jaffa. The rest of
Western Palestine, about four-fifths of the whole, would, with the
exception of Jerusalem, Bethlehem and Nazareth (to be retained
with a corridor to the sea under British mandate), be joined to
Transjordan to form an Arab state. Finally, lest anyone be in doubt
as to the continued interest of the British government in Palestine,
it was to keep yet another finger in the pie by the bland sequestra-
tion of Haifa. This was the scheme in its rudiments, and the government announced immediate acceptance of the proposals.

Ben-Gurion read the 400-page document, then sat for two days
in the public galleries of the House of Commons and House of
Lords while it was debated. He has admitted to learning a great deal
about the British character through his experiences as a witness of
the speeches there. "At times it seemed as though I was attending a
Zionist Congress," he said. Immediately afterwards, he flew to
Zurich and delivered a four-hour analysis of both the Report and
the debate to the Labour Zionists gathering in that city for the
twentieth Congress. He was moved by the reasoning, the imagina-

tion and the sympathy shown by Britain's administrators, even when they were expressing views favouring the Arabs. Churchill's speech struck him as the words of a Zionist reluctant to face the prospect of a Jewish state; and by only one speaker, Lord Samuel, 'a Jew' as he pointed out, was he moved to anger. For the former High Commissioner was the only one who sought to persuade the Jews to curtail immigration and avoid the partition of the country. As to British public opinion in general, Ben-Gurion swept away the hopes of the London Zionists of one day converting Britain's leaders to their way of thinking with the statement: "You can do many things with Englishmen, but one thing you cannot do, you cannot change them into non-Englishmen. The Englishman does not see things through Jewish eyes, he does not feel with a Jewish heart, and he does not reason with a Jewish brain."

The Arabs rejected the Report at once, and under the direction of the Mufti, who was soon to escape, a fugitive from justice, to the Lebanon, the campaign of terror was intensified. It lasted almost without intermission up to the beginning of the War.

The Report had a curious effect upon the Jewish world. When Jewry first learned of the area in which it was expected to work out operations of rescue involving millions—its immediate reaction was universal dismay. But soon afterwards a few people began to consider this idea of a 'Jewish state' and turn it into the point of departure for a new attitude to their ideal, from which the enervating, double-fronted battle the movement was fighting with the British and the Arabs would be eradicated. Not many, however, adopted this view. The majority lacked the required faith to go out and confront their destiny only twenty years after the Balfour Declaration. Had there not after all been a fruitful expansion of the National Home in collaboration with Britain, the Power which, despite its shortcomings, they trusted above all others? The movement suddenly found itself at a crossroads without being able to decide which way to turn.

Although the Peel Report was not published until July, 1937, Weizmann and some others had known months earlier of a possible plan for partition. Indeed, he had had it from Coupland in the course of a private talk when the latter divulged a suggestion from Sir Stafford Cripps for a solution on some such lines. These few therefore had had time to get used to the idea. For them it was not a bombshell dropped from the skies. And in the crucial interval between the Report's publication and the convening of Congress, Weizmann and his immediate circle showed a willingness to make the plan a basis for negotiation.

Could Weizmann have committed the entire movement? This is problematical. At this stage only a voice representing the masses of the people in Palestine itself, the people who would have to live in the tiny state, suffer its claustrophobic restrictions, accept a Zionism without Zion, could be decisive. In the *Histadruth* the consensus of opinion was against ending the Mandate at this point, for, its members maintained, Britain must be forced to fulfil her obligations until the foundations of socialism were truly laid. Opposition was centred round the powerful intellects of Berl Katznelson and Isaac Tabenkin, the latter seeing the offer as a typical British hoax to dismember the country and keep the severed bits within its grasp.

Ben-Gurion ranged himself alongside Weizmann. He was emphatic. Once the Mandatory admitted it was unworkable, he charged, the Mandate as they knew it was dead anyhow. Let them then accept the offer of independence with all its implications, and prove that by hard work and skill the soil of the tiny state could yield a living for millions. He was not surprised by Tabenkin's attitude. He felt much more keenly Katznelson's refusal to accept his appraisal of the situation, for this was the only occasion the two were in public disagreement. But the time had passed when Ben-Gurion could be influenced by his friend, and he brushed all objections aside. "A Jewish State! They, the British, said it, not us! We are vindicated before the world." He was at the helm of 400,000 people with rights to independent statehood recognised by a great tribunal. In his mind this in itself created the state. He was a step ahead of his people, but that mattered little to him. Neither did the world Zionist organisation matter. From that moment the Jews of Palestine, without realising it, had a Prime Minister of their own.

There was every justification for his conviction that the Palestine they knew had passed into history: the situation inside the country was worsening almost beyond repair. Except for some under-the-counter trade with the Jews, the Arab general strike was complete, and extended from the lowest level to the senior Arab administrative officials and the judges, both religious and civil. Essential services were disrupted; the port of Jaffa was idle, and as the defection of the Arabs left gaps, Jews rushed to fill them. They built a jetty for Tel-Aviv, that one-time strip of suburb which had grown into the commercial capital of the country with 100,000 residents. Haifa now had a first-rate, deep-water harbour, and Jewish stevedores came from the Greek ports to service it. There were two thousand miles of roads, mined by Arab guerrillas at key points. Hardly a Jew in the country was unschooled in marksmanship; and most important for its bearing on subsequent events, the Jewish preparations for self-defence proceeded apace, far in excess of anything sanctioned by the authorities. They were based on the collective villages, with associates of Tabenkin in command of shadow military formations.

Pending a political settlement, the Jewish Agency demanded that immigration continue as before, and even at the moment of the publication of the partition plan, a storm blew up. The Agency applied for 11,000 entry permits to cover a six-months period, computing the figure on the extraordinary needs of German Jewry, and on the general labour situation. It was awarded 620, of which 400 would be for German Jews and 220 under the general immigration schedule. Ben-Gurion, in London, immediately rejected the part of this insulting offer which came under the category of general immigration. This was the first open breach between the Jews and Britain. It should be observed, however, that the government continued to turn a Nelson's eye on the goings-on of the organisers of illegal immigration, even if it later took the precaution of throwing some Revisionists, including Jabotinsky's son Eri, into jail.

As Palestine slid towards catastrophe Ben-Gurion made a 'last-ditch' statement on the Jewish position. "While the Mandate lasts," he cried, "we shall fight any curtailment of the rights it accords us. We rejected the 220 certificates to remind Jewry that this matter of immigration must be fought. Let us not partition ourselves on the question of partition, but conserve our strength to fight the Mandatory power. At the time of the Balfour Declaration there were but 60,000 Jews in Palestine. Now there are 400,000. By our industry and enterprise we have absorbed them, and England too has benefited in her imperialist policy. How was she able to build the port of Haifa, the only one in the Empire with its own oil supply? It did not cost her a penny, *we* made it possible. Britain must remember that we are the deciding factor in the progress of Palestine.

The very boundaries of the country in the north were determined by the presence of our settlements there in the early days. We may be facing a war of life and death, but we are a force in Palestine and, if necessary, we shall put that force to work." Soon after this Congress met in Zurich.

It was forty years exactly since Theodor Herzl had summoned the first of those assemblies a few miles away in Basle. Many of the delegates present had marched with history from the formation of the Zionist organisation, to the possible formation of a Jewish state. At the same time Ormsby-Gore, an old comrade of Chaim Weizmann from the Zionist Commission days and now Colonial Secretary, appeared nervously before the Permanent Mandates Commission in Geneva, anxious to push the partition scheme through.

The anguish of Zionism was never more clear than at that Congress, at which the significant sessions were held in secret and each voice for or against partition came from the tribune as if spoken in a confessional.

> "Tribes of the wandering foot and weary breast
> How shall ye flee away and be at rest!
> The wild dove hath her nest, the fox his cave,
> Mankind their country—Israel but the grave."

And now, of this minute country of their longing, they were offered a minute part. Not one spokesman of the religious parties would accept it. Not one of the extreme left-wing, which wept for Jewry and for the Arabs together. Not one delegate from America. Old Ussishkin, now seventy-four, who engaged in politics on the sweet and simple assumption of the non-existence of any point of view but the Zionist maximum demand, heard the arguments of those who were pro-partition without the least glimmer of understanding. Was this Uganda come back to haunt them? Then Katznelson made a frightened man's hesitant, incoherent statement, and, finally, joined up with the 'Neinsagers' as they were called. Mrs. Golda Myerson, leader of the women's section of the *Histadruth*, also opposed partition; but her friend Remez favoured it. A telegram from South Africa protested that the proposal was even given discussion time. It was not a clear-cut debate, because those agreeing to negotiate a plan of partition wrapped their acquiescence in a tight parcel of conditions. Delegates who said 'No' begged Britain to come forward and offer them something else. Ruppin, to whom all deferred for his experience of colonisation problems, spoke in favour but without conviction. An Occupying Power engaged in a stealthy search for oil in the Negev would not, he thought, surrender its control in a hurry!

Then, like the staff of Moses outstretched to separate the waters of the Red Sea, the voice of Ben-Gurion cleared the air of indecision and divided Congress sharply into the 'Jasagers' and 'Neinsagers'. "I regard the government's declaration in favour of a Jewish State as one of the greatest acts in history," he exclaimed. "This is the beginning of redemption for which we have waited 2,000 years. We have established a great new political fact, in that our rulers have spoken to us of independence. But there is also a new damaging fact: henceforth the Mandate will not be operated."

The prophecy was to be realised sooner than he feared. Ormsby-Gore, after a grilling at the hands of the Permanent Mandates Commission, returned to London to find the enthusiasm of his colleagues in the Cabinet much diminished. The threads of Arab rebellion in the Holy Land were drawing together. Whole areas of the country were out of control, while the Arab national committees were dissolved and their leaders deported. Ormsby-Gore was sent out of the Cabinet room like a small boy with a dead mouse in his pocket. He was told to keep the Jews and Arabs talking, but not about independent states. And, as the government set to work to plumb the mind of Adolf Hitler, he sent a delaying despatch to the High Commissioner. As far as Downing Street was concerned, the partition solution to the Palestine problem was no more than a learned scrap of paper.

With ghost-ships full of Jewish derelicts floating helplessly along the Danube, with banditry enforcing its strangle-hold upon the Promised Land, Ben-Gurion, as Chairman of the Jewish Agency, refused to let the matter rest. Weizmann tiptoed discreetly from his friends in Whitehall to the colonists on guard at their stockades. For him the greatest tragedy would be open conflict between the two peoples sharing his devotion. In the mind of Ben-Gurion the war was undeclared but begun. "It is not that we regard the Mandate as our Bible," he said, "it is that the Bible is our Mandate."

6

The Scorned Ally

"A JEWISH STATE in a part of Palestine will help in the realisation of Zionism more than a British state over the whole of Palestine," Ben-Gurion told his colleagues. He was underestimating the powers of vacillation inherent in a government led by Neville Chamberlain and Lord Halifax when faced with a European situation dominated by Adolf Hitler. By autumn, 1938, Palestine was, constitutionally, suspended in mid-air, with the British government in no mood to force any kind of régime of a definite character or form upon it. This defeatism infected the whole Jewish world. The condition of their people in Central Europe, the spread of anti-Semitism over the rest of the Continent, the daily toll of lives in Palestine, the emergence of Sir Oswald Mosley's brand of Fascism in England, all these developments brought them to a fatalistic reconciliation to a pacifist settlement of their problem. Having all but given up hope of winning independence in a hate-ridden Holy Land, they restricted their claims to the needs of their brethren, degraded and stupefied, in their mass escape from Europe.

Three years before, while it was still bearable to be a Jew in Germany, the government had allowed the entry of 62,000 Jews into Palestine. Now that the Nazi policy was bent on moral extermination, and embraced Austria and the Sudetenland, the Jewish Agency begged the new Colonial Secretary, Malcolm MacDonald, to facilitate the immigration of 100,000. The Agency itself would guarantee their upkeep pending their absorption into the economy. And, as an act of sheer humanity, would he allow another 22,000 children and young people to come in? The requests were free from arrogance, and without political *arrières-*

pensées. But MacDonald turned them down, and by doing so branded hatred into the heart of every Jew in Palestine praying for the safety of his relatives. Had Britain shown at this stage and subsequently a more generous appreciation of the plight of the persecuted, there might well to this day be a British representative sitting in Government House in Jerusalem. Now Britain had cut the ground from under the feet of Chaim Weizmann and those moderates who were ready to forget statehood for the time being, even to accept a minority status indefinitely.

The government's inaction played into Ben-Gurion's hands. While political settlement hung fire, he set about establishing political facts. Why had Lord Peel awarded Galilee to the Jews? Because, he said, answering his own question, the Jews had been staking their claim to it by land-purchase and colonisation for forty years. The existence of colonies like Sejera had placed Galilee under the Jewish flag even during the period of Turkish rule. Had the Jews gone to the Negev, he was convinced, this too would have become another undisputed Jewish region. Therefore, he claimed, the time had now come to plot out new points of colonisation.

Ben-Gurion belonged to two different worlds. A part of him was chairman of the Jewish Agency, the body officially constituted to assist the government in the carrying-out of the Mandate. In this capacity he was aligned with the other international Jewish leaders engaged, with varying degrees of politeness, in negotiation with Britain. The other part of Ben-Gurion belonged to Jewish Palestine, of whose people he was the chief representative. This brought him into councils denied the Diaspora Jewish politicians—the councils of *Mapai* and *Histadruth*. In London he was overtly the collaborator, in Jerusalem he was the head of a resistance movement. In Palestine the workers pressed forward with the policy of strategic colonisation, by which hitherto uninhabited places were transformed overnight into fortified settlements. Each was given its store of arms, its emergency food-supply, its instructions for the moment when the night might be disturbed by the unannounced arrival of clandestine immigrants; and, as the confidence of the external Zionist movement dwindled, Ben-Gurion spoke as though Israel were already a nation. He exhorted his people to colonise not only the land of Israel but also the waters lapping its coasts. "This country is blessed with two seas, so that we are connected by the Mediterranean with

Europe and Africa, and by the Red Sea with Asia. Nobody can divide the sea, nobody can buy or sell it. It is as free as the human spirit." The Jews went down to the sea, and even up into the air with their own aviation company. Since the Peel Commission had discussed the proposition of a Jewish State, why should he remain secretive about his ambitions? In January 1939 Ben-Gurion went to America to ensure that finance on a new scale would be available for any eventuality.

Meanwhile, the British government had received the signal it was waiting for. Another Commission returned from the country and condemned partition as impracticable. Chamberlain then invited Jews and Arabs to a round-table conference (ominous word, in view of recent experience with India) at St. James's Palace. The Prime Minister, not yet fallen from the heights to which his famous mission to Hitler had promoted him, invited the neighbouring Arab states to send representatives also. The Jewish leaders now expected the worst. If the conference could have any definite outcome, they knew it could only be a Middle East Munich on a grand scale.

Malcolm MacDonald had no little difficulty in gathering the conference together. The Nashashibi faction among the Arabs was in open enmity with the Mufti's followers, and in a message to the Arab kings they condemned the rebellion, charging the Husseinis especially with the misappropriation of funds. At first Fakhri bey Nashashibi refused to join with the Arab Higher Committee (whose leaders, interned in the Seychelles, were now liberated by Britain to confer with the Mufti in his Lebanese retreat before the talks), although, eventually, he allowed two of his followers to participate. The Jews too were a mixed bag; and though the influence of Weizmann, Ben-Gurion and Shertok predominated, Ussishkin was there as well as Ben-Zvi, Berl Katznelson and Berl Locker. Their delegation also comprised American Jews, not yet at their peak of importance in Zionist councils; while Professor Brodetsky and all the other members of the Jewish Agency Executive, besides private individuals, were invited because of their status in the Anglo-Jewish community. Such a team could only be cemented into unity by the tragedy enveloping the millions for whom they spoke.

The round-table conference was not achieved, for the Palestine Arabs would not sit with the Jews. Then MacDonald brought Nuri

Pasha of Iraq and Ali Maher of Egypt to a meeting with the principal Jewish delegates. Lord Halifax, with R. A. Butler at his elbow, did the talking. When it was over, Ben-Gurion went straight back to the Zionist headquarters and cabled this message to the Jews of Palestine: "A scheme is being laid to liquidate the Jewish National Home and hand it over to the gang-leaders. This design will not succeed. The courage of the *Yishuv*, the plight of the Jewish people in the Diaspora, the conscience of Great Britain, the moral and political support of the civilised world, will bring the plans of our enemies to nought. Let there be no fear. The representatives of the Jewish people here are standing on guard, fully confident that every one of you will stand the supreme test in faith, unity, discipline and strength."

It was his belief that MacDonald, in bringing him to this discussion with the two Arab statesmen, had practised a deceit upon him and his colleagues. The Colonial Secretary had promised a conciliatory talk, declaring that Nuri and Ali Maher both understood that the Jews could not be expected to accept the same status in Palestine as Jewish minorities in Iraq and Egypt. He said they wanted the Palestine Arabs to come to terms with the Jews. Yet at the meeting the two Arabs backed up the Mufti's position in its entirety. Then Halifax informed the meeting of Britain's plan for peace: a maximum of 75,000 immigrants within five years, and none after that except with the Arabs' consent. Then, all being well, there would be an independent Palestinian state at the end of ten years, by which time the Jews should constitute one-third of the population. So he spoke as Hitler moved in to annex what remained of Czechoslovakia.

The proposal was received by the Jews in horrified silence. Finally, Ben-Gurion spoke: "Permit me to state that the stoppage of Jewish immigration will be impossible without the help of British bayonets. Neither will you be able to turn Palestine into an Arab state against the resistance of the Jews without the permanent presence of those bayonets."

Despite an assurance from Malcolm MacDonald that the British government had by no means spoken its last word, the Halifax formula was embodied in a White Paper. This sneaked its way through Parliament after 130 of the government's usual supporters had either voted against or abstained. It then received a hostile reception by the Permanent Mandates Commission, then in session in Geneva. In July all immigration certificates were withheld for the following six months' period as a retaliation against the growing tide of illegal entry. Two weeks before the Germans marched into Poland a Zionist Congress met to study the lessons of their defeat. The atmosphere, Weizmann himself has stated, was one of 'unreality and irrelevance'. He, the typical European upon whom darkness was to descend, was all but a broken man—nonplussed, humiliated, betrayed by the nation which, forty years before, Herzl had chosen to join the Zionists in a partnership which was now played out. The assembly thought they were back to where they had started in those early times. If only that were all! Of the 530 delegates trooping back to their homes, a quarter were not heard of again, swallowed up by the greatest catastrophe in Jewish, and human, history.

Weizmann went to London to write a letter to Neville Chamberlain. "Dear Mr. Prime Minister," it read. "In this hour of supreme crisis the consciousness that the Jews have a contribution to make to the defence of sacred values compels me to write this letter. I wish to confirm, in the most explicit manner, the declarations which I and my colleagues have made during the last months, and especially in the last week: that the Jews stand by Great Britain and will fight on the side of the democracies. Our urgent desire is to give effect to these declarations. We wish to do so in a way entirely consonant with the general scheme of British action, and therefore would place ourselves, in matters big and small, under the co-ordinating direction of His Majesty's Government. The Jewish Agency is ready to enter into immediate arrangements for utilising man-power, technical ability, resources, etc. The Jewish Agency has recently had differences in the political field with the Mandatory Power. We would like these differences to give way before the greater and more pressing necessities of the times."

David Ben-Gurion was already back in Jerusalem, occupied in the day-to-day business of the Agency on whose behalf his president was speaking. He too made a statement. "The Jews of Palestine happen to be the only community in the Middle East whose very survival is bound up with the defeat of Hitler. We shall fight the War as if there were no White Paper, and the White Paper as if there were no War." More clearly than anything else these two pronouncements foreshadowed the different paths which were to be taken by the two men in the succeeding years. Weizmann conducted himself like one of the prime ministers in exile with which London was shortly to proliferate. The other never forgot his role as a guerrilla leader, a Jewish Tito with two wars on his hands. Victory would belong to the younger man, product of a more ruthless generation of statesmen.

Poland went the way of Czechoslovakia. But the phony war which followed did not apply to Palestine. As Weizmann declared his truce, the government pressed home its defeat of Zionism. Late in February the High Commissioner, Sir Harold MacMichael, notified the Jews of an order he had received from London introducing fresh land regulations. These regulations would have the effect of only allowing them freedom to purchase territory within municipal areas, in the neighbourhood of Haifa and in a portion of the coastal plain—one-twentieth of Western Palestine. Elsewhere, they could not increase their holdings at all, unless they could show this to be necessary for the improvement of land already in their possession.

Ben-Gurion received the news with incredulity. He made straight for Government House and informed the High Commissioner that its consequences would be disastrous. Would Sir Harold postpone promulgation of the ordinance for a few days, so that he could proceed to London and endeavour to secure its annulment? He reminded Sir Harold of Chamberlain's undertaking to the Labour Party not to embark on any new steps under the terms of the White Paper, to which it had strongly objected.

"I am sure the Labour Party has not been consulted," he insisted. "I beg of you to give us a little grace."

The High Commissioner was adamant. "I cannot do it. My orders are to promulgate the ordinance by six o'clock tomorrow." They had a furious argument, and Ben-Gurion left. But he later received a telephone call at his home. It was the Chief Secretary.

"We have just received instructions to hold the matter up," he said. "What has cropped up?" Ben-Gurion was still enraged. "Do I have to tell you how the mind of your government works?" he retorted. "I expect the Labour Party has created a fuss."

The Chief Secretary asked him to be ready throughout the night to receive a call. They were expecting some clarification from

10

London. In the morning he spoke to Ben-Gurion again. They had just heard from London. The order would have to go through after all. And it was to be made retroactive to May, 1939, the date of the White Paper's publication.

So here it was. Jews might not be brought in, land might not be purchased. Even the pretence of administering the Mandate was now abandoned. The Zionist movement's proud claim of taking the people back to the neglected land was derided by these crippling new restrictions. It was a criminally foolish move on the part of a government in need of every available friend, at a time when it was ardently wooing the United States and trembling for the neutrality of Mussolini. As 100,000 Palestine Jews queued up in response to the Jewish Agency's call for national service, the feeling stirred up by this move led directly to the creation of the Stern gang.

To the High Commissioner Ben-Gurion said: "The effect of these regulations is that no Jew may acquire in Palestine a plot of land, a building, or a tree, or any right in water, except in towns and in a very small part of the country. The Land Transfer Regulations deny to Jews equality before the law and introduce racial discrimination. They confine the Jews within a small Pale of Settlement similar to that which existed in Czarist Russia before the last war, and such as now exists only under Nazi rule. They not only violate the terms of the Mandate but completely nullify its purpose . . . the policy strikes at the heart of the Jewish National Home by depriving the Jews of the right to settle on the land and compels them, as in the Diaspora, to be town-dwellers. This attempt to frustrate the age-long aspirations of the Jewish people to become rooted again in the soil of its ancient homeland is made at a time when millions of Jews are being mercilessly persecuted by a cruel enemy. . . . The Jewish people will not submit to the conversion of the National Home into a ghetto."

Now land-buying, like immigration, became one of the subterranean channels of the Jewish Agency's activities. Furthermore, a Haifa engineer named Jacob Dostrofsky,* veteran of the First World War's 40th Battalion, was called in to undertake the reorganisation of the *Haganah*. Ben-Gurion then set out for London to sharpen the other edge of his double-sided claim. He sought to

---

* Afterwards known as Dori.

obtain permission for the creation of a Jewish Allied army, composed of Palestinian, American and other volunteers. In the earlier war the enlistment of the Judeans had been largely a political stratagem. Today, he deemed it necessary to Jewish survival.

For the next seven years he was rarely to be seen in Tel-Aviv. He was to relax the control he had so long exercised over the Labour movement, and though still regarded as a *Histadruth* official (indeed, he received his salary from this source until 1948) his duties as general secretary were after 1935 divided between Remez and Sprinzak. This was still the key office of an organisation which represented more than one-half of the entire Jewish population. Temporarily robbed of its overseas citrus market, and with the restriction upon private building, both Palestine, and the *Histadruth* within it, underwent an initial period of strain due to war-time conditions. However, they recovered their balance quickly on the arrival of the reinforcements to the Middle East armies with their gargantuan consumer demands. Ben-Zvi now occupied an honoured role as chairman of the *Vaad Leumi*, the Jewish National Council, and gradually withdrew from public affairs into a life as Jewish Jerusalem's first citizen—though he was in fact to be deprived of his richly-deserved tranquillity for a long time to come. A large and diverse family bade Ben-Gurion farewell. Like families everywhere, it was to suffer great changes from the war and its aftermath.

As a result of three years of disturbances, serious political setbacks and anxious days spent waiting for news of European relatives, the Jewish community was less prepared than most for the rigours to come. Every few months it was to be roused to indignation or racked with grief as the hell-ships struggled to gain port, only to be driven back to sea, sometimes to be lost for ever or even, as occurred with one vessel, to destroy itself in suicidal protest. The White Paper flapped like an angel of death over every family circle, not excluding Ben-Gurion's, for in Warsaw there still lived, if indeed they lived, his brother Abraham's daughter and her husband and children. Palestine was shut off behind a double curtain of censorship, for to the precautions against security-leakages there were added the expurgations from the local Press of statements made in the British Parliament, editorials of respectable English newspapers, and other information thought likely to inflame the political atmosphere. And with it all *Mapai*, Ben-Gurion's party, maintained its tenuous unity with

difficulty, as Isaac Tabenkin's left-wing, with a powerful hand outstretched from Ein Harod, took to itself the grievances of the unemployed. There was plenty to occupy the thoughts of David
Ben-Gurion as he arrived in London to be confronted with the collapse of France, the entry of Mussolini into the war, and the
transformation of the Mediterranean into a principal theatre of
operations.

Chamberlain went, and Malcolm MacDonald left the Colonial
Office. This, at any rate, was some relief. On balance the new War
Cabinet was, according to the Parliamentary record of its members,
pro-Zionist. The return of Leopold Amery to the government
brought back a trusted friend. Ben-Gurion's hopes rose as in the
Bloomsbury offices of the Jewish Agency he worked out a new
programme for Zionism to help win the war, to strengthen the
Jewish position, and to break the opposition to greater immigration.

The tenor of Churchill's early 'fight on the beaches' broadcasts,
his apparent readiness to make revolutionary changes in his country's
relationship with others, made Ben-Gurion optimistic. He believed
that the slate had been wiped completely clean of the previous
Palestine policy. He defined the priorities of Zionism as, first, the
cancellation of the White Paper; secondly, the recall of Sir Harold
MacMichael, or at least an insistence on more toleration for *Haganah*,
the prevention of police outrages, the facilitation of immigration,
help for the Jews to develop Tel-Aviv as a port and the honouring
of an old promise to allow them to drain the north Galilean marshlands; his third priority was permission for the mobilisation of at
least two specifically Jewish divisions, one from Palestine, the other
from countries outside. Finally the Agency should inform Britain
that nothing short of statehood, either within the Commonwealth, as part of a Near East Confederation, or with independent
sovereignty, would satisfy the Jews.

Like all of Ben-Gurion's dreams, these demands were to him
urgent, legitimate and utterly realistic. Unfortunately, they could
only reach the Prime Minister via the frigid channels of the
Colonial Office. The new man in charge was Lord Lloyd, hardly an
ardent upholder of the Zionist cause. Ben-Gurion and Weizmann
decided to tackle him together. Their first interview was brief
and discouraging. While Ben-Gurion was favourably impressed by

the directness and intellectual honesty of the Minister, he saw that here they were dealing with a determined and resourceful antagonist. Lloyd was quick to appreciate and exploit the difference between the two men, a difference revealed in the very way they introduced the offer of a Jewish army.

Weizmann volunteered the immediate and complete participation of the Palestine Jews in the war, in whatever form the General Staff might decide. "There are no conditions attached to our offer," he said.

"We have half a million people who, if they were British by blood and language, could not be more reliable," Ben-Gurion cut in. "But the authorities must cease their present attitude. They must learn to treat our people with confidence, and," referring to the constant surveillance upon *Haganah*, "the arms searches must stop. Weapons have only been used in self-defence."

In reply to a question from Lloyd, Weizmann denied knowledge of any such organisation. But, he said, everyone, including Lord Lloyd, knew the settlements were armed. Briefly, the Minister observed that the question of the White Paper could not be opened at this time. He was visibly in a state of shock from the latest war news: Holland had fallen only a day or two earlier. In no mood to argue, he lapsed into silence, leaving Weizmann to carry on the discussion of the war in more general terms. Weizmann's politeness concealed an intense dislike of the man.

The government's hesitation to enter into a commitment with the Jews clearly derived from their fear of being drawn into a 'pact of honour' on the lines of the Balfour Declaration. They were ready, however, to raise 'Palestinian' units, in which Jews and Arabs could serve on an equal basis. Quite obviously this would restrict the Jews to an insignificant part in the war, as there was little hope of enrolling masses of Arabs for a conflict towards whose outcome they were universally apathetic, if they were not distinctly prejudiced in favour of the Germans. Ben-Gurion, as was his practice, made comprehensive notes on the interview. He concluded that Lloyd disagreed with the opinion, advanced by Weizmann and himself, that the Arabs were pro-Hitler, and for this clear error of judgment on the Minister's part he blamed the local Palestine Administration, still, he realised, as influential as ever.

The line he advised his colleagues to adopt with the British government was to warn it that it could not take the availability of the Jews, in Palestine or America, for granted. And he bombarded Lloyd with letters to this effect. He enlarged on the theme of Jewish participation, and even offered to establish a special agency under the Ministry of Economic Warfare to operate in the still neutral Balkan countries, where the Jews had strong contacts.

This was at the end of May, 1940. After Churchill's fighting broadcast of June 4th he wrote to Lloyd again: "You may find it strange coming from me, but I too happen to be a passionate British imperialist. . . . I believe the Empire stands for something much greater than itself, for a cause wider than its own frontiers. I believe the Empire is the political rallying-point of spiritual forces throughout the world. I am a convinced believer in this universal mission of the British Empire . . . and I am not a British Jew, merely a Jewish Jew."

Ben-Gurion, like so many Palestinians whose judgment of the English had previously been based on their experiences with the colonial ruling-classes brandishing the Union Jack in their faces, was revising his opinion of the nation. "Churchill's was the voice not only of a great warrior and a great statesman. It was also the voice of a man with a deep faith in the universal significance of this fight. . . . For you to be faced with the threat of destruction is a novel experience," he told Lloyd. "We have been facing this ordeal for centuries." He showed how Palestine could manufacture arms, develop a pharmaceutical industry. Lloyd seemed to enjoy receiving the letters, for early in July he asked Ben-Gurion to come and see him again. They began to talk of Italy's entry into the war. Ben-Gurion thought this must surely dissolve the government's hostility to the mobilisation of his people.

He informed the Colonial Secretary of the existence of Jewish Agency officials in Jerusalem with unique sources of information in Turkey. They believed that should an invasion of Syria take place, and the British withdraw from Palestine, the Turks would march in and annex Aleppo and Gezirah. Lloyd interposed: "And Mosul." But, said Ben-Gurion confidently, given adequate equipment, Palestine could nevertheless be held. And if the 20,000 Jewish supernumerary police were covertly transformed into a fighting force, the Arabs would not be unduly upset.

"What would then happen to our policy of parity?" queried

Lloyd. Ben-Gurion was in a bargaining mood. "We could fix a basis of 500 Arabs to 1,000 Jews," was his answer.

Just at this time Orde Wingate, a soldier with infinite faith in the capacities of the Jewish colonists, and in the justice of their cause, was worrying Ben-Gurion to persuade the government to employ him on special missions with the Zionists, and his name now cropped up.

"I know him, and I like him," observed Lloyd, "but if he goes to Palestine the Arabs will immediately be up in arms."

"It could be secret."

"He will start mobilising a Jewish Army."

"But—under orders?"

"He isn't the man to bother about orders."

"Will you then release the 'forty-three'?" (*Haganah* members imprisoned for infringing the Land Transfer Ordinances.)

"I am not going to release young Jabotinsky. He was the organiser of all the illegal immigration," said the other firmly.

"Not all of it!" was Ben-Gurion's quick, jealous answer.

"Well, you ought to know," laughed Lloyd.

Ben-Gurion was in no laughing mood. That week he wired a Zionist Convention meeting in Pittsburgh: "I have full confidence in the victory of the democracies but before that Jewish Palestine may be wiped out."

Naturally, Lord Lloyd and the rest of the government were not unaware of the value of enlisting Jewish help for the Allied cause. Churchill had every intention of making use of the Palestine settlers, and had a shrewd idea who was blocking the path. But he had not yet been in the saddle long enough for that overwhelming mastery of decision over the lesser men around him to develop. He did, however, know something of the situation in America, and that a most effective way of attacking its neutralism was through the Jews of New York. Lloyd told Ben-Gurion that either he or Weizmann should proceed to the United States. Weizmann had as it happened just returned from that country, and was now back in London engaged on chemical research for the Ministry of Supply. Ben-Gurion therefore agreed to go. But he hung on for a long time, in a vain endeavour to force a decision for the army. He also plugged the lesser issues—permission for Jewish enlistment in the R.A.F., training of 500 young men from Palestine as a cadre of officers and

N.C.O.s, raising refugee units in England and, of course, the release of the 'forty-three'.

Then Lloyd warned him that his agitation was getting him no-where: "I ought to tell you," said the Colonial Secretary at the end of August, "that while I am an 'enemy', you have even bigger 'enemies' in the War Office. I spoke on Friday evening to Anthony (Eden) and told him I was not against a Jewish unit, and suggested he should see his people at the War Office. Why is it there are so many people against you?" "Apparently it is our fault," Ben-Gurion said, "because it has already been going on for 2,000 years." "The trouble is that you are bad mixers," Lloyd complained. "If you really want victory, why can't you just enlist in the British army? Why do you need a Jewish unit?" Ben-Gurion replied, Jewish-wise, with another question: "Why don't you ask these things of the French, or the Czechs, or the Poles?"

Of course there was a political motive behind his desire for a Jewish force, he admitted. They were Jews, and wanted to fight as Jews, just as the English were English and the French French.

"Some people say that when you have a Jewish army you will increase our troubles out there," grumbled the other. Ben-Gurion countered: "The trouble we will give you will be due simply to the fact that we exist. But at present we are concerned with only one thing—victory. Although I am thinking a good deal about our future, and the future of the world, I know very well that at present there is only one paramount consideration—winning the war. But we want to make our contribution as Jews."

"Well, it depends on the War Office now."

The man who was thinking a great deal about the future of the world was also thinking a great deal about the future of Churchill. "Are you taking adequate precautions?" he asked Lloyd.

"What do you mean?"

"Assassination. It can happen, you know." The English aristocrat ushered the man from Plonsk out, with an English aristocratic smile. Ben-Gurion never saw him again. Lloyd died in February, 1941, while Ben-Gurion was in Washington.

A few days later Weizmann, bearing the draft plan for a Jewish army, was received by the Prime Minister. The plan called for the mobilisation of a maximum number of Palestinian Jews into

battalions and larger formations. It suggested circumventing the
'parity' objection by allowing the excess of Jews over Arabs to be
trained in Egypt or elsewhere. There were to be officer cadres, a
desert unit for special service, and the raising of units from among
foreign Jews in England and other countries. Churchill agreed
whole-heartedly.

Weizmann had known the Prime Minister would be in favour
of his plan, but needed the interview to strengthen his hand for a
coming meeting with Eden and General Dill, the C.I.G.S. This
followed at once, but while these two were ready to concede the
point regarding the Palestine Jews, the talk became bogged-down
in detail and the Zionist president left Whitehall without discussing
the raising of a force from the rest of the world (meaning, of course,
America). Ben-Gurion heard the news of the omission with dismay.
It was all the more lamentable as he was on the point of leaving
London to persuade American Jews to join up, and he expected to
have a concrete proposal to place before them. Now the initiative,
which was theirs by virtue of the Prime Minister's concurrence in
principle, had been thrown away.

There was little he could do at this stage. Circulating a note to his
colleagues in Great Russell Street, he made for Lisbon where through
the intervention of Lord Lloyd he was to be given a seat in a V.I.P.
plane for New York. The message read: "We should take to heart
one important principle which the English people have been teaching the world in recent months, never to accept defeat. In the face
of setbacks, evasions, whittling-down and sabotage from the War
Office and the Foreign Office, we must go on."

How startling the contrast between London and New York! In
London the daily imminence of death, the sense of pride and
purpose shared by the whole nation, and all who lived among it;
in New York the universal manifestation of fear, a people clinging
in their pacifism to their immunity from the terrors of war, but
substituting instead the terrors of peace. To plunge into the tedium
of party-meetings, of new committees composed of people strange
to him, of powerful women's groups, was almost beyond the
patience of a man whose very character was fashioned out of conflict.
It meant arguing almost from first principles, even to men of the
stature of Justice Brandeis, still the first name in American Zionism,
as it had been nearly a generation before when Ben-Gurion was

first in America on a mission little different, except in proportion, from his present one.

Time and again he was asked: Had everything been done to reach agreement with the Arabs? Was there not a way out of the impasse? Was statehood for the Jews vital? "Yes," he replied wearily, "yes and yes and yes! But now there is a war and we shall be annihilated if we are defeated. This is the new basis to which you must accustom your thinking."

Confusion, reluctance and concern lest the *Chicago-Tribune* brand the Jews as warmongers, wrung excuses out of all the Zionists he spoke to whenever he discussed their participation in the war. He told the executive of the Hadassah women's organisation, a national body of giant membership: "We need a Jewish army, recruited partly in America, to help Britain. I hope you won't let cheap pacifism stand in your way. I know what this means to you as women and Jews. There is no more sacred task at the moment than the defeat of Hitler and Nazism, and they cannot be defeated by mere words. England is paying dearly for her previous pacifism. As far back as five or six years ago I had discussions with members of the Labour Party in England. I believed they were making a fatal mistake in opposing rearmament in England. I told them this was a contradiction—pacifism and opposition to Fascism—which would not be defeated by words." A woman asked him: "What is the assurance that even with a Jewish army we shall get a Jewish state?"

"There is no assurance. It is just a matter of chance."

So it went on for months. He stayed in America till the early summer of 1941, when urgent messages summoned him back to Palestine. He was out of touch with his own party, within which two conflicting tendencies presaged momentous changes in the orientation of *Mapai*, and therefore in the political bone-structure of the Jewish community as a whole. The party they had so arduously established eleven years before, in the comparative tranquillity of a time when the community was less of a fluctuating, half-absorbed mass, was in danger. Tabenkin and his *kibbutz* group had combined with the left-wing town proletariat and threatened to take over the leadership. On the other hand, Katznelson, Golomb and those adhering to the Ben-Gurion wing, were completing negotiations for a fusion with Revisionism, and had reached a measure of agreement towards uniting *Haganah* with the more 'activist' military underground of the Right.

Either way the Labour movement was heading for a crisis, and until it was settled Jewish participation in the war, Ben-Gurion's principal aim, would remain in the balance. He came home to verify, as it were, his credit to negotiate on behalf of the Labour movement.

Jabotinsky died early in 1940, a loss from which the Revisionists could not recover. Their own underground military force, the *Irgun Zvai Leumi*, though small in size, was well-organised, aggressive, and fanatically nationalist. Its divergence from *Haganah*, apart from the now academic political issues, stemmed from its conviction that *Haganah*'s doctrine of passive defence of the Jewish position was a mistake. Just as the official Zionist movement broke the law to bring in refugees, so it should also break the law by disposing of known Arab terrorists and trouble-makers. For some of the *Irgun* even this was not enough. After the outbreak of war a few of them, under the leadership of Abraham Stern, broke away. England, they insisted, was the real enemy of Zionism, and while she was at war their duty was to harass her at every point, for a victorious England would not award them their rights to independence.

In the circumstances, some Revisionist leaders, seeing their party's positive Zionist ideals threatened by explosive inner conflict, decided it was time to effect a union with *Haganah*. Talks began between a member of the former Paris executive, Benjamin Lubotsky,* and Eliahu Golomb, who was agreeable to their aims. The talks were widened by the inclusion of Katznelson on the one side and Eri Jabotinsky, a former cell-mate of Lubotsky's, on the other. They came to an accord to synchronise political and military activities, and soon a draft was signed at Golomb's Tel-Aviv home in Rothschild Boulevard.

The *Irgun Zvai Leumi*'s commander was David Raziel, a man with little interest in politics. He worked out plans for shock-troops according to which his men would serve alongside the socialists. Simultaneously, Tabenkin and others in the settlements were creating a striking-force for *Haganah*, but it was a case of the right hand not knowing what the left-wing was doing.

The negotiations proceeded to a point of finalisation. Then,

* Afterwards known as Eliav.

suddenly, Katznelson drew back on the grounds that Ben-Gurion, who should have been party to the discussions, was out of the country. At a meeting in Golda Myerson's house, with Golomb and David Remez present, he backed out altogether. Lubotsky had, with difficulty, won the co-operation of his own colleagues. Now Katznelson said that although Ben-Gurion did not have the standing in *Mapai* which the elder Jabotinsky had enjoyed among the *Revisionists*, nevertheless it would be wise to await his return to Palestine.

Just then Raziel withdrew to take on a job with some British officers in a commando operation against Rashid Ali's rebellion in Iraq. He went on the understanding that if an opportunity were presented, he would kill the ex-Mufti of Jerusalem, who was operating against Britain from Bagdad. Raziel was himself killed, by a German bomb, near Habbaniyah. It was as well that Meridor, another Irgun member, was there to witness his death; otherwise it would have been impossible, given the attitude of the authorities to Jewish defence organisations, to prevent the growth of a legend that he had been removed by the British.

The meetings had, of course, been secret. The mood of the Labour masses was undefinable, and in the stress of war (8,000 Jews were already serving in the forces, though no commitment on a separate Jewish army had been given) the purity of their socialism and their Tolstoyan simplicity were being defiled. To restore the balance which had been disturbed by the Partition issue—in which Ben-Gurion was as emphatically for the proposal as Tabenkin was emphatically against—had proved beyond *Mapai*'s resilience. And now the *kibbutz élite* could openly challenge their old comrades of Unity of Labour (*Achdut Avoda*) not only as the untarnished champions of socialism, but also as the Jewish army in the making. By espousing the cause of the under-dog in the towns they carried the conflict into the day-to-day activities of the Labour Councils of Tel-Aviv and Haifa, refused to abide by *Histadruth* decisions, found themselves unable to toe the *Mapai* party-line and constituted a rebellious 'keep-left' group whose reputation grew under the sinister designation 'Fraction B'.

Mapai, it will be recalled, had been established through a succession of alliances. A generation before there had existed two political organisations of the Left—*Poale Zion* and *Hapoel Hatzair* (the self-styled 'non-political' agriculturists led by Sprinzak and Aharanowitz). *Poale Zion*, by the accretion of some minor groups, became *Achdut Avoda* in 1919. Only in 1930 was it able to join with *Hapoel Hatzair* to create *Mapai*. All these developments were rather marriages of convenience than fusions of ideas. The great defect of Jewish politicians is their inability to forget. Crisis invariably jerks their memory back, the old habits of vituperation revive and questions of policy become clouded in personal vendettas. So it had been when Arlosoroff died; at the time of Partition debate; and now again, owing to the White Paper and the outbreak of war.

As the months of 1940 went by it became evident that a considerable sector of the membership of the largest and most prosperous collective network, *Kibbutz Hameuchad*, were in sympathy with Tabenkin and his friend Aharon Zisling of Ein Harod, and were turning 'Fraction B' into an independent political arm. They not only talked of the democratisation of the party and the *Histadruth*; they propounded a new ideology of the unity of defence and work —meaning the development of *Haganah*'s well-trained nucleus into a political weapon. They won over the entire socialist-youth movement. They agitated for the rooting-out of such corrupt manifestations as behind-the-scenes deals with Revisionism. They chose, in fact, to make the war the occasion for a spiritual regeneration of the Left. This in itself menaced the supremacy of Ben-Gurion, Shertok, Katznelson, Kaplan and Sprinzak as the combination at the head of *Mapai*. But there was something even more fundamental behind the agitation: unwillingness to face the issue of statehood before the socialist sector of the economy was strong enough to impose a collectivist system upon the rest.

One month was all that Ben-Gurion could allow himself in Palestine. It was July, 1941. The Germans had broken with Russia, Rommel's panzers were forming their ring round Tobruk. Lord Moyne was now the Colonial Secretary and for the moment all prospects of the early creation of a Jewish contingent were dashed.

The month was long enough for Ben-Gurion to make himself undisputed master of Jewish Palestine. The country swarmed with Allied troops of every race and nationality. Business was booming, unemployment low—but the Nile and the great struggle looming up for its possession seemed near indeed. He scotched all hopes of a truce with the Revisionists. He was adamant, and told Golomb and Katznelson not to complicate the negotiations with Britain. There would be a confusion of issues, he pointed out, in which statehood, workers' solidarity and Jewish defence would get tangled in controversy.

Golomb fought hard to keep his word with the other party. But Ben-Gurion was afraid of the reaction on *Mapai*'s far left, a consideration that had not weighed so heavily with him when he himself had talked with Jabotinsky. Did he commit a grave blunder? Did he save the reputation of *Haganah*, which was soon to earn the respect of British generals? Was it a ruse to use the *Irgun Zvai Leumi* without acknowledging responsibility for its actions? Nobody could say exactly, but he certainly cleared the path for Jewish terrorism to perform its subsequent role.

Now for 'Fraction B'. Here Ben-Gurion was in agreement with his colleagues in refusing to tolerate the factionalist tendency in *Mapai*. Tabenkin and Zisling would have to be forced out, and he was ready to gamble that without them *Mapai* would retain its majority within the *Histadruth* and the allegiance of the mass of the workers. The fight for statehood, inextricably bound up with the struggle for a Jewish army, would be gravely impaired if a section of the party was against it.

Ben-Gurion had an appointment to keep with Oliver Lyttelton in Cairo, so with the party feuds still very much alive he left Palestine again. Lyttelton was in charge of political work in the Middle East, one of those despairing jobs performed by Britons in which the height of success could be no more than to turn warm hostility into cold apathy. Ben-Gurion addressed him in rough terms: "If Britain intends after the war to make Palestine an Arab State you will be unable to deliver the goods. You could only do it by shooting the Jews, for we should resist. The same applies if you try to prevent our immigration."

"I shall limit our commitment to the Arabs as much as possible," said Lyttelton. "You have achieved a great deal so far. We have doubled the number of your armed settlement police force in the last three months, and they are full-paid employees of the Mandatory. In addition, some 15,000 of your people throughout the country are being armed and trained by us." In point of fact, this statement implied the legalisation of *Haganah*.

To Lord Moyne in London, the Jewish demand for a separate force was beyond comprehension. He had his own ideas for solving the

Jewish problem, and elaborated to Ben-Gurion a plan for allocating the Jews a self-governing enclave in Europe. Moyne was annoyed at the impatience with which his hearer brushed the plan aside. "We have to find living-space for three millions!" Ben-Gurion said.

If Lloyd admitted to being an 'enemy' of Zionism, this close friend of Churchill's came under a much more sinister classification. He spoke up soon after the interview in a parliamentary debate to voice the opinion that Palestine was an Arab country and that the Jewish complication was something from which the government were in honour bound to extricate themselves.

After two years, then, the Jewish army was as far from realisation as ever. However, Churchill had given the project his support, and the Cabinet had been largely cleared of the 'White Paper gang', as Ben-Gurion termed the pre-war appeasers of the Arabs. The Middle East situation was precarious in the extreme. To Ben-Gurion, Britain's hesitation in rallying the Jewish world to her side was inexplicable. He made Weizmann the scapegoat. Jewry's premier statesman could have pulled it off, he thought, if only he would but exploit the esteem in which he was universally held. Ben-Gurion failed to recognise the sources of Weizmann's potent diplomacy. Ben-Gurion could fulminate and threaten, but Weizmann, by holding something of himself back, saved the link with the War Cabinet that must at all costs be preserved.

Ben-Gurion saw the problem in terms of black and white. He complained bitterly to his colleagues: "Five million Americans are not as important as one Egyptian king. Half a million Jews ready to fight for Britain are not as important as three million Iraqis ready to fight against her!"

Then came Pearl Harbour, and five million American Jews began to matter very much.

7

The Bevin Years

THE STORY SO far unfolded has been that of a man using speed of decision to establish his people firmly in the land of Palestine before an opposition of great intrinsic power could assert itself. That opposition drew its strength from three separate sources: the Arab people, tardily expressing a long-dormant national urge; the Mandatory government, which resented being made an appendage of Zionist colonisation and which from the thirties had assumed the role of Arab protector; and the world Jewish movement, flurried, indeterminate, dispersed, in which a hundred different voices joined to devise a political instrument geographically remote from its creative centre, and psychologically out of harmony with the left-wing tendency predominating at that centre.

Now we come to the final, most exacting stage of the long road from Plonsk. Ben-Gurion had set the pace. Ben-Gurion had won for himself the Jewish leadership. The last move was to 'Ben-Gurion-ise' the Zionist organisation and, at the crucial moment, force the accomplishment of Jewish independence. He could not do it alone; but those who were to help him most were not Jews, or at least, not individual Jews. His chief allies were to be the blundering, blustering tactics of His Majesty's Government, sinned against and sinning, and its agents in the Middle East; the millions of victims, some dead, some still living, of the battleground of Europe; and President Truman.

America's entry into the war brought some of the Jewish citizens of that country to the sudden realisation of the need to create a Jewish volunteer army, fighting under its own flag, the very point

on which Ben-Gurion had failed to convince them one year previously. The demand was blazoned forth in advertisements inserted
in the New York Press by Peter Bergson, the youthful leader of a
body known as the 'Jewish Army Committee', linked with the *Irgun
Zvai Leumi* in Palestine. (Bergson's father, Chief Rabbi Kook of
Palestine, had himself been not unsympathetic to Revisionism.) This
group proved an embarrassment to Ben-Gurion. He would have
no truck with its spurious tactics in Palestine, while association with
it in America would give his own work there an unsavoury colour-
ing. Others, however, believed it to be too powerful to be ignored;
and as a pressure-group within the Zionist structure it gradually suf-
fused all Jewish nationalist activities in America with a virulently
anti-British bias, not unlike American-Irish nationalism.

It was apparent that the new factor of American participation in
the war would harden Zionist demands and reduce Weizmann's
importance as a moderator. Britain remained as obdurate on the
question of a Jewish army as she was in upholding the immigration
policy of the 1939 White Paper. This caught Ben-Gurion on the
raw, and threw him into alliance with the ebullient, aggressive
Zionist tacticians in America. He and Weizmann took their respective points of view to an emergency conference at New York's
Biltmore Hotel in May, 1942. There, a resolution was unanimously adopted embodying maximum Zionist demands—complete
freedom for the Jewish Agency to develop Palestine 'as a Jewish
commonwealth, integrated into the structure of the new democratic
world'. At that time Weizmann offered no public objections to
the new policy, though his private misgivings were well known.

It is doubtful whether this foolhardy and pretentious resolution
carried them one step nearer their goal. Instead it had the effect of
branding the Jewish leaders in British eyes as allies of uncertain
loyalty, whose word could not be trusted. It was Ben-Gurion's
first essay at the game of power-politics, and it found him playing
on the side of inexperienced men of doubtful sincerity. Palestine
could not and would not become a wholly Jewish state, as Ben-
Gurion had readily conceded in his negotiations with the Arabs;
when he brought the 1937 Congress round to accepting some form
of partition; and when he was in London for the St. James's Conference. Sooner or later they would have to climb down, and though
Weizmann never recovered the ground he lost through the

adoption of the 'Biltmore programme', as it was called, he was subsequently to show how this gratuitous slap in the face to Britain led to further delay in the fulfilment of that part of their programme which was both practicable and equitable.

The Palestine censorship ruthlessly deleted all mention of the 'Biltmore programme' from the local Press, just as it prohibited publication of what was known of the disaster overtaking European Jewry. (The London Polish government revealed that between July and October, 1942, nearly three-quarters of Warsaw's 400,000 Jews had been liquidated.) Relations between the Mandatory and the *Yishuv* had so deteriorated that what amounted to a cold war was now in progress between them, with Shertok struggling on with the heartbreaking task of urging his people to volunteer for the Forces—on an individual basis, of course—and then having his recruiting speeches castrated by the censor.

The farcical realities of the Palestine situation did not slip past the watchful eyes of the British censor, and little except disquieting ripples reached America. Letters took several weeks, and Ben-Gurion's correspondence with his family during the major part of 1942 consisted of hurriedly pencilled notes to Paula, in a large, bold scribble. He was especially hungry for news of his son, Amos, serving with the army somewhere in the widely-expanding Middle East Command. There came a telegram in May informing him of his father's death. Though Avigdor had survived to his eighty-seventh year, occupying himself usefully until shortly before his death as a ledger-clerk in one of the *Histadruth* concerns, it was a blow. Ben-Gurion wrote home: "In my loneliness, far from home, comes this saddening news. I know how much father wanted me to be at his side in his last days. We had so much in common, he and I, though belonging to different generations. It was from him I inherited my love for the people, the land, the language of Israel. He was the leader of our work in Plonsk . . . how I remember those Zionist meetings every week with Simcha Isaac. . . ." Now Avigdor Green's seed was truly spread over the Land of Israel, with sons and grandsons in occupations ranging from the humblest to the highest.

After ten months in America, Ben-Gurion returned to Jerusalem. He reached Palestine by way of Cairo in October, 1942, soon enough to taste in full the humiliations of being a civilian Jew behind the El Alamein battleline. Every ingenuity and crudity known to a colonial bureaucracy was employed to remind the *Yishuv* that in its defiance of immigration regulations and in its policy of storing arms as a precaution against possible attack from the Arabs they were impeding the war effort of their defenders. Spies and counter-spies were busy everywhere, with the Stern gang and the *Irgun Zvai Leumi* ready to take retribution for the life of every Jew drowned on the high seas in a vain quest for shelter in the Promised Land.

Now that statehood in the whole of the country was Zionism's declared post-war aim—there being no possibility of convening Congress to ratify or reject the New York decision—Ben-Gurion had to acquaint *Mapai* with its implications. The fifth conference of the party was due to take place as he arrived. It was held at the co-operative village of Kfar Vitkin,* half-way up the coastal plain near Hadera.

His report on the Biltmore conference and its consequences was long and uneventful. Few could dispute the virtues of gaining independence; many sensed a ring of unreality in the proposal. What savoured of more immediate issues was the large number of delegates who turned up solely to register their boycott of the agenda now before them. This consisted of *Mapai*'s 'Fraction B', one-third of the total number of delegates. Their silence represented the feelings of the majority of the members of *Kibbutz Hameuchad* and the extreme left flank of the party in the towns—in fact the 'downstairs half' of Brenner House.

Ben-Gurion insisted upon absolute unity and discipline within the party. 'Fraction B' claimed they had no quarrel which would justify a split with the leadership, but they wanted redress for measures which had been taken against seven of their members who had been squeezed out of the Tel-Aviv Labour Council. On this issue a motion outlawing autonomous groups was unanimously passed, with 'Fraction B' abstaining. This broke the party and created irreparable rifts within *Kibbutz Hameuchad*.

It was the worst thing that could have happened to *Mapai*. Ben-Gurion should have learned to live with his 'Bevanites'; for Tabenkin and Zisling, who now resuscitated for their group their old name of the twenties, *Achdut Avoda*, took away with them the

* Named after Joseph Vitkin. See page 42.

cream of Israel's pioneering material. This included the most productive colonies and the striking force of *Haganah*, in fact the agricultural backbone of the *Yishuv*. Along with them went Shlomo
Kaplansky, one of the experts on colonisation; while Katznelson,
alarmed at the turn of events, went into semi-retirement. He died
two years later. To Isaac Tabenkin the *kibbutz* idea was not merely
a new and precious asset to the Jews, as it was to Ben-Gurion: it
was the highest expression of human society, and thus more important than statehood. Therefore he did not intend to see his
ambition to make the country a purely socialist commonwealth
thwarted by a party vote. There were others on the Left outside the
control of Ben-Gurion, and he joined up with them. Step-by-step
Tabenkin's resentment of his old comrade grew into hatred. Then,
almost unconsciously, he slipped into the role of Communism's
champion in Palestine.

This, however, was yet to come. For the moment Ben-Gurion's
supremacy both in the world movement and at home, as shown by
the Biltmore programme and the Kfar Vitkin purge, was confirmed.
He stood for the struggle against the White Paper as if there were no
war, and the threat he represented was put into ferocious effect as the
toll of Jewish martyrdom mounted with every passing day. Land
continued to be acquired, immigrants continued to filter in, the
caches of arms increased. The Jews were in open and secret defiance
of the law.

Sometimes the British government was guilty of incredible errors
of psychology, and talked as though the Colonial Office would be
able to toy with Palestine for ever. Early in 1943, for example, the
High Commissioner broadcast a message to the country on the
occasion of the appointment of Sir Douglas Harris, a technician long
employed on the staff of the Administration, as chief of post-war
reconstruction. Sir Harold MacMichael stressed the essentially agricultural character of the country, and the need to weed out the
mushroom industries which had grown up on war-time prosperity
and select for survival only those which might have a chance against
peacetime foreign competition. There would be a certain amount
of state control, he announced, and they would try to raise living
standards, especially of the Arab community "where much remains
to be done." Regarding loans for irrigation, building projects,
and welfare schemes, he warned that there was little hope of looking

elsewhere than in Palestine itself, for in London the possibilities of obtaining a loan for a country which had suffered less than so many others were limited.

As a proposal for the expansion of a rudimentary Arab economy, hardly affected by the war, all this may have been admirable. The Jews, with their large numbers of young men and women in the armed forces, their economy almost exclusively linked to the war effort, their leaders preaching that war's end would mean liberation for themselves and their surviving brothers in Europe, considered it an insult. Ben-Gurion made Sir Harold's broadcast the text of one of his bitterest, and most brilliant, speeches, at a 'parliament' of the *Yishuv* in March.

"The three Jewish disasters of today," he said, "are the White Paper, the war itself, and the massacre of our people in Europe. I know that among us there are those who maintain that the sole task before us is to fight Hitler and so save our nation from destruction. They advise us to leave the political future of this country to the Peace Conference. Does anybody know whether there will ever be a Peace Conference? Churchill has been meeting Roosevelt in Casablanca. That was part of the Peace Conference. So was the meeting of Cordell Hull recently with Eden and friend Halifax in Washington.

"The fate of this country is being shaped by the creation of political, military and economic facts. In accordance with the policy laid down by the 1939 White Paper, Palestine is being transformed into a bi-national state—an Anglo-Arab state with a Jewish ghetto. The government thinks it can deceive us by giving their plans the name of 'reconstruction', and springs this scheme upon us when we are playing our part, no less than Britain or Russia, in this holy war to defeat the common enemy.

"Very lively negotiations have been going on in Bagdad and Cairo, and between Jeddah and Jerusalem. No one has consulted us on them. But they ask us to co-operate in this 'reconstruction programme'. Let us analyse it: the High Commissioner speaks of developing public services, of selecting those branches of industry which have 'a reasonable chance of survival' in conditions of peace; and developing them through the continuance of government control over several branches of economic life, such as irrigation and the marketing of citrus. He warns us that the money for this will have to be found from resources locally accumulated, because 'the great majority of countries to be assisted have suffered infinitely more than Palestine'.

"The High Commissioner tells us that Palestine is essentially an agricultural country. We do not believe this. So was Britain, once. We have always given priority to agriculture; but we need to expand industry as a source of livelihood for the masses of immigrants to be absorbed. Now an 'expert' is to decide which factories are to stay and which must be closed down. The continuance of this state control after the war has another objective: to shackle Jewish initiative and strangle the National Home.

"His Excellency did not baldly tell us that irrigation, drainage and terracing schemes were expressly for the Arabs, as he did in respect of social services. It would have been superfluous to do so; for according to the Land Transfer Regulations of February, 1940, the Jews are restricted to reside in towns and in a small area along the sea-shore—places where there is no need for terracing, afforestation or drainage or whatever else he promises. Our part will be to supply Sir Douglas Harris with the money, he will apply it to reconstruction in the hill region, in the Negev plains, in the Judean and Jezreel valleys—all areas barred to us. This is the 97 per cent of the country in which we are forbidden even to rent a house.

"All this is to be done, of course, on the basis that there will be no influx of capital, and that Jewish immigration will end in conformity with the White Paper. 'There are countries which have suffered infinitely more than Palestine', says the High Commissioner. But what about the people who have suffered infinitely more than any other people!

". . . The High Commissioner's broadcast failed to mention several 'unimportant' matters. The special status of this country; the peculiar conditions prevailing in it; its association with the Jewish people in the past and the future; the special obligations undertaken by the Mandatory government; the rights of the National Home; the historic link between the Jewish people and Palestine even before the British Empire came into being; the terrible disaster that has now befallen the Jews; the reconstruction work that has already been done here and the ability displayed by the Jews to revive the desolate areas of this country, etc.

"When you have read the High Commissioner's speech, you get

the impression that the rulers of the country have never opened their Bible, never heard anything of the Balfour Declaration, never read the clauses of the Mandate, never visited a Jewish settlement, never met a Jewish pioneer, and, naturally, never heard of the existence of the Jewish Agency for Palestine which has been entrusted under the Mandate with 'assisting and taking part in the development of the country'. . . . We shall not co-operate with the White Paper government, neither today nor after the war. We shall not lend a hand to the implementation of the schemes announced last night, for all these schemes are based on the stoppage of Jewish immigration and the segregation of the Jews in a Pale of Settlement.

". . . What has been done in this country in the past sixty years in the sphere of industry and agriculture has been done by returning exiles. It was not money accumulated in the country, but pioneering capital and pioneering labour, bearing with them the vision of Jewish revival which built Petach Tikvah on the swamps of the Yarkon River, Rishon le Zion on the sand-dunes of Ain Hakoveh, Motza on the rocks of Jerusalem, and Hanita on the heights of Galilee. It was they who made fertile the neglected and desolate Jezreel valley, and created hundreds of settlements and industrial enterprises.

"As for money accumulated in this country—such a thing has never existed, it has been poured in by our own national and private funds. Palestine's soil has been neglected not because of too many people, but because of too few. This expert Sir Douglas Harris came here eight years ago as a development officer, but to this day we have not seen the villages he has developed, the swamps drained, the hills re-afforested and terraced, the irrigation schemes created. There *has* been development, accomplished not with his aid but despite obstruction from him and his colleagues!

"We shall not co-operate with this plan because we have a plan of our own, long-prepared before the government thought of its reconstruction programme. It is based on these facts.

1. Of the six and a-half million acres in this country, four and a-half are totally uncultivated. And the rest is only partially cultivated. We shall develop agriculture, crafts, industry and maritime resources.
2. There is one people in the world without a home, bound for

millennia to this land. There is no salvation for them but to
return here, and they shall return, whether they have in their
hands an official scrap of paper called an immigration certifi-
cate or not.

3. We shall get the money—either from richer Jewish communities or by an international loan. Our sufferings bring us high
   on the list.

4. Those 'realists' among us are blind. They think that a scrap of
   paper is stronger than the distress of a people, the will for
   regeneration, the longing for a homeland."

Of course, this was only partly a reply to the authorities, who were
soon to pick an occasion to avenge themselves on the arrogant,
angry, and self-confessed law-breaker. More directly this speech was
meant as a morale-raiser, in the middle of war, for a people whose
confidence in themselves and their leaders had suffered a decline.
Ben-Gurion gave the Jews what Churchill gave to the British, and
Goebbels to the Germans—the force to carry on when all appeared
lost. There was no other man in the world who could speak with
such authority on behalf of these intellectually and socially marooned
half-million in the Middle East.

The authorities acted at once. They were going to show the world,
and especially his friends in America, what this verbose historian
really was—a dangerous rabble-rouser! They staged a lavish show-
trial, and on this occasion the censors were instructed to take a
holiday. In fact American correspondents from Cairo were specifically invited to be present as the military court in Jerusalem opened
a case involving British army deserters and local Jews, a case during
which sweeping charges were made against Ben-Gurion, the
Agency, the *Histadruth* and the *Haganah* as the organisers behind a
large and wealthy arms-smuggling ring.

Since the earliest days of the Mandate, cases of illegal possession
of arms by both Jews and Arabs had been before the courts and
attracted but scant attention. This time everything was done to
elevate the proceedings to the status of a *cause célèbre*. Questions to
the accused were so framed as to point to the Agency chairman as
the master-mind, the architect of a conspiracy hostile to the Allied
war-effort in the Middle East.

Naturally, the Jews had arms, and would purchase more wherever the opportunity arose. *Haganah* was not illegal, though its existence was unproclaimed; and within its framework *Palmach* had been enlisted by the British Army to help in the Syrian campaign and other operations, having been trained and equipped for the purpose. All this was known. It was an article of Zionist faith, first established in the Sejera settlement where Ben-Gurion had laboured as a youth, that Jewish security was a Jewish concern. Was this not justified by the events of 1921, 1929 and 1936? Why, then, this elaborately-staged publicity for known facts, with a photograph of Ben-Gurion passed around the court as a prominent exhibit? The reason was clear: few officials in Palestine wished to see the Jews mobilised in their own military formations, so how better to defile that aspiration than by spreading the concept of a Jewish fifth column, of 'Nazi discipline', as the prosecutor declared!

To his own people, incensed by the trial, sickened by the anti-Semitism blatantly displayed throughout the thirty-four-day hearing, Ben-Gurion declared: "We have known other British officials than those appearing for the prosecution at this trial, officers with whom our boys have gone through fire. Threats will not influence us to surrender our right to our homeland. We continue to believe in the conscience of mankind."

Nevertheless, it would be just as well to give the conscience of mankind a few hard facts to be getting on with. The Agency pushed its demand for a Jewish Army more strongly than ever. Shertok laid before the military a plan to start a Hungarian resistance movement by dropping Jewish parachutists into that country. But few could now be found to favour an operation which would allow a wide range of responsibilities to a suspect organisation like the Jewish Agency, whose president, Chaim Weizmann, was now mourning the loss of his younger son on a mission with the R.A.F.

Then, in the summer of 1944, Churchill suddenly woke up. As the Allies crossed the Channel to storm Hitler's Europe he gave his attention to a final appeal by Weizmann to allow the Jews to serve with the Star of David shoulder flash. He asked to see a design of the proposed flag, and within two weeks the decision was made. Churchill told the House of Commons on September 28th: "The government has decided to accede to the request of the Jewish Agency for Palestine that a Jewish Brigade Group should be formed to take part in active operations. I know there are vast numbers of

Jews serving with our Forces and the American Forces throughout
all the Armies, but it seemed to me indeed appropriate that a special
Jewish unit, of that race which has suffered indescribable torments
from the Nazis, should be represented as a distinct formation among
the forces gathered for their final overthrow."

So, after five long years of agitation, Ben-Gurion's first ambition
of the war was realised. Golomb came to London and with Shertok
worked out the details at the War Office. Of the 30,000 Palestine
Jews on active service, some 5,000 were organised within the
Brigade. But a political and moral victory so late in the day could
not restore the ebbing authority of the Agency over the Jewish
community. The *Irgun Zvai Leumi* and the Stern gang were already
hard set in their own plans for achieving Zionism through armed
insurrection. In August an unsuccessful attempt was made in Jaffa
on the life of the High Commissioner, Sir Harold MacMichael.
(He was at last due for retirement.) The Administration retaliated
by deporting suspects in large numbers to the Sudan, later transferring them to Eritrea. Thereupon the Stern gang committed the
shocking crime of assassinating Lord Moyne, now Minister of State
in the Middle East, in Cairo. This at last prompted the Agency itself
to act against terrorism. It used *Haganah* on punitive raids and it
furnished the police with information for the apprehension of known
murderers.

Within the Agency serious differences developed as to the attitude
to be adopted towards the terrorists in their growing aggressiveness.
The problem was whether to root them out, or to come to terms
with them. Golomb, the head of security, believed in partial co-
operation with the government and the secret strengthening of
Haganah. Moshe Sneh, the civilian 'War-Minister' of the Agency,
thought the time had come for a show of force. Ben-Gurion was
prepared to fight, but not at this stage. These discussions created
a lamentable weakness in policy as a result of which the Agency
sometimes helped to eradicate terrorism, and sometimes quietly
assisted in covering up its traces. One minor concession on immigration, one gesture of humanity towards the refugee-boats, would
have helped it to make up its mind. But there was no gesture by the
Administration, only a series of sledge-hammer blows, inaccurate
and ill-timed, against people held in a tragic dilemma. In the general
rot the only people with a consistent policy were the terrorists. They

concluded, after a careful if one-sided study of Britain's colonial
history, that Palestine was approaching its '1776', and their tech-
nique was to persuade Britain that to stay in Palestine would prove
too costly in men, money and prestige. With a few well-placed
bombs, some carefully-planned sabotage, the selection of appropriate candidates for assassination, they hoped they would succeed
where Ben-Gurion with his threats and Weizmann with his moderation had failed.

In this atmosphere of distrust and suspicion the war in Europe
ended, and the Bevin era began. As the British electorate returned
the Labour Party to power, Moshe Shertok formally placed the
Biltmore demands before the government, together with a request
for the immediate admission of 100,000 Jewish fugitives drawn
from what was left of the wrecked communities of Europe. Ben-
Gurion turned up in the United States, on a crucial and secret
mission linked with the expectation that the White Paper would
at last be revoked.

"The British worker," he had said, "will understand our aims."
Hope ran high. No political group in the world was so irretrievably
committed to support of the Zionist programme as the British
socialists, nursed by the *Histadruth* since the days of Arlosoroff for
this moment. But Ben-Gurion was now under no illusions as to the
Arab reaction to the new flow of immigrants he legitimately
awaited. Neither did he place reliance on any people but his own
to counter their resistance. He took an engineer named Chaim
Slavin with him to America, as well as Dostrovsky, then in operational command of *Haganah*.

In New York friends provided him with a list of people prepared
to help in the event of war with the Arabs—a 'probable eventuality',
as he said. America was then in her optimistic mood of disarmament
and demobilisation, and was scrapping first-rate material and
munitions. Ben-Gurion arranged for the purchase of whatever
Slavin could lay his hands on. The latter remained in the country for
eighteen months, and for the expenditure of $800,000 brought back
war equipment worth many millions. It was brought to Palestine
secretly, or so those responsible for the trans-shipments thought.
In fact the British were not unaware of the business, but let the whole
lot through. The Jews should remember this in any assessment they
make of Britain's role during those wretched years. The stores were

taken to secret dumps and formed the basis of a Jewish armaments industry. Simultaneously, others in Europe were buying aircraft, light and heavy guns, explosives and rifles. The purchases were made principally in Czechoslovakia and France. The time was not yet ripe for bringing these latter to Palestine. They were stored in readiness for the moment of release.

Both the main American political parties lent their voices to aid the Zionist programme, and President Truman's special streak of doggedness prevailed against considerable pressure exerted in Washington for the Arabs. But Ernest Bevin proved that America had, at that time, nothing more concrete to offer towards the solution of the Arab-Jewish problem—now inextricably interwoven with the wider strategic and national problems of the whole Middle East—than advice. The man whom Dov Hos★ had enlisted to help with the reversal of the Passfield policy fifteen years before took personal command of the Palestine situation, and disabused the optimists about Labour's intentions. Crushing, though by no means silencing, the opposition within his own ranks, he fought the Jews on the immigration issue, tracked the underground escape-route down to its very source in Europe and made it doubly hard for Jews to reach the safety of the shores of Palestine. He also made the Jewish determination to resist doubly strong.

Bevin came to the Foreign Office with only the vaguest comprehension of the nature of the Middle East between the collapse of the Ottoman Empire and the outbreak of the Second World War; while of the changes wrought by the war upon the various Arab peoples and their relations with Britain he had no comprehension at all. He saw himself as inheriting a responsibility to safeguard a vital British interest. It could only be preserved by inviting the Arabs to join with him, to their mutual benefit, in upholding 'democratic civilisation', now menaced by the weight of Russian power descending from the north upon the Moslem 'roof.' In this he considered he was being impeded by a simulated American interest in Zionism, and sabotaged by an international conspiracy in which power-hungry men exploited the sufferings of their fellow-Jews to further their own ambitions.

Clearly, the most ruthless of these men was David Ben-Gurion. The next three years consisted largely of a war between the two men,

★ Hos, with his wife and daughter, was killed in a car accident in 1940.

fought with hatred and desperation on both sides. A squalid war, Churchill called it. Nothing happened to end the deadlock during the first months of the Labour Party's return to office. Bevin challenged Truman to come to serious grips with the Palestine problem by nominating American members to a new commission of enquiry. Another enquiry! The Jewish Agency chairman replied by switching into operation a long-completed plan of escape in which sixty-three weather-beaten vessels formed the armada, and the whole of Europe the Dunkirk.

In those three years 84,000 immigrants sought to cross the Mediterranean to Palestine. The scope of the plan extended from the eastern frontier of Poland through seven countries with twenty-four secret points along their borders. It was implemented by a group of young men drawn from *Haganah* who were prepared to follow Ben-Gurion to the death. They had to make painful decisions, often ending in disaster for the escapees. And it was carried out in the face of opposition by many old-fashioned Zionists less reconciled than Ben-Gurion to the use of force.

Of those sixty-three ships, fifty-seven were intercepted in transit, or rather hauled in by the Navy in pathetic scenes at the port of Haifa to provide front-page horror stories for the world's Press. Bevin went obstinately on. He was alone in his policy. He swamped Palestine with troops, so that every new military camp and installation multiplied the opportunities of the terrorist organisations for driving home their lesson that any conflict between fanatical guerrillas and perplexed officialdom must end in the humiliation of the latter.

Ben-Gurion described the Bevin policy as one of double repudiation: the scrapping of both the White Paper and Zionism at the same time. He understood his fellow-socialist's stubborn mind. The Foreign Secretary was seeking to drive a wedge between Jews and Zionists—but here again he failed because nothing brought Jews of all opinions more closely together than their collective national grief, to which the cemetery of Europe was the gigantic witness. "The Bevin policy," Ben-Gurion declared, "is a clear attempt to do away with the Jews as a nation and to recognise only the existence of dispersed Jewish communities, to be either objects of charity to other peoples, or targets for their pogroms. It intends Palestine to serve as a base for the British forces driven out by the Arabs of

Egypt, of Iraq, of Syria. It aims at turning this country into a second Malta!"

Ben-Gurion was worried by the possibility of the problem coming before the United Nations, hinted at by Bevin in his announcement of the despatch of the Anglo-American committee of enquiry. In Britain he had an enemy with whom he was comfortably familiar, but the United Nations Organisation was an unknown quantity, and in it the Arab states constituted a formidable voting bloc. Furthermore, he was able to shut off his Zionist prejudices from his general assessment of Britain, of which he was a stalwart admirer through his unqualified sympathy for the Welfare State as a domestic principle. He also believed Britain's colonial policy in Africa, the West Indies and elsewhere, expressed in the vast undertakings for their betterment then being planned by the Colonial Development Corporation, to be both generous and humane. Later, he was profoundly impressed by the departure of the British from India. To him it was a true act of socialism.

It seemed to him that with the United Nations as arbiter of the current controversy between his people and the Arabs, or his people and the British, Palestine could be reduced to a pawn among the hostile power-groups of West and East, and he shuddered at the prospect. Personally, he disliked to have to turn to the Soviet Union for support; but outwardly he displayed some bravado. Should the matter come before the United Nations, he told his friends in *Mapai*, they would state their case with neither faith nor fear. "We shall come as accusers," he asserted. "But let us bear in mind the two primary forces to decide this issue, both situated here, in Palestine. They are our own strength as a community and the determination with which we push the drive for immigration."

He could by no means take the strength of the Jews for granted. Only on one issue were they united: the claim for the immediate transfer of the 100,000 refugees. Sharp and fundamental divisions existed among the Jewish Agency executive. The London members followed the Weizmann line that *Haganah* should vindicate its name by rooting out terrorism, a view shared by the leading American Zionists with the exception of Abba Hillel Silver, now emerging as the dominant figure on that side of the Atlantic. Within Palestine itself there was no clear dividing line between legality and illegality, between *Haganah*'s permissible acts of 'resistance' and the terrorism, beyond the pale, of the *Irgun*. The Administration itself termed *Haganah* 'semi-official', and when it implored the Agency to suppress the terror it was inviting *Haganah* to do a normal policeman's job. But *Haganah* dared not act. It did not want the responsibility of fomenting a Jewish civil war, and thus leaving the community open to attacks from the third party in the triangle, the Arabs. Besides, the terrorists disposed of more support than the Agency cared to admit. They could hold up banks in broad daylight, but either through fear or sympathy not one witness would come forward to testify against them. It is a measure of Bevin's efficacy in solving the problem of Palestine that the moment he began applying himself to it, the difference between terror and 'activism' all but disappeared.

In the Y.M.C.A. building, a striking piece of architecture close to the Old City walls in Jerusalem, the Anglo-American committee heard Ben-Gurion's evidence. He was given a rough time. His introductory speech was strong though subjective (he recounted the story of his immigration forty years earlier, and the cool reception accorded him by the Love-of-Zion organisation in Odessa, see page 48). But the committee was far more interested in the relationship between the Jewish Agency and *Haganah,* and his replies to their keen interrogation lacked conviction. Whereas Weizmann a few days earlier had intimated that, should 100,000 certificates for refugees be granted, he would perhaps be prepared to forget about Jewish independence, Ben-Gurion revealed how, in his eyes, statehood was more important than the 100,000.

By the end of April, 1946, the committee had its report ready. It struck a compromise between the known British and American positions, and was obviously the product of hard bargaining between the individual members. It contained a strong recommendation for the entry of the 100,000, and an equally strong warning against the bloody consequences if statehood, in a part or the whole of Palestine, were awarded to either the Jews or Arabs.

Weizmann and Shertok saw, in the report, a welcome gleam of hope. In the abrogation of the White Paper's hated clauses and in the endorsement of Jewry's major immigration demand they had gained substantial victories, enough to give everyone concerned a fresh start in an atmosphere of tranquillity. Not so Ben-Gurion. He condemned the report in its totality. After several private discussions with some of the committee members, in Tel-Aviv and

Jerusalem, he had had the impression of having won them over to the urgency and justice of reviving the Peel partition formula, though with frontiers more generous to the Jews. He was now grievously disappointed. The recommendations, he said, would be taken by Bevin to represent not the scrapping of the White Paper, but a new edition of it.

Events confirmed these fears. Truman rushed in, supporting the plea on behalf of the 100,000. Attlee told Parliament nothing could be done until the private militias were disbanded, after which the report would have to be considered in all its implications and as a whole, with particular attention to the expense of moving that waiting mass of human beings, the technical difficulties involved, and the problem of who was going to ensure their re-establishment, without disturbances, in Palestine. But apparently the government in London alone saw any virtue in patience. Its servants in Jerusalem were moving towards their own solution. They decided to put the Jewish Agency leaders, and anyone else of importance they could lay their hands on, under lock and key, thus destroying, they hoped, the resistance in one swoop.

The plan went ludicrously awry, for Jewish intelligence among the British military was at least as well-informed as the counter-intelligence on the other side. Ben-Gurion had a meeting with George Hall, the Colonial Secretary, in the week beginning June 24th. A day later he slipped off quietly to Paris. Moshe Sneh, number one on the army's list of suspects, disappeared underground. Abba Hushi of Haifa left for the hinterland to hide among his friends the Druses. At dawn on the Saturday, Jewry's Sabbath, operations began. Moshe Shertok and David Hacohen were picked up in Tel-Aviv and taken to jail in Latrun, to be joined the next day by David Remez, Dov Joseph, Rabbi Fishman and others. Weizmann, Golda Myerson and Ben-Zvi were not among the 2,600 arrested. Kaplan, the Agency treasurer, was, like Ben-Gurion, out of the country.

Simultaneously, searches to uncover weapons, root out suspects, and terrify the Jews into submission were instituted in the towns and the settlements. About 30 little collectives had their menfolk carted off, not without the use of rifle-butts to tear their protesting women away from them. Ein Harod offered a particularly un-edifying example of the evil merry-go-round in motion. A good haul of rifles, mortars, machine-guns, grenades, and ammunition was unearthed, but nearly all from one *kibbutz*, Yagur, near Haifa, where tear-gas was used to overcome passive resistance from the settlers. They were caged in their hundreds far down south, but as none would divulge his name on interrogation, the round-up was largely a waste of time. The *Irgun Zvai Leumi* and the Stern gang, whose members were old hands at meeting the first sign of trouble with the disappearing trick, were wholly spared the indignities and discomforts of it all.

Weizmann was due to leave to have an eye operation in London, so Palestinian Jewry was left without a top-calibre spokesman. The British occupation of the Jewish Agency's headquarters in Jerusalem did not impede Moshe Sneh in his work of activism, which was carried on in association with an all-party council of seven known as 'Committee X'. Its activities were, of course, secret, and it never burdened Weizmann's conscience with its operational details. Ben-Gurion, however, in radio contact with *Haganah* from his room at the Parc Monceau Hotel in Paris, was kept informed of every new development.

Throughout the year *Irgun*, the Sternists and 'Committee X' maintained close liaison. Sometimes, when a particularly dangerous operation was on the tapis, they pooled their knowledge and even their personnel. This was undoubtedly the case with the plot to blow up the civil and military headquarters of the Administration in the King David Hotel. The project had been mooted months before, but Sneh and Israel Galili, the men responsible for *Haganah* policy, kept putting it off as a dangerous exploit of unwarranted seriousness. The relationship between *Haganah* and the *Irgun* on this occasion, as indeed on all others, was stiff and unfriendly, and it is difficult to trace the original sponsor of the attack. Certainly, the job was done by the *Irgun* alone, though, according to Menachem Beigin, leader of that body, only after a specific order had been received from *Haganah*.

To add to the obscurity surrounding the explosion's authorship, a crucial change had taken place in *Haganah*'s leadership between the making of the decision and its actual implementation. With Ben-Gurion out of the country and no other high officer left with freedom of movement and speech, Weizmann tried to force the activists to abandon their tactics. Just before leaving for Britain he sent an emissary to Sneh with an ultimatum. This envoy, Meyer Weisgal, an American citizen who was assisting Weizmann in the establishment of an institute of science at Rehovoth, carried an order from Weizmann that all active resistance against the British should cease, pending a meeting of the Executive to discuss the future conduct of the struggle. Should Sneh refuse, Weizmann would resign the presidency, publicly announcing his reasons. Sneh was unwilling to decide alone on how to reply. At a meeting of 'Committee X' he laid Weizmann's ultimatum before the members, and asked that it be rejected. Only one man beside himself—the representative of the regenerated *Achdut Avoda*—voted in favour of rejection.

On July 16th Sneh resigned from *Haganah*, and made his preparations to leave the country. On the 22nd the Administration's wing of the King David Hotel blew up, causing the loss of ninety-one British, Arab and Jewish lives, with many more injured. The following day Sneh boarded a French vessel, the *André Lebon*. He made for Paris, where a meeting of those leaders not in prison was to take place. Here the Weizmann policy was endorsed.

The King David operation was worked out with meticulous care. Elaborate precautions were taken to avoid bloodshed. Had the wing been sliced away without loss of life the event, by its very daring, would have earned prestige for the *Yishuv*, because where innocent lives are not involved a military feat can win recognition on the strength of its spectacular cunning and prowess alone. Instead, it took on the character of a brutal massacre, and the Agency acted accordingly. Denying any responsibility for the affair, it condemned it as a dastardly crime. The removal of Sneh at this fortuitous moment left the impression that he was personally and exclusively involved, and was being punished accordingly. The detention of Shertok and the others in Latrun, and the 'confinement' of Ben-Gurion in Paris lent veracity to the pronouncement. But the urbane Sneh, whose outward charm conceals a shrewdly realistic brain, was not the man to carry sole responsibility for such an operation, and, in the circumstances, his claim that he was used as a scapegoat carries conviction.

By assuring himself the so-called 'defence' portfolio in the Agency, and by presenting himself as an activist who would not carry operations beyond the decent limitations imposed by the war against the White Paper, Ben-Gurion brought about a complete break with the *Irgun* and Sternists. This, they claimed, was the third occasion on which he had done them down, recalling bitterly the abortive pact with Jabotinsky, and the intervention which, in 1941, had ended the projects for coalition with Golomb* and Katznelson. Henceforth, he could pull his own chestnuts out of the fire.

At this point it is not unlikely that, through the revulsion caused in Palestine at the outrage, and the Jews' fear of indiscriminate reprisals from the infuriated general commanding hard-pressed troops, the terrorists would have been grateful for an opportunity to cease their ugly work, temporarily at least. It would have needed an act of statesmanship on the part of the government, not at all beyond its capacities. Such an act might well have taken the form of an interim announcement on the Anglo-American proposals, to show that at least they were the subject of honest study. Britain, however, taught the world that obstinacy was a game she too could play. British policy towards the refugees was stiffened.

Immigrants who reached the coasts of Palestine were now deprived of the privilege of being interned in the land of their dreams. They were dragged off the Haifa quayside and carried to new barbed wire existences in Cyprus; and as brutalities on the part of some individuals in the C.I.D. and the army's special services came to light, the hostility of the Jewish community turned to loathing and disgust. The terrorists had no time now for the mealy-mouthed hyprocrisy of *Haganah*. If their policy of death for death met with obstruction on its part, they would, they said, turn their bullets against Jewish treachery. The ordinary Jews in the street saw in them the terrible instrument of righteous retribution, and not surprisingly endeavoured to elude their wrath.

Looking out over the Bois de Boulogne, a sanctuary of midsummer calm, Ben-Gurion faced his young staff waiting the next move in perplexity. The war was on—against Britain, against the terrorists, but were they free to fight it? Men and women in their thirties, they were intellectuals turned farm-labourers turned *maquisards*. For years they had accepted life as being inextricably bound up with the importance of outmanœuvring officialdom. But how long would it go on? "You are all much younger than I,"

* Golomb died in 1945.

Ben-Gurion told them, "but I too will live to see the Jewish state, and in four to five years at that!" Of course, they believed him. It was their Churchill speaking, and their Moses. Their reverence for him was not far short of idolatry.

Nevertheless, the achievement of independence was now fraught with greater obstacles than at any other period of Zionist colonisation in Palestine. Let us examine, briefly, the balance of forces as they stood after the Second World War. The Jewish people in the world were, as Weizmann put it, numerically reduced and intellectually impoverished. There were about six millions fewer of them than before—eleven millions as against seventeen in 1939. It was precisely among those six millions that religious sentiment and national consciousness, kept strong by centuries of persecution, had created the idea of Zionism and the necessity of achieving it in the shortest space of time. From among their ranks the successive waves of immigration had come, each contributing its own special talents, each transplanting its own special strength. Now the movement in the Diaspora had shifted its gravitational centre to America, where sentiment, rather than a sense of survival, was its prime motivating force. Moreover, Zionism had lost its most faithful sympathiser, Great Britain. What had begun a generation earlier as a partnership was now twisted into a relentless conflict of interests with the atmosphere between them poisoned by ambuscade, blockade, diplomatic manœuvring and murder.

The Middle East, of which Palestine formed so vital a part, was no longer a strategic backwater relegated to Britain's suzerainty, and the Suez Canal was no longer a comparatively neglected waterway. Embedded within the region lay a new and coveted prime material, oil, in almost-unlimited supply, without which it now seemed that not only the wars and the diplomacy, but the very economics, of other countries could not be carried on. In brief the area had been brought within the sphere of the larger conflicts of the new masters of the globe's destiny—America and the Soviet Union. As these two wooed the friendship of the Arab world, the Jews, in the act of being lightly sacrificed by Britain, became of no great ultimate significance.

The Arab peoples were themselves making rapid headway under their suddenly-achieved importance. Six of them were nations, free in fact or in principle, and together were formed into a league solidly opposed to the realisation of Jewish ambitions, and aware of their own weight as a pressure-group among the nations.

All these factors made for a truly formidable opposition. With what could the Jews counteract it? First, by their own achievements in Palestine. They had gathered together 600,000 of their people, anchored to a comparatively advanced economy, with their own secret army well-trained in peace and tested in war. They had poured their devotion into the hard soil of Palestine and turned their own areas into the most productive. The wise purchase of land, made with an eye to the strategy of defence, had entrenched them firmly along the Mediterranean littoral. In their natural, human instinct to save the remnants of their people in the one country where Jewish refugees were assured of a welcome, they enjoyed the moral support of the world, a Christian world sharing collective culpability for the magnitude of Germany's crime. American Jewry stepped forward as a rich and powerful ally. It was so situated in New York and elsewhere as to wield appreciable influence on the shape of American policy.

Finally, the Jews had their desperation, a mighty weapon in the hands of people with little to lose but the prospect of extinction, and with survival and self-respect to gain in the one land where they had any right at all, shadowy though their opponents might deem that right.

The *Irgun* had succumbed to that desperation. Its leaders were young men without roots in the country, for their blood had not gone into the building of Petach Tikvah or into the drainage of the Jezreel valley. Its rank and file were frequently not European at all, but Oriental Jews from outside the main Zionist stream, without knowledge of, or sympathy for, its Russian and Polish sources.

Ben-Gurion controlled this sense of desperation like a tap. He viewed it simply as one of many factors, if historically the latest and most compelling, in Zionism. The instruments of redemption were the sword *and* the plough, not, as Beigin believed, the sword alone, and not, as Weizmann preached, the plough alone. Far-seeing, intrepid men had come to the country in its beginnings as he had done, to prepare it and themselves for the desperate needs such as now faced them in 1946. Such a man could be affected but little by the temporising of a government, whose Foreign Secretary was too proud to admit failure.

Britain was heartily reluctant to take the problem to the United
Nations, as a new Colonial Secretary, Creech-Jones, openly confessed to the Jews. The government warded off the evil moment by
refurbishing the Anglo-American proposals, coupling them with a
promise of ultimate autonomy for the entire population, and
presenting them afresh to the Jews and Arabs. By this time Palestine
was hardly being administered at all, merely garrisoned. The revised
plan found adherents in neither camp, while the accompanying
invitation to a new London conference was understandably declined
by the Jewish leaders, deprived of the advice, but aware of the bargaining power, of their colleagues in internment. In November
these latter were quietly released; but the conference, which had
meanwhile opened with exploratory talks with representatives of
the Arab states, was put off till January. Before this the Zionist
Congress was due to meet, for the first time in seven years.

On one important issue Weizmann had been right, Ben-Gurion
wrong. This was in the Biltmore programme of 1942, reiterated
three years later in London, for a Jewish state to cover the whole of
Palestine. The realities now showed these demands to be flamboyant
and fanciful. Weizmann had known this then, but had not spoken
up. In 1946 Ben-Gurion saw it too, and at a meeting in his Paris
hide-out the Biltmore programme was shorn down to a demand
for statehood in a partitioned Palestine—the formula agreed upon
was 'Peel plus the Negev'. This retreat incurred the anger of Abba
Hillel Silver, of Cleveland, Ohio, who charged the Executive with
exceeding its powers, with sacrificing part of the sacred soil of
Palestine, with compromising itself *vis-à-vis* the British—guilty, he
emphasised, of a black oppression 'unheard of except in the acts of
Hitler and Mussolini'. It was Britain, not the Jews, who had to
climb down, said Silver; and she would do so quickly enough if
America would only apply economic sanctions towards the Mandatory: to be precise, shelve Britain's request for a loan.

Ben-Gurion would not go as far as Silver. Nevertheless, he had
long decided (since 1938, in fact) that Chaim Weizmann was past
making a contribution to a Zionist victory. The old man was sick, in
heart and body, and found no place in the new climate of Bevinist
repudiation and Jewish resistance. The Congress about to take place
would round off a fifty years' struggle and complete the circle in
Basle. Ben-Gurion determined that this time their venerable leader

was not 'going to get away with it'. He could not trust Weizmann to go back to Whitehall as an accurate ambassador. And what Weizmann said all the other London men believed. Therefore, to rid the movement of the Weizmann incubus of moderation (characterised by a formal claim to statehood which camouflaged a practical readiness to continue with Britain on a promise of freer immigration) Ben Gurion allied himself with Silver and his supporters.

That December they convened in Basle. Controversy was bitter, ostensibly as to whether they should accept the government's renewed invitation to talks. In fact, Chaim Weizmann, president of the Jewish Agency and the Zionist Organisation, was in the dock. Again, as so frequently before, the old captain towered above his mutinous crew. Throughout his career his failing had been lack of decision, but this he more than atoned for in his majesty of stature, his refusal to sink to the labyrinthine tactics of the party men.

Four hundred delegates, from sixty-one countries, with two thousand visitors, including members of the Diplomatic Corps (but no Englishmen), heard him address this twenty-second Congress, the last of an era, in the great Mustermesse, Basle's Exhibition Hall. "I am seventy-three," he said, reading deliberately from his notes, "and this is probably the last time I shall speak to you. Remember it is easy to preach resistance from New York. It is easier to swim in the sea than in a bath-tub. You American Jews woke up too late. The United States will not fight Britain on the Palestine issue." He attacked Silver, whose espousal of Moshe Sneh in the councils of the Executive brought him into tacit acceptance of near-terrorist methods. From the rear of the hall there were rumblings of protest as the Americans wilted under the taunts of a tongue which could be as bitter as any. Looking up from his prepared speech he called back at them: "There is a drop of my blood in every house in Tel-Aviv, in every barn in Nahalal (a Jezreel settlement). Don't try and compare our position with the Boers or the Irish!"

He could not sway them. Bevin had got under their skin. Ben-Gurion only attacked the speech obliquely, by barely referring to Weizmann's defence. There was strong opposition within *Mapai* against dropping the old pilot, and Eliezer Kaplan openly canvassed support for Weizmann among his fellow-socialists in the Executive. He was largely successful, though in the outcome the scales slightly tipped against the London talks, and therefore against Weizmann.

The socialists were principally afraid of what was, in effect, a bid by the Silverites to make New York the centre of the movement with themselves at the helm. This in any case happened, though its effect was mitigated by an arrangement whereby the man from Cleveland would be 'head of the American section' of the Agency, and Ben-Gurion the world chairman. It was an uneasy alliance, but it ensured the rejection of any solution other than statehood in a part of the country at least, and it prevented the complete arrogation of power by non-Palestinians, which would have been a retrograde step the left-wing could hardly be expected to tolerate. A further safeguard for the Jerusalem socialists was the presence in America of Moshe Shertok ; and it was in him, rather than in Silver, that Ben-Gurion placed his reliance.

Defeated and disillusioned, Weizmann returned home. He would not stay the Congress out, yet if he had done so he would have learned that the new Executive, having sacrificed the leader, followed his policy and did in fact decide to go to London. This much Ben-Gurion, spurred on by Kaplan, had extracted from Silver. So much for the democratic will in the hyper-democratic movement of Zionism!

Off they went to their various posts: Ben-Gurion to London, Sneh to Paris and to the direction of the Continental escape-route, Silver to New York, Shertok to Washington. The stage was set, the actors in their places, and up went the curtain for the last act in the drama.

Creech-Jones was new to the Colonial Office, but not to Zionism. His voice had often been heard on Jewish platforms in the years when Labour had volunteered abundant lip-service to the cause. He and the Jews talked together like a sorely-tried family conspiring against its tyrannical and rough-mouthed head who is heaping dishonour upon its name. Parallel talks were in progress with the Arabs in St. James's Palace, scene of so many ill-fated conferences between Britain and the representatives of argumentative colonial races. The dismissal of Weizmann and the growing criticism in the British Press at the conduct of Palestine affairs brought a new atmosphere to the discussions. Creech-Jones was anxious to reach a political settlement. He told Berl Locker and Nahum Goldmann, of the Agency, that he would himself sponsor a scheme to partition Palestine. The trouble was Bevin. He seemed to listen to nobody except Harold Beeley—the 'unavoidable'—whose dread of Russia, dislike of the Americans and respect for the Arabs was the determining factor in the Foreign Office policy for the Middle East.

At the first meeting which Bevin attended the Jews received a shock. Their arch-enemy loped and tottered into Creech-Jones's office like an exhausted man. Only when he was seated and supported by the table did he look the party-boss. He blinked suspiciously at the Agency men, at Ben-Gurion, ready for a fight, at Goldmann, Locker and Professor Brodetsky, hoping against hope that all would end in a dramatic peace gesture from the government. Those were the gloomy days of Britain's fuel-cuts, and the large room was eerily lit by candles. To Bevin his antagonists seemed no different from the troublesome Jews, whom he hated, of his own Labour Party. Among his respectful retinue hovered Sir Douglas Harris, their old neighbour from Jerusalem now supposedly engaged on the 'reconstruction' of Palestine.

Creech-Jones thought a way out of the impasse could be found if the Jews would shelve their political demands for a period of five years, in return for which the White Paper and land-purchase veto would not be enforced. But Bevin refused to countenance the suggestion. Protesting his good intentions, he seemed mainly to be looking for sympathy in his own difficulties. He was against racialism, he said, and if the Jews would only leave him in peace he could compose their differences with the Arabs. The meeting broke up cold and pessimistic.

Ben-Gurion asked Bevin if he might see him alone. The Foreign Secretary agreed. Nevertheless, he brought Beeley along with him. "Why don't you believe we are honest about our policy?" Bevin asked. "We have no selfish intentions. It's peace and stability in the Middle East we are looking for, no more." The other said bluntly: "Tell me frankly what you want. Perhaps we Jews would be willing to help. Perhaps our interests coincide." As it happened, the interests of these two men did coincide, in part, at least. Ben-Gurion mentioned the possibility of British bases in the Negev, as an alternative to Suez, and they discussed the chances of finding oil in the Negev, that expanse of desert in the south of Palestine. Bevin's mind was significantly impressed; and at a subsequent meeting with the Arabs he advanced a large part of Ben-Gurion's argument as his own. The Arabs left him in no doubt as to their reaction.

These talks were officially labelled 'informal'. What was 'formal' took place between the British government and the Arab states, with the belated participation of the Mufti's Palestinian supporters. When this last-named delegation arrived, Ben-Gurion chose to drop out of the picture. He returned home, to be informed by the High Commissioner of the government's intention to impose martial law upon the Jews. Only stiff action by the Agency could prevent it. This, thought Ben-Gurion, was where he came in. Did the High Commissioner realise what the crushing of terrorism would involve? At the least, a split in the Agency Executive; at the most, an internecine struggle among the Jews during which their resources, their creative energies, and perhaps their youth too, would be consigned to Moloch. If there was any dirty work to be done, let the government do it. Events moved rapidly to their climax. Boat-loads continued to arrive, quietly aided on their way by several European governments, notably the French. The Administration barricaded itself in the business centre of Jerusalem, newspaper correspondents swarmed into the country, and British families and other civilians were, amid their protests, evacuated home.

Ben-Gurion spoke over the radio. "We shall continue negotiations with the government," he declared, "but we are quite sure we shall accept nothing that is not just, practicable and lasting."

Bevin produced a plan. It proposed British trusteeship for another five years, free immigration for 96,000 Jews during two years, and, at the end of five years, a bi-national, independent Palestine, in which the Jews and Arabs could fight out the immigration issue between themselves. Twenty months earlier the Anglo-American committee had talked of 100,000 'immediately'. An offer which the Jews might gladly have considered in 1945 stank to high heaven in 1947. Ben-Gurion turned it down. Bevin threw his hands up in a final gesture of defeat and told everyone concerned that he was handing the baby over to the United Nations. It was a piece of histrionics. There was no doubt in his mind that where he had failed the pooled political brains of fifty-six other nations could not succeed.

The United Nations General Assembly was especially convened, at Britain's request, on April 28th, 1947, and despite Bevin's efforts to inject the virus of defeatism into the discussion, there was immediate evidence of the influence of fresh minds upon the old problem. The most important turn in events was a statement by the Soviet Union's Andrei Gromyko, which foreshadowed a new approach cutting across the power-relationships as stabilised since the end of the war. The Jews had not expected much help from Russia, a country where Zionism had for thirty years been a proscribed movement, where Jews were still forbidden to speak Hebrew and denied contact with their brethren in the rest of the world.

It may be that the Palestine issue was the weakest link in the Anglo-American alliance and Russia was seeking to split the Atlantic Powers via Jerusalem—the official Jewish leaders at any rate were past praying for Russia's help out of humanity alone—but the result was the same. Gromyko argued the justice of Jewry's claim to statehood. He was not immediately ready to offer precise recommendations, but Ben-Gurion, who arrived in New York to prepare the strategy with Hillel Silver and Shertok, learned in the course of a talk with Gromyko of Moscow's intention to support the Jews at the expense of Britain. This was not exactly what Ben-Gurion wanted (a Soviet 'big brother'), and he began wondering what effect this sudden endorsement of Zionism might have in Palestine.

A tussle on procedure found the American delegation apprehensively looking to Britain for guidance. The Assembly refused an Arab proposal to debate the question of immediate independence for Palestine. Luckily for the Jews, it granted the Agency leaders a hearing before the Political Committee. Ben-Gurion's arrival in the lobbies to give his evidence caused something of a stir. The man looked oddly out of harmony with the atmosphere of international diplomacy, more like a rebel emerging from some rural hide-out than the representative of what he affirmed was one of the world's oldest nations. In fact, the puzzle of who was who was a problem to many delegates. The Argentinian representative, to everyone's amusement and his own embarrassment, took Ben-Gurion for the leader of the Palestine Arab delegation!

The Jewish pressure-groups had a field day. Britain's growing discomfiture at the course taken by the debate gave them plenty of ammunition, which proved especially effective with Irish Democrats, and Senator Howard MacGrath had the statements of the three Jewish leaders inserted in the Congressional Record. Peter Bergson's Committee of Hebrew Liberation, nailing the names of several distinguished if uninformed American politicians to its banner, also busied itself behind the scenes. Much play was made by the Yugoslavs, not yet disentangled from the Eastern power bloc, of the existence in Palestine of an army 100,000 strong to maintain order in a country whose total population was less than two millions.

Such were the preliminaries. The outcome was the creation of an eleven-member special investigation committee, nicely balanced with two Asian representatives, two from the British Commonwealth, two Western and two Eastern Europeans, and three South Americans. Ben-Gurion then left the international political responsibility in the hands of Shertok and Silver, the one capable, the other eager, and flew to Jerusalem. He saw that the deadlock was now at an end, that whatever decision the committee made would be irrevocable.

Yet the turn of events gave him no grounds for self-congratulation. He could not assess the new Russian factor. Should they achieve their state, would the Jews find they had changed one master for another, and so rendered independence chimerical? Reviewing developments at a meeting in Jerusalem, he let fall a curious and ambiguous phrase: "We must not ignore realities. The United Nations will not acquiesce to the whole of Palestine becoming a Jewish state. It may be necessary to leave part of the country under a Mandatory régime, while other parts become ours forthwith."

Was this an invitation to Britain not to clear out completely? Did it presage an alliance with London? Was it a hint to Gromyko not to expect, in the manner of Napoleon III, a *pourboire* for coming to their aid? Ben-Gurion subsequently denied such a construction, but it was the general interpretation placed on a sentence that was hurriedly disavowed by other *Mapai* people as a personal viewpoint expressed by their leader.

Whether this sentiment was his own opinion or not, it escaped him after a quick look at the *Yishuv* had revealed the people's inadequacies as they clamoured for independence. The wide array of parties in the 600,000 strong community testified to their rifts and disagreements. Seven years of prolonged absence abroad had made him unaware of the scars on the face of his people, which on closer scrutiny was the face of a tired and intolerant community unsettled within itself. As for *Mapai*, the Gromyko speech now deprived it of one of the main props of its political credo: the justification which Soviet anti-Zionism had given it for keeping its socialism moderate and western-orientated. But Gromyko now made Jewish statehood acceptable to the Jewish communists and other groups of the extreme Left which had long been suffering from the unease of deviationism. Now they could with a clear conscience join up with *Achdut Avoda*. They did not move right in the process; instead they pulled *Achdut Avoda*, dominant in the *kibbutzim*, leftwards with them, and carried the *Palmach* into their political camp. And Moshe Sneh came along with them. For two years he had favoured an approach to the Soviet Union for help against Britain, and open rebellion against the Mandatory. Not unreasonably he felt his own day was now beginning to dawn.

This meant that in the coming struggle Ben-Gurion would not have the whole-hearted allegiance of *Palmach*, the Jews' largest fully-trained armed force. Nor did his troubles end there. At the other extreme the *Irgun* and Stern gang were independent forces beyond the Jewish Agency's discipline. Their progenitor, Revisionism, was of no consequence now, but they had new sponsors of substance in the Conservative 'General Zionists', composed of the middle-class businessmen from Tel-Aviv and the other urban centres along the maritime plain. In external alliance with Silver, in league at home with Beigin, this group constituted the powerful anti-socialist phalanx of the *Yishuv*. The 'General Zionist' leaders, Israel Rokach, Mayor of Tel-Aviv, and Peretz Bernstein, editor of a Conservative paper, had additional grievances of their own, and were boycotting the Jewish 'parliament' of which Ben-Zvi was the president and Remez the chairman, and whose members constituted a Jewish National Council.

With some justification, then, Ben-Gurion looked upon independence—as its outlines loomed ahead— as an awesome prospect. His own following was undoubtedly the largest in the country. Yet a coalition of all the other forces could overwhelm him. In those fateful days his leadership of the world movement could not be disputed; in Palestine alone his support was ebbing away.

In that torrid summer of 1947, the conflicting impulses in Palestine rode blindly on. That summer saw the tragic mockery of the river-boat *Exodus 1947*, creaking with its load of 4,500 displaced persons forcibly returned, under the eyes of an incredulous world,

to Germany. The *Irgun* raided Acre jail, liberating their own men and
bands of Arab criminals besides. Curfews were imposed and lifted.
Two English sergeants were hanged by the *Irgun*, in reprisal for the
execution of their own members. Rokach and other Conservatives
were arrested just as they gave their promise to help in restraining the
terrorists. And through it all Unscop (the designation by which the
United Nations investigators were to go down in history) patiently
continued the search for truth, at times bringing the dispute back to
its ancient fundamentals with such force that the clattering twentieth
century dissolved into a myth. There was a testy duologue between
Sir Abdur Rahman, an Indian Moslem, and Ben-Gurion which
went as follows:

Abdur Rahman: "Who was in possession and occupation of
Palestine, as it is known today, before the Israelites?"

Ben-Gurion: "There were a large number of people who came
here—there are many names. The names are supplied in our
Bible."

Abdur Rahman: "All of them have died out?"

Ben-Gurion: "Yes, all of them."

Abdur Rahman: "All of them, and their descendants have died
out?"

Ben-Gurion: "Yes, they disappeared."

Abdur Rahman: "And the *fellahin* who exist in Palestine today,
are they descendants?"

Ben-Gurion: "I do not think so."

Abdur Rahman: "Do you know that Abraham had two wives—
at least, two wives with whom we are concerned—Hagar and
Sarah? Sarah was the first, and Hagar was the second. Ishmael was
the son of Hagar; Isaac was the son of Sarah. Is that correct?"

Ben-Gurion: "Yes."

Abdur Rahman: "Now it was predicted in the Bible—when I
refer to the Bible I mean the Old Testament, I do not refer to the
New Testament at all—it was predicted in the Old Testament that
twelve tribes would spring from Israel."

Ben-Gurion: "It is said in the Bible, with regard to these two
children, that 'to Isaac and the seed of Isaac I will give this land'."

Abdur Rahman: "When did the Jews leave Palestine?"

Ben-Gurion: "They never left it."

Abdur Rahman: "They have always been here?"

Ben-Gurion: "Yes, except in the period of the Crusades, when all Jews were entirely exterminated."

Abdur Rahman: "When was that?"

Ben-Gurion: "You know it was the 10th, 11th and 12th centuries."

Abdur Rahman: "Did Titus deal very cruelly with the Jews?"

Ben-Gurion: "You can rely only on the historical documents which exist. I mean, that he was cruel. He destroyed the Temple, expelled their leaders, put them to death in circuses in Rome, sold them as slaves."

Abdur Rahman: "And that was the first century A.D.?"

Ben-Gurion: "Yes, but he did not expel all the Jews—some sixty years after that the Jews made war on the Romans, and 600,000 Jews were killed by the Roman legions."

Abdur Rahman: "When was that."

Ben-Gurion: "That was in A.D. 130."

Unscop's recommendations consisted of two solutions: a majority report, signed by seven members (Canada, Czechoslovakia, Guatemala, Netherlands, Peru, Sweden and Uruguay), proposed the division of Palestine within two years into a Jewish state, an Arab state, and an autonomous province of Jerusalem. In the interim Britain, possibly assisted by another U.N. member, was to continue the administration of the country, in the course of which 150,000 Jews were to be admitted. Land restrictions were to be abolished within the area of the contemplated Jewish state. This was to include the coastal plain extending from fifteen miles south of Tel-Aviv to a point just north of Haifa, eastern Galilee, almost the entire Negev. It was approximately the Jewish formula of Peel plus the Negev, but without western Galilee.

The minority report was signed by India, Iran and Yugoslavia, and advanced a federalist solution with immigration to continue up to the limits of Palestine's absorptive capacity, perhaps until the number of Jews reached level with the Arabs. The Australian member lent his name to neither solution.

The Jews were satisfied with the majority's view, though sceptical of its ever being implemented. The Arabs rejected both formulae, and expressed their disapproval in renewed attacks upon the Jews, which brought retaliation from *Haganah*. The prospects of winning the General Assembly's approval for the majority scheme seemed good.

Despite the amazing union of opinion between America and Russia, Bevin fought a stubborn rearguard action at Lake Success to stall the inexorable march of events. His spokesman declared Britain's inability, either single-handed or with the help of other nations, to assist in implementing the plan as it had failed to secure the agreement of both contestants. She would evacuate the country as soon as possible, but could not guarantee any date in advance. She would hand over her authority to a body nominated by the United Nations, but to no one else, and not until the final transfer of power on a day to be notified.

This Ben-Gurion described as a deliberate attempt to create a political and psychological vacuum in Palestine. It warned him that the transitional period might be one of complete chaos, though he still could not believe that a country whose record for conscientious administration surpassed that of any since the Roman Empire, would so debase itself. "Britain has virtually declared she will not implement any United Nations decision not conforming with her own present policy," he protested. "The Jews are ready to establish a Provisional Government in the transition period so as to carry out those decisions as far as Jewish aspirations go." He ordered the total mobilisation of Jewish man-power and the call-up of young men and women to *Haganah*.

The Assembly's final vote took place on November 29th, 1947, a day to be coupled for its significance in modern Jewish history with only one other—November 2nd, 1917, when Lord Balfour issued the Declaration inaugurating the modern Zionist era. Four British Dominions could not find it in their hearts to underline Creech-Jones's disapproval by joining him in abstention, and by thirty-three votes against thirteen the British were curtly ordered to quit the country by August 1st, 1948, so as to make way for two independent states, Arab and Jewish, which must come into existence not later than two months afterwards. Britain thereupon announced that she would terminate the Mandate on May 15th, and her troops would be out of the country by the required date, August 1st. The die was cast.

The decision found Ben-Gurion at his post in Jerusalem, far from the scene of diplomatic victory, which was described by Trygve Lie as the 'first rounded positive achievement of this session'. From his window in the Agency headquarters he could see the cheering throng charge along the highway, called to this day King George V Avenue in honour of the monarch whose servant Lord Balfour had been, waving their flags, dancing their national *hora*. Independence was theirs at last. What would they make of it, he wondered, as he thought of their divergencies, their small numbers, the patchwork quilt into which the map of Palestine was to be transformed, with the Jewish thousands left a minority in the Arab state, and this Jerusalem, their Holy City, a new Danzig with one-sixth of his people segregated within its limits?

"This decision," he announced, "represents a great moral victory of the very conception of the United Nations, the idea of inter-national co-operation in the cause of peace, justice and equality over the world. The Jewish people will gratefully remember the efforts of the two Great Powers, the U.S.A. and the Soviet Union, as well as the endeavours of many other states, which have brought it about. The co-operation of America and Russia in the solution of the Palestine problem is bound to be an example of encouragement to all those who believe, in common with the Jewish people, in the possi-bility of permanent co-operation between East and West and the furtherance of permanent peace in the world.

"The decision to establish a Jewish state imposes a heavy re-sponsibility on the *Yishuv* and the entire Jewish people. It is, in fact, a challenge to all scattered communities of Israel to bring forth the great strength, spiritual and material, necessary for building a Jewish state for the absorption of large numbers from Europe and the Orient, and elsewhere; for the development of our wastelands, and for the creation of an independent Jewish society which will express the great ideals of the prophets of Israel. At this great hour for the Jewish people it will not disappoint its historic destiny."

The State would not be established by words. Britain was not going to help. The Arabs were determined to frustrate it. The Jews' physical strength was minute. How, then, would it be achieved? Ben-Gurion believed it could be accomplished peacefully if the United Nations, having made the decision, now assumed the re-sponsibility of carrying it out. But the United Nations failed to measure up to the test. An international police force was proposed, but it did not materialise. A Jewish militia was authorised, but

13

Britain would not sanction its creation while she was still in nominal charge—an act of wilfulness which did not go unremarked by the nations in assembly.

Nevertheless, *Haganah* came out into the open, and was immediately in action against Arab irregulars who managed to cross the borders despite the costly look-out apparatus. They were on a mission of conquest at the behest of Haj Amin el Husseini. To the alarm of Musa Alami and other Palestine Arabs, the ex-Mufti from his exile arrogated to himself leadership of the war against the United Nations, enlisting as his Commander-in-Chief Fawzi el Kaukji, a notorious brigand active during the 1936 disturbances, though now without his agility of those days.

"Law and order," Mr. Bevin claimed, "is still an exclusive British responsibility." In the name of law and order the strangest things began to happen. The British continued to disarm *Haganah* soldiers and put them in jail—or sometimes hand them over to the Arabs. The U.S.A. announced an embargo on arms to the Middle East, to prevent Jews and Arabs from gaining the possession of the means for their mutual annihilation. If this was intended as a hint to Britain it was not taken up, for Bevin went on selling arms to the Arab states because of what he fondly termed treaty-obligations. He had no treaty-obligations towards Fawzi el Kaukji, but this difficulty was circumvented when the civil administration, tidying up affairs, decided the time was appropriate for handing over to the Supreme Moslem Council a sum of £300,000 in settlement of old debts—this sum went straight into the Mufti's war-fund. While 100,000 crack troops maintained law and order, the number of Arabs and Jews who succeeded in killing each other in the three months ended February, 1948, was at least 1,200.

The United Nations had planned to make Jerusalem their own special and sacred trust, and the city took on a new look and a new smell—those of a battlefield. The *Palestine Post* building went up in smoke, as did a section of the main Jewish thoroughfare, Ben-Yehuda Street, with the loss of many innocent lives. The British claimed that during these explosions they were crouched within their own compound; and doubtless they were, except for a few adventurers who had been lured to desertion and sabotage by offers of fabulous pay from the Arabs. With the roadway and water-line from Tel-Aviv blocked, the last impression which the people of Jerusalem had of the neutrality of Britain and of the world's anxiety for the sacred city was that of a starvation diet, the crackle of machine-gun fire and the reeking odour of unflushed toilets.

With the fate of Jerusalem in the balance, Ben-Gurion set up the nucleus of an administration in Tel-Aviv. By a supreme effort of concentration he applied himself to learning the logistics of war. One by one he called the members of *Haganah*'s High Command to his home, and interrogated each for several hours. At his side was Israel Galili, his deputy in matters of defence. Galili was a young and immensely likeable member of Na'an *kibbutz*, within the *Meuchad* network, where he was a fellow-pioneer with Ben-Gurion's nephew, son of his brother Abraham Green. Ben-Gurion was coming fresh to tactical problems that had been familiar for years to Galili, a leading personality in the new Tabenkin-Sneh political line-up.

Ben-Gurion wanted to know what their chances were. The High Command told him that their only hope lay in the concentration of their people and their strength along the coast and in a lower Galilee redoubt. If they remained dispersed over the country in their isolated settlements the pioneers would be overrun and perhaps massacred. As for Jerusalem, it was hardly defensible and they should pray for the intervention of the United Nations, perhaps by declaring it an open city. Equipment was already being purchased from whomsoever would sell, but the most favourable contacts were in Czechoslovakia and France. They expected deliveries by air of small artillery pieces, of which they at present had none, though there were sufficient stocks of rifles and sten-guns for the whole of *Palmach* and for part of the 30,000 men enrolled in *Haganah* and not yet on full-time duty. There were a few old-fashioned British reconnaissance planes, salted away at Afikim *kibbutz* in the Vale of Jezreel. Fighters had been purchased in Europe but not yet delivered. Whether they would arrive at all was problematic.

Ben-Gurion neither asked for, nor was he given, details of the operational potential of the *Irgun* and the Stern gang. But the High Command knew that *Irgun*'s friends in America had piled up stocks of arms and would be sending them across. They knew of the *Irgun*'s operational plans but had no control over them. A final summing-up of the situation entitled them to believe they could hold out against the local guerrillas, even put them to flight should they venture too close. But this could not be the case if the Arab states kept their promise and invaded the country to prevent its partition. Then the outlook would be serious indeed. All this, however, was in the realms of guesswork. The immediate responsibility was to keep the highways clear and provide Jewish centres off the coast road, far away to the north and south of Jerusalem, with food.

Ben-Gurion was an apt pupil. Having assimilated the military situation he took a look at the diplomatic barometer. Here, too, they faced squalls. America, corner-stone of the struggle for statehood at Lake Success, was in the process of changing her mind. Palestine as it degenerated into anarchy looked ugly from Washington, where the President was being jostled into a frame of mind bordering on panic by his military experts who enumerated the enemies they would encounter were partition enforced. The day after Chaim Weizmann received Truman's personal assurance that he would not go back on his word, on March 19th, Ambassador Warren Austen spoke up at Lake Success and performed a political somersault. He proposed the shelving of partition and its replacement by a scheme of Trusteeship over an undivided Palestine.

Pressure was brought upon Ben-Gurion from all sides not to defy America by declaring the Jewish state established on the day of the Mandate's termination—May 15th. Nahum Goldmann flew in with the most discouraging intelligence. There was angry conflict, he revealed, between the Zionist leaders and the United States government. Trusteeship would not necessarily imply the abandonment of their hopes; a foolhardy proclamation decidedly would. But what was certain was that America was in deadly earnest about not wishing to face the consequences of a Middle Eastern conflagration. If the Jews went ahead, she could not save them from destruction. Shertok wired the same advice, and Kaplan added his own plea. Only Abba Hillel Silver, who in addition to being a Jewish leader was also a Republican from the Middle West, thought they should push the issue through.

During March the ring around Jerusalem tightened. Another of those mysterious explosions occurred, this time rocking the Jewish Agency headquarters. Ben-Zvi was among the lucky ones to escape being killed as his office caved in on him. Nevertheless, the cause to which his life had been unobtrusively devoted claimed its sacrifice in the end: his son Eli was killed while in action against the Arabs. Soon afterwards a convoy of doctors and nurses, on its way from the centre of Jerusalem to the University and hospital isolated on Mount Scopus, was intercepted and destroyed. Among the seventy Jews left to die was the young scientist engaged to Ben-Gurion's younger daughter, Renaana. Such incidents helped to turn some part of Ben-Gurion to granite. He could not be budged. He would proclaim independence on the day the Union Jack disappeared below the skyline.

It was a month of costly reverses for the Jewish convoys hastening from point to point with food and arms. The loss of a convoy meant the loss also of splendid young men, the flower of the pioneers. Suddenly, a bright episode came to lift the drooping spirits of the Jews. El Kaukji, swooping down from the hills with his men in a vainglorious attempt to seize Haifa, encountered Jews ready to give battle. He was repulsed.

But the first great test of this informal war was around beleaguered Jerusalem. Ben-Gurion had installed Dov Joseph, member of the Agency Executive and a prominent lawyer, as military governor. His stocks of food dwindled; civilian morale was low; religious extremists, without interest in the Zionist struggle, constituted a grave problem. The local commander, David Shaltiel, was in urgent need of ammunition and among his other problems had to cope with four separately identifiable groups among the defenders. There was a tendency in *Haganah* to evade the problem of Jerusalem. It would not be theirs anyway in the final settlement, they protested to Ben-Gurion, as, at the end of March, they informed him they could no longer get through to the city. They toyed with the idea of giving Jerusalem up as a burden too costly to carry.

They found they were talking to an obsessed man. He could see nothing but victory, and would surrender nothing without a struggle. He ordered the concentration of all available men and arms and the assembly of convoys. Some 1,500 men were involved, many of them armed with rifles still sticky from the packing in which they had been flown from Europe a few hours before. The operation entailed the use of half the Jews' total fire-power and the cream of their fighting forces, but it gave them a series of comforting victories along the route. Between Tel-Aviv and Jerusalem stood the heights of Castel, the point at which the Arabs brought most Jewish traffic to grief. *Palmach*, operating from Jerusalem, wrested the heights from its stubborn defenders, at the same time securing a prize kill in the Arab commander of the Jerusalem front. Thereafter Castel changed hands several times, but the larger part of the convoys got through. As a result of this first major Jewish operation the 100,000-strong population of Jerusalem was saved from the alternatives of starvation or surrender, while the sight of trucks streaming along the road from Tel-Aviv 45 miles away gave them enough moral strength to carry them over the remaining months of their ordeal. This success gave Ben-Gurion renewed confidence in the people. It was the first indication that as a military leader he could show the same power of decision, the same ruthlessness and the same imagination, as he had shown in the political struggle. For these qualities his people were much more grateful in war than they were in peace.

British authority was washed away in the stormy days of April, and the intricate machinery of government, developed over long and painful years, disintegrated into fragments reminiscent of the traces left in Spain of its ancient Moorish occupier—deserted blockhouses, munitions turned to old iron, the charred ends of burnt documents in the wind. But now the situation took on a spectacular transformation. All that the Jews had intended since November was to hold fast, yet the attacking forces melted away almost before their eyes. Haifa was taken in the very presence of the British while a large part of the Arab population fled. Tiberias had fallen three days earlier, and the Jews swung first into Rosh Pinna, then into Safed. All the crucial highways were cleared except one— the Tel-Aviv–Jerusalem road.

In Jerusalem Shaltiel was in nominal command only. On one side *Irgun* and Stern fought how and where they chose; on the other *Palmach* refused to exploit advantages they thought would entail heavy casualties. The *Irgun* informed Shaltiel they intended taking Deir Yassin, a village just outside the city. The locality was not without importance, but could not be decisive for the permanent opening of the highway, as it was too far off the main road. Shaltiel realised it was pointless to veto the operation, for the *Irgun* would go ahead anyway. They went in, to encounter unexpected resistance, and after four or five hours found themselves with their wounded in a tight corner. They sent back a call for help. This was answered by a small detachment of *Palmach*, which with its superior weapons cleared the village of resistance. Then it left. What then occurred is a dark and disfiguring episode in this story, clouding the valour earned by these Jews, unschooled in the arts of generalship but resolute in the defence of the home they had created for themselves and which was legalised by the supreme international authority. The *Irgun* killed 250 men, women and children. They brought some sample corpses back to Jerusalem, to vaunt their capabilities.

Two thousand years before, Jerusalem had been conquered by the Romans, not because the Jews were defeated but because of internal differences among the defenders. *Haganah* could easily slip into that very error again. Shaltiel dared not punish the assassins, as his instincts ordered. He suffered the humiliation of this, but held the city.

This episode the Arabs will always recall as the first stirrings of Jewry as a reborn nation. No matter how short the war, the memory will be long. It foreshadowed days of cruelty ahead, vindictiveness within the border and without, especially for David Ben-Gurion, who in Tel-Aviv assumed personal command of his people's struggle as Premier and Minister of Defence. He knew how much of Jewry's tragic past was the result of its own inner frailties. Forty-three years before he had come to the country with the dream of building a homeland. It was dreamed by many, but translated into a habit of life by only a few. Then he made the decision to turn the homeland into a state, and then to defend it. It was he, again, who gave his people the heart to fight. Such has been his intervention in the course of history while Britain shrugged a responsibility off her shoulders, and the United Nations fumbled for their next move. Force had been used to destroy the Jews, and had been met by force. Ben-Gurion, with statehood won, wrote a new chapter in the chronicle of a nation's history broken off since the day Bar-Cochba kindled momentarily the spark of independence eighteen centuries before. Would he succeed where that old predecessor had failed?

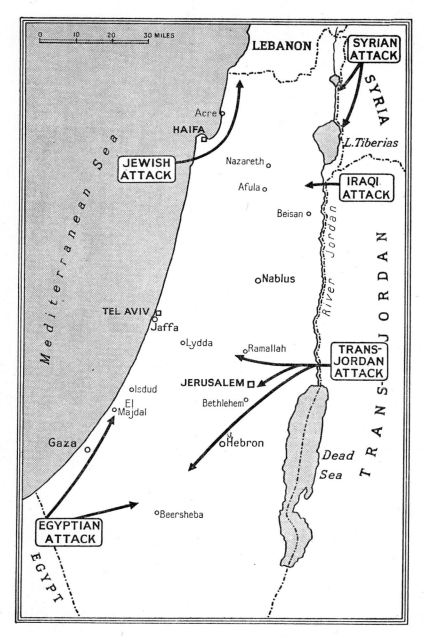

The Arab Invasion

8

Hour of Triumph

BRITISH RULE OVER Palestine was due to dissolve officially at midnight on May 14th, 1948. At four o'clock on that day, a Friday, the Jewish anthem echoed through a low, white building in the all-Jewish city of Tel-Aviv; and David Ben-Gurion, witnessed by a small audience of one hundred people, read in his soft, steady voice the Proclamation of the Independence of the Jewish nation as a state to be called Israel. The Proclamation was at once a Bill of Jewish Rights, a statement of ethical principles and a resolution to serve the community of peoples. At dusk it would be the Sabbath, so the sixty-two years old leader had not waited for the formal termination of the Mandate.

Above him hung a portrait of Theodor Herzl, whose vision was commemorated in the 1,027-word declaration. Thirty-six representatives of all political parties filed past the table to sign after him, last of all Moshe Shertok, who had just crossed the Atlantic, still enveloped in the atmosphere of indecision from New York—indecision which, however, could not survive long in the neighbourhood of Ben-Gurion. The thirty-six were, with the country's leader, to comprise a Provisional State Council, a committee of public safety to protect the destinies of the minute republic of 650,000 souls until times were calmer and a general election could take place. One of their leaders, whose name many had hoped would be the first on the list, was absent. Plead as he rightfully could that his omission was necessitated by tasks that still required him elsewhere, it was taken by the man at the helm, and those moved by his impulse, to signify absence from duty at the moment of supreme test. This missing name was that of Chaim Weizmann, heir to the mantle of Theodor Herzl. Unlike many others, he would come, as he had oft averred; and then he would be embraced by Ben-Gurion as their first President. The moment, however, could not be stayed. By the time Chaim Weizmann joined his people a new phase in their history had noisily passed him by, and he could only experience its distant echoes.

The building had once been the home of Meir Dizengoff, founder of this city, and was now its art museum. Efforts to keep the gathering a secret had been of no avail. Word went round of the historic event due to take place there, and excited, cheering crowds pressed as close to the doorways as the bristling sten-guns of the sentries would permit. Then the new state was toasted throughout the night. In Jerusalem, few heard the Proclamation over the radio because the electric current had gone dead, but when the news eventually came through to the 100,000 isolated Jews tensely expecting it, the same wild scenes of excitement were enacted—dancing in the streets and the exchanges of incoherent congratulations.

At five a.m. the next day Ben-Gurion went to what, but yesterday, had been an illegal broadcasting station and spoke a message to America. As he spoke the morning sky was disturbed by the zoom of aeroplanes rising from the south—Spitfires, come to bomb Tel-Aviv. They struck the power station and airport. War then was upon them. The Arab states, scorning the offers of Jewish friendship and the edict of the nations, had not made empty threats. They were determined that his Israel should not live. It was going to be war indeed, not the petty skirmishings of guerrillas. And he had no army to oppose them, only his own guerrillas, some of whom accepted his orders and some of whom did not. His people had no planes, no anti-aircraft artillery, nothing yet except this Declaration, and their own faith. He saw the anxious faces of the citizens of Tel-Aviv, their dancing stilled, as he went to inspect the damage from this first raid, and snatch a few hours' sleep. He was proud to observe that there was no panic.

Ben-Gurion's voice had a greater resonance than those meagre bombs. His announcement of the Jewish state's rebirth, two thousand years after the Hasmoneans had been made to lower the flag of freedom, echoed in the hearts of millions of his co-religionists overseas. It was an event that made them both humble and proud, and its implications sometimes filled them with foreboding. The dispersed people, as it prayed and hoped and doubted, recognised that from this May 14th a new factor had entered their lives; from now on they must always be conscious of the new paths which were being beaten out of the ancient tracks of the Bible.

Statesmen of all nations were deliberating the future of Palestine in a committee of the United Nations then meeting at Lake Success. But now they ceased to plan and prepared to wait. Christians, Moslems, agnostics, they could not but see that an old Book was taking on renewed life. Israel, once just a religious term or a vaguely racial one, was now a polity. It could be loved, or hated, or despised; but not ignored. Some doubted whether the assertion of independence was just. Was it timely? Was it realistic? Was it worthwhile? Few of those experienced statesmen dared at that moment to hazard an opinion. Only the enthusiasts and the opponents spoke up, and they were the least trusted.

So much for the external reaction to the announcement. In Palestine the Jews received Ben-Gurion's words as if they were logical, righteous and necessary. What were they offered as the alternative to statehood? More discussion, more indecision. Bombs, explosions, killings, restrictions—they had had them all before. Now they had them still, but with freedom to defend themselves, and to strike back. With but a few exceptions, all of the thirty-six to sign the Proclamation with Ben-Gurion were born in his corner of Europe, and were of his generation. The course upon which they were embarked had been charted by powers stronger than they. Czarism had compelled them to escape from the Jewish Pale of Settlement, the nineteenth century brought them to nationalism, their religion brought them to this land; their neighbour's attitude to their coming had induced them to use the sword as well as the plough, and that of their British masters set them to breaking the law, just as Hitler taught them to break it often and without compunction. For Ben-Zvi, as for Remez, Zisling, Kaplan, Nir, and the others whose signatures completed the document of independence, the issues were as straightforward as that.

As they prepared that Friday to greet their new dawn, Sir Alan Cunningham, last High Commissioner of Palestine, left his official hill-top residence in Jerusalem and quietly slipped out of the country on to the cruiser *Euryalus*, standing by in Haifa Bay to take him home. Physical contact with the Palestine problem had not

failed to reduce him, as it had so many other Englishmen, to an enervating perplexity which led to misguided intentions, misplaced
effort, an automatic distrust of idealists and a sense of inadequacy.
He was soured by Zionism and was glad to be rid of it. Indeed, the
same could be said of the politicians in London, a city which was
that day taking on the dreamy air which is its own advance notice
to itself that it is about to close down for a long week-end. It was
Whitsuntide, yet formality demanded a statement in the House of
Commons. When Mr. A. V. Alexander, the Minister of Defence,
rose to deliver the appropriate obituary, barely a handful of members
were present to receive the information that an area of 10,000 square
miles, familiarly coloured red on the map, was no longer a part of
the Empire. There was one hour's desultory debate, the Minister
occupying solitary prominence on the front bench. British policy
now, he said, was to effect a complete evacuation by August 1st.
The last word of this last chapter of British rule, begun with such
glory and promise with General Allenby's humble entry on foot
into Jerusalem thirty years earlier, was entitled to be spoken with
more grandiloquence. But there was none ready to do so.

Jerusalem minus Sir Alan Cunningham, and Jerusalem plus its
new status as a *corpus separatum* in the trust of the United Nations,
showed little visible change: it was pock-marked, besieged, dry.
The United Nations had allocated the Holy City a new governor,
but he was still languidly packing his bags in Philadelphia, while the
city of his charge every so often became alive as one side or the other
made a sortie to wrest this building or that sector from the enemy.
In the ancient walled city the Arabs were closing relentlessly in;
elsewhere Jews clung to what they held. Among all the problems
facing the new Prime Minister, that of Jerusalem held high priority.
He had accepted, not without great hesitation, the principle of its
internationalisation, but already Abdullah's Arab Legion (or did
it belong to that other gentleman innocently quartered on the *Euryalus*?) had all but taken the Old City and was rapidly isolating the
all-Jewish new section in preparation for the final blow. The Arabs
did not accept partition, and they rejected the internationalisation
of Jerusalem along with it. This hallowed place was the Zion of
Zionism. Could a Jewish Prime Minister betray it, desert its great
Jewish population? Along the highway from Tel-Aviv raged a
battle on whose outcome the coveted prize, now reduced to a

vacuum beyond the politicians' reach, depended. Whether it stood or fell need not crucially affect the outcome of this war, yet its occupation by the enemy would cost him much of the loyalty and trust he commanded in this new country.

The Arabs were strong in Latrun, in the Valley of Ajalon, where Joshua, by commanding the sun to stand still, had routed the Canaanites. Now, as then, freedom of access to Jerusalem turned upon its possession. Ben-Gurion ordered its capture, a shade prematurely in the view of his military advisers. A brigade of troops, largely composed of young men and women liberated from their Cyprus internment but two days before, closed in combat with the Arab Legion, financed, trained and commanded by the British. The Jews, led by Colonel Marcus, an American, were driven back by massed artillery. Then the *Palmach* went in, and the battle raged on. Though the operation came to grief, it served two crucial purposes. A portion of the widely-extended Legion was drawn away and so reduced the threat to Jewish-held positions in Jerusalem, and two small villages, gateway to the Jerusalem foothills, were taken and held. Through them poured mule-trains, engineers, and a pioneer corps of old, bearded labourers. They laid a water-pipe, brought cement and flour. And while some of them clambered along the slopes to carry succour to the city, others, working day and night in the lee of the battle, pieced together an alternative route to Zion—the Burma Road, it was called—barely more than a track of filled-in gullies, but sufficient to maintain a corridor of life between the beleaguered population and the great base of Jewish resistance in Tel-Aviv. To this day Latrun is in Arab hands, a dagger pointing to the seashore beyond the Jewish lowlands, poised to cut Israel in half. Jerusalem itself is more secure, for a new road was planned almost at once, and completed before the end of that eventful year.

Courage does not account for much if it is not attended by good fortune. Ben-Gurion, a man of the Bible, also needed the sun to stand still. Perhaps the miracle, though far from Gibeon, was repeated for him. On May 14th he read his Proclamation to the world. Could he and his few inexperienced comrades have been sure on that day that their abilities extended to the organisation of the 650,000 inhabitants into the nucleus of a nation? Could they impose their discipline, ensure the supply of bread and water, buy

arms and bring them into the country? Could they devise a constitution, repulse the enemy springing from Egypt and Syria and the
Lebanon and Transjordan and Iraq, could they collect taxes and
deliver mail? Nobody knew for certain.

But the following day they knew. Warren Austen, Sir Alexander
Cadogan, and a line of Arab delegates at Lake Success believed the
announcement of independence to be an empty but dangerous
gesture, and they so informed the Jewish Agency men in New York.
But they were reckoning without the unpredictable Harry Truman, the little man from Missouri, who may not even have known
the names of the Jewish leaders but who cared more for the interests
of the Democratic Party than for those of Anglo-American strategists and the oil-men. Night fell upon Tel-Aviv but the sun kept
shining in Washington. On May 15th Truman announced his
government's recognition of the Israeli state. What an event of good
fortune to enrich Ben-Gurion's first day as Prime Minister!
Shortly afterwards the Russians followed suit, and with the two
most powerful nations declared as Israel's friends, Ben-Gurion went
confidently forward to drive the enemy from his frontiers.

He was faced with one crippling obstruction to the adoption and
sustainment of a plan of defence. This was the lack of a properly
organised army, owing allegiance to the government alone; an
army inflexible in discipline, standardised in form and apolitical in
conduct. It was an immediate obsession with him, though he stood
almost alone in his belief that its formation could not await easier
times, along with the formulation of other laws. For while Ben-
Gurion could already think in terms of a state, his people, in those
early days, were not attuned to being citizens of a state, and their
military pattern automatically followed from this lack of respect for
authority. *Haganah*, though nominally non-political, was nothing
without the *Palmach*, a shock brigade in which every commander
was a political commissar as well as being a soldier, and with its
separate General Staff responsible only to itself. The *Irgun Zvai
Leumi* under their own leader, the Stern gang under theirs, had not
recognised Ben-Gurion before the declaration of independence and
their view of him remained essentially unchanged. Simultaneously,
then, with the prosecution of the war, he sought to make himself, as
Minister of Defence, absolute ruler of his forces. Taking no heed of
individual susceptibilities, he abolished the all-party High Command

of *Haganah* and made Jaacov Dori of Haifa and Igal Yadin, a Jerusalem-born archæologist thirty-two years of age, his Chief of Staff and Chief of Operations respectively.

These were non-political men, a fact that impressed itself upon Ben-Gurion as of vital importance. Despite their unquestioned military experience, neither had the influence with *Haganah* of Israel Galili, the leader of *Palmach* and a highly-vocal lieutenant of Tabenkin and Sneh in the left-wing *Mapam*. Galili, as Deputy Minister of Defence, now occupied the role previously filled by Eliahu Golomb —Jewish Palestine's undisputed authority on security matters, the military brain through which the Jewish Agency had carried on its resistance movement. Suddenly the machinery designed to translate Galili's ideas into action was swept aside, and precisely at the moment when plans prepared over the years were to be put into operation. He was left at Headquarters without a clear job of work to do, so that between him and his chief an atmosphere of mutual hostility was quick to develop.

Of course, Ben-Gurion did not at once find the opportunity to amalgamate and regroup his diverse soldiery. With the enemy at their gates, a paper edict was about the only step he could take. Then there was the political status of Jerusalem to cloud the situation further: it was outside the jurisdiction of Israel, and therefore its defenders were not legally his responsibility. So for the present they continued as they were, on all fronts, with every new exploit of the *Palmach* fostering the legend of its invincibility, and raising the prestige of the political leaders, those rebellious old comrades of Ben-Gurion, who were behind it.

Palmach had proved superb against the Arab irregulars in the first phase of war. It comprised 3,000 troops all told, scattered in front-line positions throughout the country. The *Irgun* and Sternists together amounted to some 2,000, fighting with fanatical, if sometimes ill-placed, courage. *Haganah* started with about 30,000, most of them part-timers, but was rapidly expanding and it discharged the usual military duties in outstations and behind the lines. Each of these four units included women in their numbers. Closing in on them were the standing armies of six established nations comprising a total population of 28 millions, their military forces at varying degrees of readiness, but all of which had been openly equipped over the years with weapons from sources denied the

Jews. Ben-Gurion had little choice of strategy. It required no
military genius to appreciate that at this stage of Jewish unprepared-
ness he could but restrict operations to maintaining the Jewish
positions, to endeavouring to fill the gaps within the state left open
by the withdrawal of the British, and to safeguard the integrity of
Zionist colonisation everywhere. Yet these organised nations, all of
whose Biblical forebears had waged war upon Israel, although
never simultaneously, would not allow this to be a waiting game.
The Jews held the sea-shore, and Egypt knew that by sealing off the
coast, starvation would complete the work begun by guns. Farouk's
admirals were not quick enough however. In the open roadstead
and in Mediterranean ports lurked thirty shipments of food and
arms for the Jewish state. Most of them reached Haifa and Tel-Aviv
during the night of May 14–15th; the weapons paid for by American
committees, the food by moneys released by the British Treasury
out of Jewish assets in London and mostly purchased in England. The
delay was to prove fatal to the Egyptians.

Weeks before, the *Haganah* High Command had advised Ben-
Gurion to preserve their strength by evacuating whatever was
untenable. He could not be persuaded. Every inch of Jewish soil,
robbed from the encroaching desert, was precious, and to be
defended. Once evacuation began, he said, there would be no halting
it. He saw each isolated point as a miniature Tobruk worrying their
enemy's rear.

One such outpost, the Etzion group of villages south of Jerusalem
between Hebron and Bethlehem, was overrun very early, resulting
in added pressure upon the Old City, and rendering the plight of
its 400 Jewish defenders all but hopeless. The four Etzion collectives
had held out against attack by Transjordan's Arab Legion supported
by many hundreds of irregulars for two months. Ben-Gurion's reply
was a grim decision to order a sortie from new Jerusalem to capture
the Old City. It would entail heavy losses, its success was by no
means assured, and it could not appreciably affect the outcome of
the war. Colonel Shaltiel received the order, but sought to have it
countermanded. To him the Old City had sentimental, religious
value, no more; and he had few enough men as it was, without
taking on a costly task just to prove Jewry's devotion to a mound of
holy rubble.

Meanwhile, the Egyptians moved up towards Tel-Aviv in two

columns based upon Gaza and Majdal, only a few miles down the coast. They were also pressing north from Beersheba, to add their own contribution to the artillery ceaselessly trained upon Jerusalem by Abdullah's legionaries. The Lebanese and Syrians sought, though without success, to penetrate western Galilee; and the latter, assisted by Iraqi aircraft, pressed against the Jordan valley settlements. It was a case of Molotov cocktails in the *kibbutzim* against tanks. The slender waist of Jewish territory was narrowest at Nathanya, barely ten kilometres from Tulkarm, where the apex of an arrow composed of Palestine Arabs and irregulars was seeking to pierce its way to the coast and cut the state in two.

Soon, Ben-Gurion promised, guns and aircraft in quantity would arrive for the Jews. These were there within ten days; but even before that the Arabs displayed neither fighting spirit nor co-ordinated strategy. On May 18th the Jews captured Acre and cleared all western Galilee as far as the Lebanese frontier, and beyond. Jewish fighter planes went into action above Tel-Aviv and swept the skies of the Egyptians, whose land forces too were checked, not far from Majdal. A half-dozen settlements in the Negev were cut off, but managed to hold out as supplies reached them by air-lift. Soon eastern Galilee was cleared too. Wherever the Jews penetrated a position they discovered their most effective weapon to be panic. As before May 15th, so now, the local population took flight in their hundreds of thousands, increasing the general misery of the debacle and constituting a terrible legacy of victimisation in their leaders' futile war. King Abdullah, tormented by the fear that in this staggering welter of knock-out blows his own legion might not be secure, contracted their extended line to the static Jerusalem front.

In a small *pension* in Ramat Gan, a garden-city on the outskirts of Tel-Aviv favoured as the residential centre of prosperous Jewish businessmen, Ben-Gurion pored over a large map. As news of each success came through he saw that by force of arms the Jews could fix the frontiers of his state where Their Excellencies at Lake Success, by talking, had failed. He moved his troops into the offensive. The enemy was repulsed but by no means destroyed. Given time, he would return. Ben-Gurion sent his newly-acquired planes, piloted in large measure by Jewish volunteers from England, America and South Africa, to bomb the enemy's rear positions, as far as Amman and Damascus. Sending word to Shaltiel in Jerusalem, he said he was awaiting news of the capture of the Old City.

Here the Arab Legion was almost at brigade strength. And the handful of tenacious Jews locked within it were squeezed into a corner, keeping up the struggle despite the presence among them of the 'native' Jews who belonged in spirit to the pre-Zionist days of piety. These latter saw in the continuance of the battle only the systematic destruction of their medieval synagogues, and so they agitated for surrender. The Old City was located in a dip of land and might have been taken by the Jews with comparative ease from the elevated northern suburb of Sheik Jarrah, site of the Hebrew University, but this had been lost by its *Irgun* defenders. Another point of approach had been barred by the fall of the Etzion block and the concentration of the Legion outside Ramat Rachel, the nearest *kibbutz* to the city limits.

Only through Zion Gate, therefore, could a relief column force its way. Shaltiel had a bitter argument with the *Palmach* commander over who was to take on the deadly assignment. *Haganah* disposed of the larger number of men, while *Palmach* had the arms. Finally, a *Palmach* platoon went in and cut its way through to Zion Gate. An undertaking of extreme daring, it was carried out with reluctance. Another dash and the assailants would have broken a path through to what remained of the Jewish garrison, now under merciless fire from the battlements beside the Mosque of Omar. But it seemed too costly an enterprise. The *Palmach* advanced no further, and on May 28th the last Jewish pocket of resistance succumbed.

Strategically, this was to prove a greater set-back than was at first apparent, for the Arab Legion—and in Ben-Gurion's eyes therefore the British—were ceded a position of strength flush against the Jewish portion of the city. For long afterwards the Jews in the New City were to have their sleep disturbed by artillery and 'infiltrees', while the frontier of Israel established that day right through the heart of Jerusalem, proved a source of constant nerve-racking friction. With his plan foiled the Premier's resentment centred upon his commanders in Jerusalem. As the United Nations made ready to impose their mediation and bring the fighting to a close, he decided to use the break to eradicate factionalism in the army and relieve rival units of their propensity for private vendetta.

The Powers represented at Lake Success, alarmed at a situation which had all the symptoms of a major conflagration, and recognising Palestine as the courtroom in which their own efficacy as a conciliatory body was on trial, set to work to order a truce. They despatched Count Folke Bernadotte, of the Swedish Royal House, as their Middle-East peace-maker. However, the intentions of the members of the Security Council were a more important factor than Bernadotte's own personal efforts, which transpired to be high-minded but *désorienté*. Warren Austen of the U.S.A. wriggled uncomfortably beneath the burden unloaded on to his shoulders by his President's unexpected recognition of Israel, while Andrei Gromyko pressed for a cease-fire. The combatants themselves knew this could only be a matter of days away, and fought fiercely to gain last-minute advantages before it would take effect.

By June 11th, the day Bernadotte persuaded the antagonists to silence their weapons for a period of four weeks, 'without prejudice', in the words of the Security Council Resolution, 'to the rights, claims and positions of either Arabs or Jews', one of the most spectacular political hazards of recent times had succeeded. Instead of driving the Jews into the sea, the Arab armies had achieved no more than the concentration of their strength around the area assigned to Israel by the famous decision of November 29th, 1947. No significant position had been surrendered; but contrariwise, western Galilee, assigned in the partition scheme to the Arabs, was under Jewish control. An Israeli air force was exerting a more than perceptible influence on the course of operations. The Jews had tanks and guns, and a small navy. Even at the conflict's peak 5,000 new immigrants entered the country, vanguard of a great human torrent. And during the first twenty-six days of their independence the Jews established six more agricultural settlements, high up in Galilee and in the desert battlefield of the south. Ben-Gurion, the obscure East-European socialist with a talent for quoting complete chapters of the Bible and who yet could hardly bring himself to cross the threshold of a synagogue, became one of the world's best-known figures, and this despite the failure of most foreign correspondents in Palestine to secure an interview with him.

A few days before the cease-fire took effect, a transport laden to the scuppers with personnel and munitions, and bearing the name *Altalena* (a pseudonym once used by Vladimir Jabotinsky) set sail from Port de Bouc, near Marseilles, bound for Tel-Aviv. It was no ordinary arms-ship. Its cargo was reputed to be worth five million dollars, raised by subscriptions in America. The vessel had been ready for sailing since the previous December, and Israel Galili had long been in negotiation with its owners regarding a share-out of its formidable load. These owners were the *Irgun*, whose leader, Menachem Beigin, a thin-faced, studious-looking man, was directing its course from Tel-Aviv. He condemned the truce as a "submission to shame," and had, therefore, little to lose in defying it, and much political capital to gain. Beigin has claimed that a tithe of the *Altalena's* contents would have completely reversed the setbacks in the Jerusalem sector, from Latrun to the Old City and even as far north as Ramallah. He might well have been proved correct in this assessment.

As it steamed towards the coast, Ben-Gurion, who was now learning of the *Altalena,* its owners and its cargo, for the first time, watched the ship's progress with trepidation. Among the terms of the cease-fire extracted by the U.N. mediator was an undertaking from each side not to reinforce its strength by the importation of fresh war-material. A week earlier he and his government would have greeted its arrival with relief and joy. Today, Ben-Gurion considered it as a torpedo aimed at the very heart of his authority as head of the state and Minister of Defence. But not all the members of the emergency Cabinet (thirteen men of all parties drawn from among the Provisional State Council) felt as strongly as he. The two members of the religious *Mizrachi* party, in the way that the religious have, in Zionism, of playing a purely political game, and Isaac Gruenbaum, a so-called 'Radical', felt that here was a gift from heaven, to be received in gratitude, and not subjected to the morality dictated by a hypocritical world which had left them to fend as best they could in circumstances of desperation.

Ben-Gurion saw in the truce a vital breathing-space in which to steady his army before the ramshackle Arab steamroller could get moving. There were also all kinds of domestic affairs to organise which could not be delayed. In the eyes of the *Irgun*, however, the only task which could not be delayed was the clearance of the 'homeland'—and this included all Jerusalem and Transjordan—from the 'invader'. Count Bernadotte, they said, was no impartial mediator but a puppet of the British, who were so manipulating the strings as to win key territorial concessions for their Arab friends, with Whitehall in inevitable military control. In any case, these militants argued, the *Altalena*'s cargo was intended for Jerusalem which was outside Ben-Gurion's sphere of authority. There, no truce signed by him or his representatives could be binding.

The Premier warned the *Irgun* that their line of argument constituted sabotage and treason. If Israel was to be accepted by other nations as a state, it must offer evidence of its readiness to be bound by international law, and itself show respect for international mediation. "We shall regard as a traitor anyone attempting to break the discipline of the state," he said, "and we shall mete out to him the treatment accorded in times of emergency to an enemy within the ranks." This was a new tone to adopt towards the *Irgun* who in the past had been protected by woolly apologists of their motives and towards whom not even Ben-Gurion could take a completely unsympathetic stand during the Mandate. Some of Beigin's supporters counselled submission, but others, fighting with the regular forces outside of Jerusalem, deserted. Beigin, no coward, was himself rowed out to the *Altalena*, and joined on the bridge its captain, twenty-five-year-old Munroe Fine, of Chicago.

To the north of Tel-Aviv lies the neat and prosperous agricultural co-operative known as Kfar Vitkin. Here on June 21st a tank landing-craft took off 600 men and 150 women from the *Altalena*, and they swiftly disappeared to pre-arranged hiding-places. But the arms could not be discharged without skilled lighter-men, or unloading gear. The ship moved down the coast, a few hundred yards from the port of Tel-Aviv. How *Irgun* intended to unload it was a mystery, because Ben-Gurion had already instructed Colonel Ben-Gal in charge of *Haganah* units encamped on the beaches to take all measures necessary to prevent the cargo's entry into Israel. Ben-Gal signalled the ship not to attempt a landing. It was more a plea than a command. Irgunists also were at the water-front, and they invited the vessel to come closer. This in any case was impossible, for the *Altalena* had now grounded, and *Irgun*'s white hope turned into a floundering, helpless white elephant. The messages between beach and vessel sped back and forth. The tank landing-craft tried a test landing, was turned back with casualties. On the beach fighting developed between the two factions—confused, hysterical and uncontrolled fighting. Now *Haganah* shore-batteries, receiving their orders direct from H.Q. at Ramat Gan, opened up against the

Altalena and she crackled and burst into flame. Those aboard who could, jumped clear, excepting Beigin and Fine, ready it seemed for a Viking's funeral. Seizing a beach pleasure-boat, some daring *Irgun* men rowed out and pulled the two off, leaving twelve dead aboard. From the Kaete Dan Hotel nearby, U.N. truce observers watched the grim episode work itself out to its tragic conclusion. No one knew whether a ship had merely been set alight or the first shot in a civil war fired. It looked like the latter. Among the dead was Abraham Stavsky, the man who had been on trial for the murder, fifteen years earlier to the day, of Chaim Arlosoroff on the self-same, ill-fated spot.

On the water-front *Irgun* moved in to attack their fellow-Jews. Ben-Gurion summoned the *Palmach* brigade from the Latrun sector to come in and quell the uprising. By the evening of June 22nd both sides had had enough of the futile strife, in which no one quite knew who was shooting whom. At a hurriedly-convened street-corner meeting a cease-fire was eventually arranged. *Haganah* agreed to evacuate the beach, leaving *Irgun* to gaze upon the burning coffin of their hopes as it shone out on the dark waters.

Ben-Gurion acted promptly. He rooted out Irgunists throughout the country and put them under lock and key. But Beigin was wasting no time either, and he was back, aggressive as ever, to give his version of the incident in a broadcast over his party's transmitter. To a nation for whom every cartridge might mean the balance between survival and disaster, he gave a massive assessment, not necessarily corresponding to the truth, of what had been lost: four million rounds of ammunition, 5,000 rifles, 1,000 grenades, 300 Bren guns, 400 aerial bombs, nine tanks, fifty anti-tank guns. He told of his efforts to come to agreement with the government over the disposal of the hoard, and he was especially bitter towards Shertok who, he said, had been so hypocritical as to say the government had planned to make the cargo over to Bernadotte for U.N. supervision.

"Irgun soldiers will not be a party to fratricidal warfare, but neither will they accept the discipline of Ben-Gurion's army any longer. Within the state-area we shall continue our political activities. Our fighting strength we shall conserve for the enemy outside." It was his directive to his followers to quit Israel and join the organisation on the Jerusalem front.

With the exploding *Altalena* still glaring its fiery warning in the harbour, Ben-Gurion went the following day to face an angry meeting of the State Council. His men were still busy rounding up Irgunists because at such a moment of violent emotion he could not afford to underestimate their strength or demagogy. Neither did he misjudge public feeling, and ugly charges of 'dictatorship' and 'Ben-Gurionism' were being whispered among his political adversaries, even among those sharing office and responsibility with him. In fact, as a result of the *Altalena* they ceased being whispers.

At Ben-Gurion's strong-arm policy towards men the Jews preferred to consider patriots rather than rebels, conflict within the Cabinet came to an abrupt head. Two ministers of the clerical wing resigned, alleging that Ben-Gurion, in a fury of vengeance, was seeking to resolve in a matter of days the problems of disbanding a resistance movement which, under similar conditions in 1945, had taken many months in France and Belgium. The two ministers were Rabbi Fishman,★ Minister of Religion, and Moshe Shapiro, Minister of Health and Immigration. As they left the Cabinet office in the old German Templars' colony of Sarona on the edge of Tel-Aviv, they expected three other Ministers to follow them. But they were alone. The gesture was typical of Zionist politics, where the threat of resignation was a time-honoured bargaining counter but one which in the atmosphere of war and statehood became hollow in the extreme.

Ben-Gurion let them go. He was more concerned at the appeal issued by the *Irgun* from Jerusalem summoning the population to throw off the oppressor. He told the State Council: "This armed resistance to government authority is the bitterest blow our state has yet faced. Indeed, much more than the existence of the state is threatened. At this moment the capacity of the Jews to defend their future is menaced." He spoke of his determination to honour international pledges freely entered into, but sought to mollify his resentful hearers by issuing a warning to Bernadotte of Israel's refusal to accept peace at any price. Mediation would be pointless, he declared, if Bernadotte brought back from his visits to Arab capitals proposals which excluded the acceptance of a Jewish state with unrestricted immigration.

"We have to prepare both for peace and war. We have no

★ Subsequently Maimon.

guarantee that the truce will last out twenty-eight days. This month, what remains of the British Army in Israel will be leaving Haifa; and it is possible this will herald a large-scale attack by our enemies, particularly in that area, by sea, land and air." Such articulation of a general mood won the day for Ben-Gurion. His vote of confidence was overwhelming, carried by twenty-four votes to four, with five abstentions. The régime was saved. The two protesting Ministers, learning that they had not started a general walk-out of non-socialists from the coalition, hurried to retrieve their portfolios. It was the beginning of a long career of dramatic exits on the part of Rabbi Fishman, for whom Ben-Gurion had a strong private affection. The Prime Minister tolerantly referred to him as the 'Minister of Resignation'.

The most acceptable interpretation of the *Altalena* affair must stand somewhere between the *Irgun*'s and the official version of the incident. Beigin insisted the government was prepared to treat with him and trick Bernadotte; and it is a fact that the Jews, like their enemies, broke the strict letter of the truce whenever the mediator's back was turned. It was a case of double-dealing, said Beigin, fully in keeping with the *Mapai* leader's traditional attitude towards Revisionism. When Ben-Gurion detected the *Irgun*'s reluctance to hand over the shipload entire, he determined that neither of them should have it.

In reality Beigin's venture into gun-running was a model of ineptitude and muddle. He made the blunder of thinking in terms of world Zionism, not in terms of statehood. He believed Ben-Gurion could not but defer to the displeasure of the *Irgun*'s formidable supporters among the Jews of America. The British dared not ignore them, but Ben-Gurion chose to cut clean from that bad past. He concluded, and rightly, that the Jews would be stronger by sacrificing the weapons than by smuggling them in. By making a virtue out of necessity he thus smashed a revolt, won the esteem of the outside world (including Britain) and gave his people their first lesson in national responsibility. It was a stroke of political genius.

The reactions were discernible all the way from Jerusalem to New York. The old London myth of *Irgun*'s strength, which had been assiduously circulated by the military and had even permeated the Foreign Office, was exploded. Even Ernest Bevin saw how the conditions of 1946, when *Haganah* refused to denounce the terrorists to the British forces, no longer applied. At Lake Success Sir Alexander Cadogan greeted Aubrey Eban, 'the representative of the Jewish authorities', as he quaintly described him, with slightly greater respect.

How did the American Jews accept the new situation? There the annual Zionist fund-raising appeal, which that year was to find 120 million dollars for the Israeli Treasury, could now strike out in earnest against supporters of the unofficial organisations operating with their collecting boxes on behalf of the *Irgun*. There was some protest at first. Delegates turning up for official fund-raising conventions had to be separated by police cordons from the picket-lines formed by Beigin's high-school supporters in New York; and young *Betarim* (Revisionist scouts) even went so far as to seize the Israel Government's offices on East 66th Street and stage a memorial service for Stavsky and the others killed on the *Altalena*. But it all simmered down in the end, with the return of Ben Hecht and Louis Bromfield to the literary pursuits for which they were better adapted.

Now for the unified army. Ben-Gurion plus a six-man committee devised an oath of allegiance and promised the jailed Irgunists an amnesty if they consented to bind themselves by it. Hundreds did so and before long were back at their duties. As Supreme Commander the Premier himself administered the oath to Brigadier Dori, the Chief of Staff, and Colonel Yadin, Chief of Operations. They repeated after him: "I swear on my honour to give allegiance to the State of Israel, its laws and competent authorities, to accept unconditionally and without question the discipline of the Defence Army of Israel, to obey all orders and instructions given by its commanders and to devote all my strength and, if need be, give my life, in defence of my country and its freedom."

Obedience cannot be commanded by an oath, however solemn. The continued presence at General Headquarters of Galili was a galling reminder to Ben-Gurion of his inability to extend his authority as far as the left-wing shock troops in his army—the *Palmach*. Galili knew the Premier wanted him to go, but he stood his ground, believing that Ben-Gurion would not dare dismiss him without valid reason, for this would bring the resentment of high officers in his embryo army upon the Premier. *Palmach's* strength

inside G.H.Q. lay through Galili. It had no reason to go to the
civilian branch of the Ministry of Defence, under Levi Eshkol (see
p. 85), for pay or rations, since its own lines of communication
stretched back to a little General Staff of its own, comprising nine
men and a woman. It was deployed in three Brigades, one of which
was commanded by a son of Tabenkin of Ein Harod. It scorned the
conventional army discipline of the old capitalist nations and
recognised no differential rates of pay.

During June Ben-Gurion suggested to Galili that he substitute
his place at the Ministry of Defence for another, concerned with
administration rather than with military problems. As far as Galili
was concerned, it was the *coup de grâce*. Humiliated, and justifiably
aggrieved, he went back to his *kibbutz*. His departure was a shock
to the entire army, including Dori and Yadin. Behind the polite
dismissal they thought they detected the hand of *Mapai* politicians,
anxious for their future should the war end on a crescendo of
glory for *Palmach* which *Mapam* could use for electoral purposes.

Palmach swore allegiance, not dreaming that the next step was to
be its abolition and absorption into the conscript army. A *corps
d'élite*, aggressive, exclusive, heady with victory, it remained a law
unto itself. Ben-Gurion grew impatient with these desert knights of
socialism skirmishing on the perimeter of his state. He was on the
point of bringing them into line when more urgent matters intervened. The Arabs had licked their wounds and were ready to spring
again, so that when July 9th came they showed no eagerness to
prolong the four-weeks' truce. But as, with a newly-enlisted ally,
Saudi Arabia, they entered the field to recover their sunken martial
reputations, Ben-Gurion once more took the initiative.

On the first day, his forces captured Lydda airport, and with it
eight neighbouring villages. In their new armoured vehicles the Jews
at last entered Ramleh and Lydda town. A week later Nazareth fell,
to troops moving in from Sejera. Further south the corridor to
Jerusalem was broadened by the ejection of the enemy from every
strong-point except Latrun. Jewish aircraft bombed Cairo, Damascus, and the Egyptian bases at Rafa and El Arish. Most of the Israeli
population had no idea they possessed a navy, and when a flotilla
emerged to shell Tyre in the Lebanon their confidence soared.
Armoured columns broke the Egyptian line guarding the way to the
Negev, and contact with the southern settlements was restored. By

this time the Israelis held nearly 5,000 prisoners and occupied a considerable part of what the United Nations had proposed should be a Palestinian Arab state. Organisation completely vanished from Kaukji's irregular forces, the Arab Legion sustained a severe shaking and any pretence of co-ordination among the various Arab commands evaporated. The ten-day offensive had so prospered that the Jews were confident of their ability to recapture the Old City and make themselves masters of the entire country within a month. But, to their frustration, Bernadotte, who had been away on a hurried errand to the Security Council, rushed back into the storm to proclaim a general cease-fire.

This was in mid-July. What now worried the Jews was whether Bernadotte, in his anxiety to achieve a military and political settlement, would nullify their victories by forcing upon them a series of territorial rectifications before the front-line was transformed into a frontier. There was justification for this fear. They knew he favoured handing the whole of Jerusalem over to Transjordan, because the division of the country as contemplated by the United Nations in 1947 had been rendered void by the Arab invasion of the Jewish area and their refusal to set up an autonomous administration in what remained. He also wanted the Jews to withdraw from the Negev, where their occupation was being contested, and to have instead the whole of Galilee, where they had been victorious.

Such a solution could hardly commend itself to a people who "in establishing their state, within a semi-circle of gun-fire, had given a convincing demonstration of their skill and tenacity." In these words Bernadotte described the happenings of the past two months, adding a warning to the Arabs that if they did not resign themselves to the presence of Israel they would be "pursuing the reckless course of defying the United Nations," with all that this entailed. The solution did not commend itself to the Arabs either. Abdullah's allies were indignant that Transjordan should receive such rich plums as the result of a war into which all the Arabs had rashly and disastrously tossed their wealth and reputation. Obviously, the mediator would have to think again, and he went off to Rhodes, far from all these conflicting pressures, to do so. The new session of the General Assembly met that September in Paris. Bernadotte sent it a report recommending that the Jews should surrender not the whole of the Negev in payment for their acquisition of Galilee but

only that part of it below a line from Majdal to Faluja held by the
Egyptians; and advocating a return to the internationalisation of
Jerusalem, rather than the city's cession to the Transjordanian King.

Ben-Gurion was not going to surrender easily his position in
Jerusalem, stoically held against almost hopeless odds. He, not the
United Nations, had saved the Jews there from annihilation. He
declared the New City occupied territory, to be the subject of fresh
proposals when his enemies came to accept Israel's existence and
meet him at a peace-conference.

The King of Transjordan was a pensioner of the Foreign Office,
Egypt was the most important overseas garrison of the British army,
and the Jews felt that whatever the shapes into which the U.N.
mediator cut about the remnant of Palestine not occupied by them,
the result would be the same: Britain, the Power responsible in their
eyes for so much of their recent misfortune, who could have stayed
Arab tanks and aircraft but had not done so, would be there on
their very doorstep. This did not in itself incur Ben-Gurion's
wholehearted condemnation; even before Israel's establishment he
had in that famous off-the-record statement which had been the
subject of strong disavowal by his *Mapai* followers, intimated his
readiness to accept the existence of British influence upon his
neighbours, which as he saw it would not necessarily be replaced by
something better. But on the subject of Great Britain he was practically in a minority of one in his country. There were people so
crazed with hatred for the former Mandatory that they regarded
the presence of the Swede among them as an invitation to express
their objection to British aspirations on the Jordan or in the Negev.
Whether real or imaginary, they thought their objections sufficient
to warrant his assassination.

On September 16th Ben-Gurion received a telephone message
from Jerusalem that the mediator had been struck down. The assassination had taken place while Bernadotte was on his way to an
appointment with Dov Joseph, the Military Governor. The work of
a tommy-gun in the hands of a uniformed man brought the
shattering realisation to the Prime Minister that Israel did not yet
qualify as a nation, as he himself understood the term. The habit of
terror is a difficult one to outgrow. Responsibility for the crime was
admitted by a group dubbing itself the 'Fatherland Front', which
according to government information was a survival of the

apparently defunct Stern gang. The news swept across a dismayed Israel. Women wept in the streets.

Suspicion was, not unnaturally, directed towards Beigin. He denied all complicity, and there was no doubt of his organisation's innocence of this crime. Nevertheless, Ben-Gurion delivered an ultimatum to the *Irgun* commander: "Disband your organisation, surrender your arms within twenty-four hours, and submit to the laws of Israel, or the army will act against you." This of course referred only to Jerusalem, since elsewhere the *Irgun* now accepted the régime. Beigin capitulated within the allotted time-span. The assassins could not be traced. But hundreds of known Sternists, including their two leaders, were arrested. After a protracted trial the leaders were found guilty of 'terrorist activities', and sentenced to long terms of imprisonment. Even then they were given a chance to mend their ways and accept the State. But a pardon from Ben-Gurion was more than they could stomach; and, spurning the offer, they were led away. Many Sternists escaped from jail soon afterwards. Nathan Friedmann-Yellin, their leader, was amnestied in 1949, on his election to Parliament, but soon faded out of public life.

Bernadotte's murder drew attention with startling ruthlessness to the crack in Israel's armour—contempt for authority. Ben-Gurion was Prime Minister of a country still in a condition of semi-anarchy. A state without a postal service or proper communications, its internal administration in disarray—this he could accept temporarily as the sorrowful legacy of Britain's abdication. Not so the lack of self-discipline. Statehood was a phantom unless government was strong. But government could not be strong if the ultimate safeguard of law, the army, was still partially outside his control. He had subjected the *Irgun*, outlawed the Stern gang, brought *Haganah* under national jurisdiction. Only one element remained: the *Palmach*.

Early in October, Egyptian armoured units began to harass the supply convoys which, according to the truce, Israel was allowed to send down to the settlements isolated in the south. *Palmach* units were ordered into the Negev to intercept the enemy, and while they were away Ben-Gurion abolished their headquarters. This swift and simple act found the men down south off their guard. So, at all events, did they maintain. As a matter of fact Ben-Gurion had already ceased to recognize the separateness of *Palmach*. Almost one month earlier, he had called a meeting of *Palmach* officers at Naan,

Galili's *kibbutz,* and informed them that their independence constituted a grave danger to the integrity of the army and the state,
and could not be tolerated. Nevertheless they now felt themselves
in a dilemma; either they had to register a protest by refusing
to obey orders and thus abandon these forward points of Jewish
colonisation which, for almost a year, had been sustained by their
own spirit, and had been the sharpest thorn in the flesh of the
Egyptian invaders; or they had to carry out their instructions
which were to seize the opportunity of clearing the region of the
enemy. To follow the first course would be a terrible betrayal of
trust, while to accept Ben-Gurion's decapitation of their military
machine was to surrender the dream of crowning military achievement by political supremacy. To their eternal credit they chose the
second course, and remained in the field to chop up their adversary's
lines, capture Beersheba and remove the southern threat to the
Jerusalem corridor. Ben-Gurion's conduct against the *Palmach* remains as perhaps the most unpopular of his actions in all the five
and a half years of his first term of office as Prime Minister. Unlike
the *Irgun* and the Stern gang, *Palmach* had been a constructive, not a
disintegrating force. Its members represented the very best elements
in Zionism—self-sacrifice in pioneering against the desert and the
marshlands which were the inheritance of centuries of neglect.
They represented the idealism of the *kibbutz* movement, the heroism of undaunted defence. Ben-Gurion might have built his army
around *Palmach*, not the reverse. The chief defect of its members was
an almost incredible naïveté in political behaviour. Because over
the years *Mapai* had lost its revolutionary gravitation, the pro-
genitors of *Palmach* were trapped into a role of impotence, answering antagonism with greater antagonism. Having decided that Ben-
Gurion was a ruthless, power-hungry renegade from socialism, they
chose to remain in sulky opposition; whereas by pocketing a particle of their theories with their pride, they might have moved the
unformed Jewish society a long way towards the equalitarian system
of their dreams.

The war was all but over. Egypt, numerically Israel's most
powerful enemy, suffered a defeat and it would be long before its
memory would be erased. That defeat brought turmoil, revolution
and a dynastic collapse in Cairo. The Prime Minister, Nokrashy, was
assassinated, the king sent packing. Fawzi el Kaukji, the Mufti's own

general, was completely routed in the last two days of October and driven with his men in ignominious flight across the frontier. The repercussions of their own calamitous participation in the war were to be felt for a long time to come in Lebanon and Syria, and more governments tottered as their leaders or would-be leaders faced the firing squad or were driven into exile. Abdullah of Transjordan looked like riding the disaster, but he too was not to outlive the effect of Israel's creation and was shot down in the Old City of Jerusalem three years after its proud occupation by his men.

Such were the thunder-claps characterising the next four years of stormy weather in the Middle East, though first of all Ben-Gurion's champion in the White House was to give a diplomatic crown to the victory the Jews had won in the field. Truman, at the end of 1948 confirmed in a second term of office as President of the U.S.A., declared there could be no alteration of the frontiers without Israel's consent. This meant the repudiation of Bernadotte's final report, and acceptance of Jewish conquests in both the Negev and Galilee. Nevertheless, the Egyptians made one last attempt to change the dispositions in the Negev, with the object of retrieving their large forces enclosed in Faluja and reducing the extent of Jewish occupation there. Wheeling east from the Gaza area they occupied some important heights dominating the most southerly Jewish settlement, and moved north again. This time they were out-manœuvred by an Israeli column from Beersheba which, to the accompaniment of an air and sea bombardment, inflicted such damage that the enemy had to turn back. The Egyptians were then pursued across their frontier, and well beyond.

As an epilogue to this transfer of power in Palestine from British to Jewish hands, there was the final and perhaps most inglorious intervention of Bevin in the story of Zionism. Hot on the tracks of the retreating Egyptians, the Jews penetrated deep into their territory. The Foreign Secretary then persuaded America to administer a stern warning to Israel against carrying the war to the Nile. More than this, he went through a routine of testing out the terms of the Anglo-Egyptian Defence Treaty (not invoked by his ally). Above the fluid battle-line on the frontier R.A.F. fighter reconnaissance planes took off to photograph the Jewish positions. Five of them were shot down. The Israelis withdrew their forces, a cease-fire was imposed, and Egypt consented to discuss an armistice. As for Bevin, he stood among the ruins of his policy like a jungle-elephant caught uncomprehendingly in the hunter's trap. Bowing to the inevitable, he announced to a wrathful British public that the "Jewish authorities in Palestine" were a government. Britain would accord it *de facto* recognition.

David Ben-Gurion saw out that historic year as the most powerful figure in the entire Middle East south of Turkey. As a war leader his failing was impulsiveness: and even the last operation in the Negev was saved by the restraint urged upon him by his General Staff. He wanted, simultaneously with the Negev campaign, to clear the enemy out of the Samarian massif, a huge Arab bulge all but dividing Israel in two. He was told that they had the strength for one operation only; and in fact the right-wing members of the coalition preferred to consolidate in the mountainous centre rather than to collect thousands of arid acres in the south, a *terra incognita* of dubious value. But to counterbalance his impetuosity he had an unerring instinct for the right goal, and an iron will which made it impossible for him to be deflected from that goal. Having created his army, he allowed nothing to stand in the way of its proper equipment and not for a day would he surrender to anyone the close guardianship of its interests.

That *terra incognita* had been an object of fascinated study by Ben-Gurion for years, and he would not have it disparaged. Firmly believing the Biblical references to its wealth in copper and iron, as well as its ancient fertility, he saw the economic future of his country assured in the Negev. Modern technology, in his simple faith, would find a way of restoring it to its previous importance. It possessed an outlet to the Red Sea, a strip of shore eight miles wide and Israel's gateway to the awakening Orient.

That gateway was as yet unclaimed. He determined to plant his flag there. He and Yadin went through archæological surveys which revealed an ancient path leading to Akaba from Sodom, on the Dead Sea. In March, 1949, a column of troops slowly travelled down that 120-mile long ravine without opposition. Ben-Gurion called it 'Operation Fact'. In his Tel-Aviv office two days later he was handed a telegram. It read: "Greetings from Elath." Proudly he showed it to Zeev Sharef, Secretary to the Cabinet. "Let's go down and have a look," he said. They took plane as far as Sodom, then travelled through the choking dust by car till they came to the

8. With Chief-of-Staff Igal Yadin at Elath, southernmost tip of the Negev, 1950

10. With Albert Einstein at Princeton, 1951

9. Arrival in Boston, 1951

shimmering Red Sea, back-door of the Jewish state. The blinding desolation of the once-fruitful Holy Land made him morose. The two returned by air, breaking the journey at Akron, where the military had laid an air-strip.

"What solution does the Secretary of the Cabinet propose for the Negev?" Ben-Gurion asked his weary companion. "The only solution I can think of at this minute is to get a man behind a table and make him think of a solution," Sharef replied.

Ben-Gurion himself became that man. Establishing a government department for Negev development, he pressed Kaplan, his Finance Minister, for money to open the area up. "It is senseless," protested the sorely-tired Kaplan, "there is no money at this stage to waste on such adventures!"

The Premier got his money. Great roads were constructed, with long avenues of trees to prevent the encroachment of the desert as the hot gales whipped the sand up in their wake. Immigrants volunteering to work in the south received homes immediately, while others had to wait in camps. Fifty new settlements at the rate of ten a year, the construction of an entirely new town in Beersheba containing 30,000 inhabitants, the sinking of vast funds in mining projects—all these reminded Israel that Ben-Gurion assigned his nation a great new pioneering era in its desolate expanses.

To summarise the twelve months which elapsed since that fateful Friday in May is to point to a one-man revolution by which the complex of states known as the Middle East was transformed by its newest and smallest constituent. Because of Ben-Gurion's will and constancy an invader immensely superior in numbers and experience had been crushed. In the process he had forged a motley band of soldier-farmers, Oriental slum-dwellers from the so-called holy cities, and Jews made refugees by the hostility and apathy of the European atmosphere, into an army—clothed, equipped, organised; a navy and air force were produced, born war-fledged. The ink of his Proclamation of Statehood was barely dry when ships packed with candidates for the new nationality docked along the coast. He quelled dissident groups riding aggressively to power on the immaturity of the government.

Sixty-one days of war sufficed to force Egyptian representatives to sign an armistice with the Jews, requiring the surrender of a vast region for which Ben-Gurion then had not people but plans; and

15

the Jewish army opened their ring at Faluja to enable King Farouk's élite troops to file back to their home base. Soon Transjordan was to come to terms, then Lebanon, then Syria.

Britain too was ready to make her peace with Ben-Gurion, and wished the state well by a generous settlement of financial claims arising from Mandatory transactions. When a free election took place in Israel the captaincy of the *Mapai* leader was confirmed, so that in February, 1949, the 'Committee of Public Safety' gave way to a popularly-elected government, and out of the volumes of Erskine May a parliament was founded, containing conservatives and communists, Arabs and Oriental Jews. On the first anniversary of May 14th, 1948, the Premier could inform his people that Israel's flag was unfurled at Flushing Meadow to mark her entry into the community of peoples as the fifty-ninth member of the United Nations. Commercial treaties had been negotiated with several European Powers, a loan from the Export-Import Bank had been granted; while the ingathering of Jewish exiles within their Land of Promise, that phenomenon of population-growth which was to give them all so much heart-ache and so much joy, had, with the arrival of 200,000 immigrants, begun.

These were achievements indeed. Yet Ben-Gurion's greatest period was still before him. His mission was the fulfilment of Zionism, and this only began with the possession of the homeland. For five more years he was to carry the nation into new realms of expression; and when, sated with politics, he laid down the burden of office, it was to return to the simple life of the pioneer, as he had in Sejera a half-century before, but this time in the virgin south where Israel might wrestle with her future by repairing the omissions of the past.

9

Between East and West

First General Election – Ben-Gurion and Sharett – Foreign policy – Attack on Mapam – Slansky trial – Complications with world Jewry – Isolation of Israel – Effect of the Korean War – Arab States and Israel – Ben-Gurion and Menachem Beigin – Ben-Gurion and the New Asia

THE PROJECTION OF the Jewish people into statehood carried with it responsibilities for which the new nation was wholly unprepared. Constitutional problems could be smoothed out by time and experience; economic progress depended upon capital investment, the introduction of new skills, the continuance of agricultural colonisation hardly different from Zionist tradition. But in the conduct of their affairs with other states, the people were given no time to learn. Foreign policy was an immediate problem which had suddenly descended on men who had never before met statesmen as equals; and as Jewish diplomats set up their Missions in foreign capitals, Ben-Gurion and his colleagues set about defining their relations with the Powers. The new government was fully aware that it was only partially a free agent and that the Powers themselves had still to adjust their thinking to the existence of a nation not only singular in the Middle-East but far different in content and aspiration from the older nations of the world.

Early in 1949, the general election, which had had to await the termination of hostilities, at last took place, a khaki election with the whole nation still under arms. Its result was not consoling to the party leader who had been charged with the *Yishuv*'s destinies during the last fourteen difficult years of the Mandatory period and with carrying it over great obstacles to independence. Twenty-one parties sought the favours of less than half a million voters at the polls. Nine of them did not secure enough votes to send even one member to the 120-man Parliament. Ben-Gurion's *Mapai* was awarded forty-six seats, a little above one-third. *Mapam*, the left-wing socialists, won nineteen. An alliance of all the religious parties secured sixteen seats for this incalculable centre group. The next most important group was the party of Menachem Beigin, calling itself *Herut* (Freedom), comprised of *Irgun* members and Jabotinsky's Revisionists. This proved to be a significant force, gaining eleven per cent of the total votes cast and fourteen seats. There were seven conservative General Zionists, five left-of-centre liberals designated 'Progressives', and three Communists. Three Arabs sat in the chamber and eleven women. Chaim Weizmann was elected, against insignificant opposition, President of the State. Joseph Sprinzak, no longer the figure of prominence he had been in the *Mapai* of the thirties, became Speaker of the House and the President's Deputy.

Ben-Gurion had not been repudiated. But neither was he unquestionably vindicated. He believed he had earned the right to be accepted as the national leader. Instead, only the old guard of *Mapai* stood by him. This was in part due to voting by proportional representation, and for a party list rather than an individual. To rule, he would require a coalition, but for unwavering loyalty he could only rely on his own comrades, who drew their power from the wide influence they exerted within the *Histadruth*.

And so it came about that the men guiding the country in its early, hesitant years were cautious social-democrats entrenched in their key positions because the newly-created state was largely an off-shoot of a process they themselves had created years before. After Ben-Gurion the dominant personalities were Eliezer Kaplan, the Finance Minister, Moshe Sharett (Hebraicised from Shertok), Foreign Minister, and David Remez, Minister of Communications. These controlled foreign and fiscal policy. In theory, they may have believed in the socialist society. In practice, they preferred to go on as before, a capitalist society with their own impersonal *Histadruth*, unassailably established in industry, agriculture, social welfare and education, the mightiest capitalist of them all.

Israel was a ready-made paradise for the bureaucrats operating this machine. The men administering the workers' undertakings, nearly all of them of a pioneer generation which had started life on the ground floor of the national edifice when practical Zionism was the proud calling of the hardy and the idealist, now constituted the aristocracy of the nation. They were also the only full-time politicians in the country. Nominally, many of them were members of *kibbutzim* (where they would return for occasional week-ends), but their work kept them in the chief cities of Tel-Aviv and Haifa, wielding enormous power. They were chosen less for their prowess than for their party faith. The pattern was not unknown in other countries; only here the texture was closer knit.

Government by *Histadruth* meant the Welfare State at home. What did it imply abroad? Ironically, it ensured a 'Bevinist' foreign policy—a tendency to preserve the status quo, association with the West, a conservative approach in diplomacy, a refusal, polite but firm, to be led along the path of the 'People's Democracies' into the Soviet camp. No one was better fitted to carry out this programme than Sharett, appointed by Ben-Gurion the first Foreign Minister of the State of Israel.

What separated Ben-Gurion from Sharett was a difference in perspective. Ben-Gurion examined every act of foreign policy to see whether it would assist or retard the consolidation of the country. Sharett worked from the standpoint of the outside world. Would this move or that cause Israel to be more liked or less? Ben-Gurion believed Israel would get herself accepted by the magnitude of her achievements. Sharett had the task of explaining away her deficiencies to the shrewd observers he met in his Foreign Ministry or at the United Nations. Ben-Gurion was a lone wolf, unversed in diplomacy, and unapproachable except to the group of young men around him. Sharett was sophisticated, witty, subtle. Ben-Gurion shunned the limelight, was a poor conversationalist. Sharett thrived on publicity, never made a miscalculation on what constituted good taste, and could penetrate deep into the foreigner's mind. Ben-Gurion was made of rougher material. He was abrupt and rarely took pains to explain himself. He was a man of history (and he did not consider history an exact science) motivated by the lessons of the past, and the ancient past at that. The other thought in terms of the day-to-day present, elevating a diplomatic Note to the majesty of holy writ. Through twenty years of close collaboration they did not become friends. For the greater part they were complementary, understanding each other's mind perfectly. Sometimes they clashed.

The most serious difference was over the question of Jerusalem. In December, 1949, America and Britain could not prevent the passing of a U.N. resolution for its internationalisation in the face of a determined move by the Russian, the Arab and the Catholic blocs. Ben-Gurion retorted by defying the vote and transferring the government and his office to the Holy City. But Sharett temporised

over taking the Foreign Ministry away from Tel-Aviv, because the
foreign Missions located there informed him they would not follow
the move to Jerusalem. In the end the Prime Minister impatiently
told his Foreign Minister to ignore them and move, or he would
take over the portfolio himself. This was in 1953, and by the time
Sharett said good-bye to his beloved Tel-Aviv, America and Britain
too were wavering in their support of the incorporation of the
modern city into Israel. Sharett does not share Ben-Gurion's mystical
veneration for Jerusalem, which has always loomed as a spiritual and
moral stronghold, though in terms of Zionist pioneering a backwater. And it stands deep in an enclave of Arab territory. The capital,
Sharett said, should be more secure. On the contrary, replied
Ben-Gurion, by advancing our capital to Jerusalem we are making
the enemy less secure.

During the days of the emergency the coalition had been truly
national, containing representatives of all groups from the right-
wing General Zionists to the quasi-Communist *Mapam*. Not so now.
The Premier managed to bring together a coalition embracing seven
members of his Labour Party, three from the Religious Front, a
Progressive, and a representative, who later became identified with
Labour, of the Sephardi Jews, the Levantine, non-European branch
of the race. This was a shaky team, for the Religious Front held the
power to keep the government in office or let it tumble. It used its
position to press for concessions in matters of orthodoxy, and fought
to impose church authority upon the secular. *Mapam*, insistent upon a
foreign policy which it termed neutral but which was in fact merely
that of a tame satellite in the shadow of the U.S.S.R., would not
come in. Neither would the General Zionists, whose price for participation in the government was a freer economy, cleared of the con-
trols so dear to the doctrinaire socialists. With all these Ben-Gurion
wished to work, for he considered the country in no less of an emergency now than before. But he would not surrender any of the most
important portfolios to men either to the left or right of his own
Mapai. He therefore had to string along with the least demanding
groups in the *Knesset* (Parliament) to form a weak government whose
life was punctuated by one heart attack after another. A second election took place in 1951, but the balance of forces hardly changed,
neither did the Cabinet. The General Zionists improved their position enormously at the expense of *Herut* and the Progressives, while

Mapam dropped to third place. Against this domestic background the foreign policy of Ben-Gurion and Sharett proceeded fairly smoothly, until in 1952 Israel was jolted from its platitudinous declarations of goodwill to all men into a world of reality.

The *Knesset* is a unicameral parliament occupying a compact, narrow building with a curved stonework façade in Jerusalem's King George V Avenue. Intended for the head office of a bank, the structure was hurriedly requisitioned after December, 1949, to take the *Knesset*, which had hitherto met in a Tel-Aviv cinema. This was a demonstration against the United Nations for having brought the issue of Jewish control over the New City back to the level of international controversy. Ben-Gurion has fought many battles there, but few were as bitter, or as momentous for the future of the embryo state, at the sitting of November 25th, 1952, when he delivered the political knock-out blow to the United Workers Party, *Mapam*. Outside, and oblivious of the drizzling rain, a large crowd was massed. For the loudspeakers designed to carry voices to every corner of the makeshift chamber carried them into the streets as well. Corridors, aisles and a small visitors' gallery were packed.

Throughout the nation consternation was spreading under the impact of an event then taking place far away in central Europe. The trial that month in Prague of fourteen leading Communists, eleven of them Jews, was turning the very creed of this nation's statehood, Zionism, into a weapon in the cold war; and Israel herself was being arraigned before a court which for gruesomeness probably knew no parallel in the history of justice. Czechoslovakia was a country but lately noted for its friendship towards Israel. It was among the first to join Israel in commercial treaty. It had supplied many valued immigrants.

The Premier was in his usual place at the centre table reserved for the Cabinet. His presence in the chamber was rare. When he did come, he seemed to fill it. Beside him was the dapper Foreign Minister, who the day before had, in this assembly, assailed the proceedings in Prague as a "judicial plot, an exhibition of moral suicide and self-degradation to shock every person still believing in the sanctity and spiritual worth of the human personality"—strong words from one better cultivated in the art of diplomacy and the science of being non-committal than any man of prominence in Israel. The debate betrayed a tendency, not unusual in countries older than Israel, for all sides of the House to draw political capital from the situation as well as establishing their attitudes to it. In Prague one after another of the accused had confessed to subversive dealings with Israelis, with members of the world Zionist movement, with bourgeois Jewish nationalists and saboteurs seeking to undermine the economy of Czechoslovakia and chain it to America. Twelve of the fourteen were sentenced to death.

In the Jewish state many thousands of citizens, their ears glued to their radios, heard with horror the week-long testimony as both prosecution and accused turned Zionism into one of the seven deadly sins of capitalist reaction against the international working class. To many of those listening in the communal dining-halls, at certain club-rooms in Tel-Aviv, and in the water-front cafés of Haifa, every word broadcast delivered a wound. They were the members of *Mapam*. And when the voice of Mordecai Oren, a key prosecution witness, came over the air, it was the most painful stab of all. Oren was one of their own leaders, sent by them a year earlier on a mission of goodwill to Berlin—city of anathema to all Jewry—as a delegate to the Cominform-sponsored Peace Congress. They were hearing his voice for the first time since his unexplained disappearance without trace in Czechoslovakia soon afterwards. To all Israel, with the exception of the small Communist party, the Prague trial had come as an almost personal disaster. But theirs was the greatest agony.

Now their parliamentary leaders, ranged on the *Mapam* benches, were searching their hearts for a reconciliation of the principles of Zionism, for which they were ready to die, with the policies of the Soviet system, for whose success they wished ardently to live. To-day, they were reduced to what for doctrinaire ideologists must surely be the greatest desolation of all—a party without a line.

Ben-Gurion fidgeted impatiently as Esther Wilenska, one of the three Communists present (two other representatives were even at that moment in Moscow), invoked the Prague trial as a devout Jew would the God-given *Torah* to prove the government was abetting the Atlantic Powers for a future war against Russia. General Zionist Peretz Bernstein followed. He spoke, not surprisingly, with the self-righteousness of the innocent and the wise—his party had been in opposition for four years. Bernstein nevertheless was able to point to the gravest feature of the trial of the Clementis-Slansky group: it had been staged in a country whose succour had been crucial in the war years of 1948 and 1949. True, Communist Czechoslovakia discontinued the warm endorsement of Jewish independence characteristic of the Beneš régime; but it had at least shown no open hostility. Now Israel's most favourable contact behind the Iron Curtain was baring its dragon's fangs.

It was a sullen, distressed Ben-Gurion who mounted the tribune to face the *Mapam* members. The men and women in front of him were, by a strange irony, the ones who as individuals were dear to him. Were they not from the settlements, peasant-farmer Jews, an élite among the nation, loving their country devotedly? Had they not, in their *Palmach* days, provided a cadre of commandos that had laid the enemy low, so low that what had been boasted of as an Arab military parade was turned into an Arab national debacle? Zionism could always count on people such as these to colonise the northern swamps and the southern deserts. What poets and Hebrew intellectuals Israel possessed came from their ranks. He thought of them as the new Jews of his aspirations, idealists spurning material gain, sacrificing themselves to the reconstruction of the homeland. He had always wanted them to work with him in his government—and he knew they wanted it too. Yet instead the administration had stumbled along year after year on the basis of a fragile coalition, achieved in desperation, of his own Labour Party and the rabbis, some of whom were so fanatically religious as to oppose the very principle of a statehood that was man-made, not divinely ordered. On domestic issues the parties of the Left, banded together as they already were in the *Histadruth*, might have agreed. Only foreign policy divided them. *Mapam*, puritanical, intellectually introspective, had been unable to exorcise its fascination for the Soviet system. Hatred of England and America turned its members into slavish worshippers of Moscow. Though their devotion had been scorned, they yielded to none in their adherence to the faith.

Now Ben-Gurion had had enough. Statehood was based on reciprocal needs and responsibilities. A *kibbutz* could afford to be purist, to wall itself in behind a stockade shutting out not only Arab snipers but the corrupt world with them, and give itself over to Marxist meditation, so that every daily custom, beginning with the sharing out of the tobacco ration, was elevated into an article of faith. The new Israel had other, more complicated needs. She must seek foreign capital for development, obtain immigrants to reclaim and settle her empty regions. She had both to save and be saved. She was one nation among many.

"Why are you so two-faced?" he questioned them shrilly. "If the Prague régime is good for Czechoslovakia, surely it must also be good for Israel? And in Prague Zionism has been branded counter-revolutionary, a channel of American espionage, as testified by one of your own members. In that case you, socialist-Zionists, are also counter-revolutionaries. You should be banned in this country. You deny the morality of accepting foreign aid to buy tractors, but you are not against accepting those tractors for your settlements. You venerate the name of Chaim Weizmann (the first President had recently died), yet according to a Soviet encyclopaedia he was an imperialist agent. You do not accept the confession of Mordecai Oren, but you are satisfied the men convicted on the strength of that confession are guilty."

He paused for a moment amid the whisperings of the spectators' gallery, the shuffling of unhappy *Mapam* feet. In this debate Ben-Gurion was taking the plunge. He was abandoning for ever the hope, fondly entertained in the past, of building a government of all the Zionist forces of the left-wing. And with that hope was going another, greater in aspiration though dimmer even in memory, of producing in Israel the blue-print for a harmonious relationship between the East and the West—which could be adapted to the entire Asian world.

Referring to the distinction which a more moderate section within *Mapam* was trying to make between the guilt of Clementis, the former Czechoslovak Foreign Minister, and the innocence of their own party comrade Oren, Ben-Gurion told parliament that Clementis had helped Israel more than Oren, and he recalled tributes which *Mapam* had paid Clementis in the past, when the party had attacked the government for voting against him when he had been a candidate for the presidency of the U.N. General Assembly.

"At least the Communists here are consistent," the Premier cried. "They have always toed the Moscow line in its attitude to Israel, as when Russia supported the internationalisation of Jerusalem and their switch after she opposed it. But what of you, members of *Mapam*! How can you recognise the anti-Zionist aspects of this so-called trial, yet deny its blatant anti-Semitic features?"

This debate in the *Knesset* was no doctrinaire affair. In an atmo-

sphere of heightening drama one member after another spoke of
personal experiences, interviews, correspondence with some of the
accused, or their accusers. Few of the leading Central European
Communists, if they are Jews, are without relatives or former friends
in Israel. Rudolf Slansky, who until his fall from power was the
Czechoslovak Communist Party's general secretary, and his ten
Jewish co-defendants could never have been Zionists. They would
probably be alive today, and in Israel, had they been. In reality
they had, during the period when they exercised such great authority
in their country, implemented all agreements officially concluded
with Israel with rigorous exactitude. Some 30,000 Jews had been
permitted to leave Czechoslovakia out of the 55,000 left in the country
at the time of the Communist *coup* in February, 1948. Most of those
remaining elected to do so because they were anti-Zionists untouched
by Jewish sentiment, and apostles of the new Gottwald régime.
Right up to 1951 the Czechoslovak government continued to make
declarations friendly to Israel, though indigenous Communist Jewish
organisations waged their own private war against the new state
and those Czech citizens who expressed a desire to emigrate there.

Having won the support of the large majority of members for
his motion condemning the Prague trial as 'foul and dangerous anti-
Israel and anti-Jewish propaganda' Ben-Gurion left the Chamber
for his office a hundred yards away, to pursue the destruction of
Mapam by methods other than parliamentary debate. As in the
military struggle, so in politics, he went into the attack while the
enemy was off his guard. He wrote a series of articles in *Davar* (Ben-
Gurion hates newspapers yet takes a delight in contributing to them)
in which he laid bare the hopeless dilemma of left-wing international-
ist Zionists in a national Jewish state. He gave vent to all his resentment against the group which, by its narrow-mindedness and
pedantry, had prevented Israel from building up a strong workers'
party of the prestige and responsibility of British Labour, and as
solidly representative of the masses. The war was carried into the
collectives and the trades councils. *Mapai* supporters were drafted
into the settlements of *Kibbutz Hameuchad* in order to defeat
Mapam's hegemony within the network.

Ben-Gurion might have spared himself the effort. Soon afterwards *Mapam* disintegrated beneath the pressure of developments
graver for Israel than even the Prague trial. In his death agonies, the

man in the Kremlin and the rulers of the Soviet Union chose to single out Zionism, not as an enemy of its system, but as *the* enemy. Allegations of this Jewish movement's sinister role as an agent of America's plan for world-domination poured from the capitals of the Soviet's satellites: a group of Jewish doctors in Moscow were said to have attempted the assassination of Russia's military leaders, and a propaganda-war of dimensions hitherto unknown in peacetime was unleashed against Ben-Gurion's tiny state.

Here, a peculiar, complicating factor in the workings of Israel's foreign policy should be mentioned. It is the tendency of the individual Jewish communities in the western world, and particularly in America, to become quickly alarmed by acts of hostility towards Israel without first digesting their purport or analysing their character. The Prague purge and the ensuing manifestations of an incoherent anti-Jewish line in Moscow inspired Americans to launch a retaliatory attack upon the Communist world; Jewish leaders charged the governments of eastern Europe with contemplating a scale of persecution for which there was hardly a shred of evidence. The reason for this reaction was twofold: the genuine anxiety of American Jews to assert their Americanism as an inevitable counterpart to their Jewishness found stronger expression than ever before when the Republicans captured Congress, and discarded Truman's pro-Israel policy; and further, the reaction sprang from the knowledge that the pro-Israel fund-raising movement was lagging after years of mechanical if lavish philanthropy. One way to revitalise it would be by showing the Jewish world that Israel must be given the resources to prepare for the early, perhaps immediate, reception of new waves of refugees. Jews in America are private citizens and do not speak with the responsibility of officialdom. They certainly do not speak in the name of the Israel government. Yet they create the impression of being the spokesmen abroad of Israel, and utilise mass techniques in which the quality of subtlety, in the belief that the end justifies the means, is absent.

Jewish public opinion abroad has been of no small service to the state of Israel and no one more than Ben-Gurion has been grateful for the goodwill it has won. But this crisis provided an example of the boomerang effect the external Jewish world could have upon the state's international position. The statements by some American Jewish leaders, widely disseminated as they were, apparently stung

Russia deeply and she reacted. Russia, however, could exert no pressure upon American Jews. She could upon Israel. She waited for a pretext to administer a crushing reproof to the State. This soon occurred. A bomb explosion shook the Soviet Legation in Tel-Aviv at 10 p.m. on February 9th, 1953, injuring three members of the Legation staff, including the Minister's wife. Moscow replied by breaking off diplomatic relations with the Jewish State, thus returning full circle to the traditional policy preceding Gromyko's sudden espousal of the Zionist cause in 1947. It was the climax of a series of diplomatic failures for Israel.

The Arabs, militarily much stronger than in 1948, and thirsting for revenge, now had the monopoly of Russia's goodwill in the Middle East. Arms were already pouring into the area, sold, as it were, over the counter by Britain and France to whoever had the money to buy; but Israel could not compete against the combined purchases of her neighbours. The new Secretary of State in Washington, Foster Dulles, was anxious to complete a strategic belt from Spain through Egypt and Pakistan to Japan and supported Arab claims against both Israel and Britain. Discounting the multifarious Jewish communities overseas erring on the side of enthusiasm, the Jewish state was isolated. Ben-Gurion had long known this, and had warned his people that the benevolent atmosphere in which they had established themselves could not last. Sooner or later they would be sacrificed to higher considerations of the cold war. The crisis had come sooner.

His was a pauper state dependent upon financial and political goodwill from outside, and had but little influence on such events. They did, however, drive home one important lesson: excessive party polemic was a luxury Israel could not afford, however much the old Zionist movement seemed to thrive on it. Ben-Gurion was a socialist in theory; he was a member of *Mapai* nominally. What was he in fact? He was the first, perhaps at that time the only, nonpartisan figure in Israel's public life. He thought in terms of the nation, both that part of it concentrated within the frontiers of the state and that part of it dispersed over the five continents. Jews everywhere, except the few fanatical politicians with long memories on both the Right and the Left, now accepted him personally as their leader. As 1953 dawned he used this position to perform the difficult act of consolidating his life's work. He persuaded his following in

Mapai to share office and responsibility with the Conservatives, who now had 20 seats in the House, and, with a working majority for such a coalition assured, he invited the smaller fry to join him or to ignore his offer at their peril. The Religious groups, who were hardly at peace with each other, could be relied upon to reach a conscience-salving formula for clinging to office, and he expressly vetoed participation by Beigin's *Herut* or the Communists.

As for *Mapam*, the distress it suffered as a result of the mutual antagonism of the Communist and the Jewish worlds broke the party into four distinct factions, of which the one led by Moshe Sneh all but identified itself with Communism pure and simple, to the point of anti-Zionism. The star of this supercilious strong-man waned and ended in a fall which was cataclysmic for a politician of such elastic ideological allegiances. A more than competent parliamentarian, Sneh might have been Israel's Prime Minister today had he not gambled so heavily on the chances of *Palmach's* thrusting *Mapam* to power in 1948. But the most forlorn picture was presented by the old-guard socialists like Zisling and Tabenkin, who had clung to the ivory-castle brand of Zionism produced by the *kibbutzim*. Their life's work dashed, they found no peace even in the domestic fastness of Ein Harod, archetype of Israel's proud *kibbutz* movement and their home. The global conflict dividing Left and near-Left shook that remote shrine of pioneering idealism to the roots of its Zionist foundations. *Mapai* members refused to eat or work with those of *Mapam*, and vice-versa. Zisling and Tabenkin, its founders, were asked to leave with their followers; and when they refused disorders broke out, involving the humiliation of police intervention. Eventually, this *kibbutz* was divided up, as were a dozen others throughout the country.

For five years Ben-Gurion kept a map of that part of the globe extending eastward from the Atlantic to the Pacific Oceans on his office wall with the surface of Israel darkened over. Thus every visitor to the Premier was made to realise what he had so often said, that Israel was a lone and separate state. He left the daily workings of foreign policy to Sharett, for once Ben-Gurion had found a faithful servant he had little wish to interfere in his department. Nevertheless, from time to time he issued broad enunciations describing the background against which that foreign policy was carried out. And this background was always the great land and population mass in the midst of which his country stood like a conspicuous, carelessly thrown, though easily obliterated, ink-blot.

Other countries had protectors, allies, regional partners, to reinforce their strength. But Israel was in a category by herself. Almost all nations, if they are not strong in themselves, draw strength from the community of interests they enjoy with neighbours, or with other nations of the same faith, or the same language, or the same race. Belgium, Luxembourg and the Netherlands become, as Benelux, a power of some significance in Western Europe, as do Sweden and Norway and Denmark and Iceland in the shape of a Scandinavian bloc. New Zealand shares in the privileges of a vast Commonwealth. Italy and Spain are linked by the Catholic faith, and this also brings them close to the South American countries, and to France. The Arabs are united in a formidable League. When Czechoslovakia loosed its war of nerves against Israel, it meant that the whole of the Slav world, with the potentialities of 250 million inhabitants behind it, was expressing enmity towards one tiny country containing a million and a-half citizens, and against a people who claimed fellowship with two and a-half million Jews enclosed, inarticulate, behind the Iron Curtain, and who were themselves only secure in the countries of their residence if they continued to behave as though Israel had never been born.

The complete isolation of Israel from the nations of the world was plainly delineated for the first time by the East European developments, but Ben-Gurion did not wait till 1952 to adjust his foreign policy accordingly. From his first day of office he sought to establish friendly contacts with groups within other nations, below government level but having the power to influence their country's attitude towards Israel. This in many respects was but an extension of his work as chairman of the Jewish Agency Executive before 1948, when the Palestine Jewish community lacked national standing and did its negotiating of foreign business in the ante-rooms, rather than the chancelleries, of the world's capitals. The existence of a vocal Jewish community five millions strong in America has been of enormous importance to Israel; and in other countries, such as Great Britain, the Argentine, France and South Africa, Jews have also exercised a considerable, though necessarily lesser, influence. Israel's interests did not thrive in the West and suffer in the East by accident. The Premier was convinced that the aspirations of his country could best be understood in those lands where free communities of Jews flourish. (One of his great disappointments had been the refusal of the Kremlin to allow him to speak directly to the Soviet Union's Jewish minority, which is subjected to spiritual asphyxiation and denied all Zionist activity or participation in the Hebrew cultural movement.)

The advantage of maintaining close relations with world Jewry is manifest: it means that Israel can explain her need for manpower, and include an invitation, as the phrase goes, 'to be ingathered' along with that explanation; it offers the state a shortcut to an influential hearing in other countries, facilitating the full presentation of Israel's case on topical issues in their parliaments and Press. An Israel-conscious Jewish community is a special-interest group no less than the Liverpool Catholics in Britain or the associations of war veterans in the United States, whose susceptibilities, not to mention their voting potential, no politician in democratic countries can afford to ignore.

Handicapped as he was from the outset of Israel's independence by the realities of the East-West schism, Ben-Gurion nevertheless made valiant efforts during the first four and a-half years of his Premiership to come to terms with eastern Europe. In the early stages that group of states gave Israel every indication of support. Soviet Russia was, with the United States, the first Power to accord her diplomatic recognition, immediately on her establishment; and Czechoslovakia followed three days later—eight months before Great Britain's Ernest Bevin found himself ready for such a step. The Kremlin's attitude was based upon an assumption which was destined to be a blunder. Its espousal of the principle of Jewish independence, an act which took the Jewish Communist Party in Palestine by complete surprise, was dictated by a conviction that a people bearing ill-will towards Britain (and the Jews could not easily forget the rough handling received from Mr. Bevin in the transitional period) would become hostile to the West. Moscow in fact saw in Israel a bridge-head for Soviet penetration of the Middle East. The Zionists in Palestine admitted to natural sympathies with the Soviet régime, because that régime represented the reversal of all they detested in Czarism, under which so many of them had lived and suffered in their youth. Ben-Gurion despatched a strong team of left-wingers as envoys to each of the eastern capitals—Golda Myerson to Moscow,

12. With Earl Mountbatten during his official visit to Israel as C. in C. Mediterranean, 1952

11. With Secretary-of-State Dean Acheson, 1951

13. With President Weizmann and Dr. James McDonald, the American Ambassador, 1951

14. Mr. and Mrs. Ben-Gurion surrounded by members of the Press, Jerusalem, 1952

Avriel, his young lieutenant of the Paris days, to Prague, and a supporter of *Mapam* to Warsaw. He was sweet reasonableness itself in his statements relating to the Communist constellation. "It is our policy to promote friendship and reciprocity with every peace-loving country," he said, "without prying into its internal constitution."

Furthermore, by virtue of their traditional Zionist faith, their desire for emigration out of the European continent and its unhappy associations, the Jewish communities of these countries constituted the most promising immigration-source for Israel. For a generation the experiment in Palestine had thrived on a partnership of Jewish man-power from eastern Europe (excluding Russia) and Jewish financial support from western Europe and America.

During three long years Israel haggled, argued, pleaded with the rulers of the 'People's Democracies' to grant exit-visas to their Jews, for Ben-Gurion was determined above all else to keep immigration flowing. The bid to ingather the European communities was prompted by a combination of humanitarian and political motives. On the one hand, the reunion of families long divided by the war and its aftermath was an instinctive need. On the other hand, population-growth was, and continues to be, the very basis of Jewish statehood, for the number of people in Israel available to settle the empty expanses in the State, and thus stake the claim of ownership over them, is even now, after the doubling of the original Jewish population, inadequate.

Although in the case of Soviet Russia his efforts were met by a flat refusal, they were not unattended by success in the satellites. It was the cry 'Let my people go' echoing down the anguished centuries. The new Moses proved as tenacious as the old, and Canaan had lost none of its magic appeal. From Poland in the north, to Yugoslavia and Bulgaria in the south-east, and by a series of hard bargains in which the dollar proved as almighty under Communist régimes as elsewhere, Jews were grudgingly permitted to come home. In Rumania the formidable Anna Pauker exploited her Jewish hostages with a callousness of which the Pharaohs might have been proud. She granted visas to the aged, the incapacitated, the misfits, the social derelicts who were a liability to her régime. She imprisoned leading Zionists, some two hundred of Rumanian Jewry's most intelligent and devoted servants, so that, unregulated, the human

16

material passing through her clutches at Constanza was at best the shattered remnant of a once proud and multitudinous community. Then she herself fell from power. Hungary proved even more flint-hearted. There, as in Russia, Communism has clamped tight the gates of escape except for some three thousand who were ransomed for dollars. Altogether about 400,000 of Europe's remaining Jews were, at phenomenal cost, brought within the confines of the state. Behind them stalked the ghosts of six million others, for whom Jewish independence had been achieved a decade too late.

At first the indifference of the East European governments to the success or failure of the Israeli state had but a neutral effect on Ben-Gurion's relations with his Arab neighbours. But later, as anti-Zionist utterances in eastern Europe poured like lava out of a smoking mountain, an immediate reaction was registered on the sensitive pattern of the Middle East. Israel and six Arab countries are still technically at war, and both sides in this conflict lobby on the international scene to advance their own points of view, or to retard the aspirations of the other. Ben-Gurion, with his East European policy collapsing about him, saw at once a new and pressing danger from the Moslem world. Indeed, espousal of the Arab cause was the Communists' logical next step. Here was fertile ground to work on, for since the end of the Second World War Middle Eastern tensions had become a permanent feature of the international landscape. The emergence of Israel served to deepen animosities and endanger the age-old social pattern within the Moslem world, though not to change the basic nationalist fabric of the problem.

Israel's difficulties with her neighbours might well be a matter of history by now had not the Korean war forced every small nation out of its safe harbour of neutrality towards the East-West conflict. Israel's own position *vis-à-vis* Korea was the only one possible for a democratic country owing its existence to, and reposing its hopes for survival in, the authority of the United Nations. Moshe Sharett had in New York voted in favour of international action against the North Koreans. He supported the crossing of the 38th Parallel and he enthusiastically endorsed India's efforts at mediation. He was, in fact, anxious for negotiation to be triumphant in settling a dispute which engendered such animosities between the rival power systems as were bound to embarrass a nation desperately anxious to remain friendly with both sides. The Arab states, in whom the

quality of embarrassment is less strongly developed, varied in their
immediate impulses but soon settled down to following the line
towards the Korean conflict laid down by Egypt, then being ruled
by the Wafd. This line made their support of the United Nations,
which implied support of the Anglo-American defence strategy
wherever régimes were deemed to be threatened by Communism,
conditional upon the realisation of their local political aspirations:
in the case of Egypt, the complete ejection of the British; in the case
of Syria, Iraq and the Lebanon as well as Egypt, the reversal of the
situation caused by the creation of Israel in so far as this affected
displaced Arabs, Jerusalem, and the frontiers of the Jewish state. In
theory this should have led the western Powers to the conclusion
that as regards these particular Middle East nations Israel was the
one certain ally, the others at best luke-warm fair-weather friends.
This was not in fact their reaction. They took their friend for granted;
and the others they sought to coax and bribe into their camp, to this
day without marked success.

David Ben-Gurion is a firm believer in the necessity of a Jewish-
Arab alliance, and is convinced that when conditions are ripe it will
come. By such an alliance he means much more than an arrangement
to refrain from waging war. He envisages its basis to be a programme
of mutual self-help, though on the surface Israel has much more to
gain from the resolution of outstanding problems than the Arabs.
In his view Israel would provide technical and scientific assistance to
her neighbours and export manufactured goods to them, receiving
in return agricultural produce. He would also be willing to allow
the kingdom of Jordan the use of a port in Israel, probably Haifa,
but this would depend on certain frontier adjustments, minor in
themselves, but which would eliminate the harassing detours necessitated in Israel's communications system by the vagaries of the truce-
situation. In fact, King Abdullah, a monarch much admired in
Israel, had gone so far as to enter into secret negotiations with Ben-
Gurion early in 1950—secret, that is, as far as anything could be
kept secret in the talkative, suspicious atmosphere of the Middle
East. The negotiations collapsed through premature publicity, and
Abdullah paid for his deviation from Arab League policy with his
life. This was in July, 1951, four days after the same fate had befallen
Riadh es-Solh, the pro-western Lebanese Premier who had planned
with Abdullah in Amman a policy involving peace with Israel and

co-operation among other Arab moderates for an understanding with the West.

After Abdullah's death no Arab would dare negotiate with Ben-Gurion. Consequently, the Premier's pessimism over the intentions of the Arab world grew. He quarrelled with his first Finance Minister, Eliezer Kaplan, because of the demands he made as Defence Minister for the allocation of money out of the state's meagre coffers for strengthening the army. This subject of security is central to all Ben-Gurion's thinking. "Even in the days of the First Temple, and the Second," he has written, "security was not a simple problem. Then, as now, the land was small. Then, as now, the people was a small one, and on all sides it was surrounded by many nations, some of them great and strong and avid for conquest. But they differed one from the other in language, culture and religion, and their differences enabled smaller and weaker neighbours to exist and retain their independence. In those days the land of Israel was never encircled by one single nation. But today the state is girdled by a tight ring, a bloc that is likely to grow, for it may be assumed that Tunis, Algeria and Morocco will also become autonomous sooner or later and be admitted, with Libya, to the United Nations. The Christian states of the world do not form a united front on any issue. Not so the Moslem states, where the feeling for national unity is quite strong, if not equally strong in all. Although Turkey looks upon itself as the associate and partner of the countries of Western Europe, most Islamic countries join forces in many political fields. The principal ones which are not Arabic-speaking, Pakistan, Persia, Afghanistan and Indonesia, occupy an area of 1,800,000 square miles. Their total population exceeds 185 millions. They give their co-operation to the Arab League states in the United Nations and support them as a matter of course in questions which are not crucial to themselves, usually including their attitude towards Israel. This is the sweep of the problem of security and of politics which the Arab countries present to the young state of Israel."

Naturally, the Arab states interpret the situation altogether differently. In their view Israel has been wedged between them by the power of limitless money in the hands of men who have almost limitless influence in America, England and the United Nations. They maintain that Israel, despite her constant protestations of goodwill and peace, cannot possibly sustain the number she hopes eventually to absorb—it has been variously assessed from two to five millions—within her present limits. Indeed, their argument goes, has she not already caused a tragic refugee problem of large dimensions among the former Arab citizens of Palestine? She aspires to develop the country by stealing the waters of the Jordan, while the territory covered by the northern marshlands which she is in process of draining is historically Syria's.

The Arabs are now ready to accept an Israel restricted within the frontiers laid down by the United Nations when partition of Palestine was recommended in the General Assembly of November, 1947. But they were not prepared to accept it then, and in fact, were they able to reach agreement among themselves and had they confidence in their own internal situation, they would not accept it now. Israel, they feel, has expanded despite United Nations resolutions regarding the repatriation of refugees and the internationalisation of Jerusalem. They have forgotten that it was their own defiance of the United Nations, which they carried to the length of waging war upon Israel, which brought them to their present straits. Even the wealthy, corrupt and entrenched Arab nobility, even the feudalistic and fanatical *mullahs*, when they name Islam's greatest menace do not speak of Communism, or Soviet expansion, or British imperialism, but of Israel and the world Zionist organisation with its headquarters in New York and its fist in the treasure-chest of the United States of America.

Whenever a new man emerged among the Arabs Ben-Gurion put out feelers for the settlement of their differences. The secret history of his administration records near-successful attempts at reaching agreement not only with Abdullah of Jordan but also with Husni Zaim of Syria, a short-lived dictator who had risen to power on the wave of unrest and jockeying for position which followed that country's defeat by the Jewish forces. Ben-Gurion's party, *Mapai*, proudly points to a long record, going back to the days of the second Jewish settlement period of 1906, of political work among the Arabs, and some of its members have a deep understanding of the Arab mentality. While it was apparent, at the time of writing, that Communist infiltration in the Middle East was of minor proportions, ultra-nationalist elements such as the Moslem Brotherhood in Egypt and the followers of Mullah Kashani in Persia have been

known to make use of Communist agitators in the pursuit of their
political aims. The ex-Mufti of Jerusalem, Haj Amin el Husseini,
with his own reasons for disliking not only Israel but the Arab rulers
as well, has been adapting Communism to his own ends, just as he
once used German and Italian fascism, and he appears to have been
singled out by Moscow as its most promising vehicle in the Arab
world. He is in touch with Communists in every country where pan-
Islamism and hatred of western 'imperialism' go hand in hand.

Ever since the word Korea struck the newspaper headlines, a
defence arrangement for the Middle East has loomed large in the
calculations of Anglo-American strategists, and, correspondingly,
the Arabs have known that they dispose of considerable bargaining
power with the western allies. In the case of the Lebanon, a country
Ben-Gurion insists has no cause for maintaining a state of war with
Israel, public feeling undoubtedly favours an arrangement for entering the western camp. For the most part Jordan feels the same, for,
as a state, it too has benefited territorially by the Arab-Israel war,
though the 400,000 Palestine refugees in its midst, a most articulate
section of the population, nourish determined hostility to the two
chief western powers. Egypt managed to keep Foster Dulles in a
state of titillating expectancy but made no practical moves to help
him with his plans until the negotiation, in July, 1954, of the
Anglo-Egyptian agreement to evacuate the Suez garrison. Iraq
has always been conformist to Arab League policy towards Israel;
and when the Foreign Office, goaded by an exasperated House of
Commons, demanded the reopening of the pipe-line to Anglo-
Iranian's oil refinery at Haifa, she wore Britain down with her
obstinacy. Silhouetted against the Mediterranean sky the great
cylinders of that refinery are now about as extinct as a Cornish tin-
mine.

Refusing obstinately to talk peace with Israel, this group of
countries has obstructed traffic through the Suez Canal, denied
bases to the western Powers, withheld aid from the United Nations
in Korea, and indeed made little effort to alleviate the plight of the
Arab refugees. Yet they sought and received modern war equipment
from England, France and America of an importance vastly outstripping the military might of Israel, whose own rearmament can
be achieved only at the cost of retarding still further her urgent and
expensive development programme. Today, the balance of power

in the Middle East is heavily loaded against Israel. She disposes of an excellent army, well-trained, intelligent, and prepared to defend the state and the cause identified with it. It is nevertheless difficult to see what this will avail against a synchronised attack, launched by air, sea and land, of nations sharing the humiliation of a combined defeat, better led than previously, and far less arrogant.

Ben-Gurion made his willingness to fit into an arrangement of regional defence all too plain, though he would prefer such a scheme to be the responsibility of Britain rather than America. Here indeed is a change in his ideas. For years he castigated Britain for appeasing the Arab world at the cost of the Jews. From 1949 onward the State Department, not the Foreign Office, became the object of his distrust, and this despite the enmity of Britain's ally across the Jordan. The American method of 'hard-ware' aid as a substitute for Britain's posting overseas of large troop detachments is the source of that anxiety. Money and equipment in the hands of his neighbours endanger his country's security; western troops in the area are an insurance against a possible second round of war. Not that he has lost faith in his people's ability to repeat their successes. Once, when his neighbour from the north-east looked darkly at Jewish reclamation work in the Huleh marshlands, asserting that there was no room in the Middle East for both Israel and Syria, the lively Jewish Premier retorted: "Let me assure Colonel Shishekli that Damascus is no further from Galilee than Galilee is from Damascus."

Despite the blackening clouds in the international firmament, the state of Israel pulled off a major diplomatic stroke during 1952—one of enormous economic advantage. Thanks to the good offices of the British government and the quite outstanding negotiating prowess of Dr. Nahum Goldmann, an agreement was signed in Luxembourg —where Israelis could meet with Germans in an atmosphere of mutual detachment—for the payment by West Germany of material reparations for the crimes of spoliation committed during the Nazi régime upon hundreds of thousands of Jewish survivors, now mostly citizens of Israel. Machinery and raw materials were promised to the value of 715 million dollars, to be spread over a period not exceeding fourteen years, and to be paid by Germany as its recognition of culpability. The character of the agreement was unique; so was the reaction of the Israeli people towards its negotiation. All the western governments, and their public opinion, welcomed it.

In Arab capitals it provoked such violent protest that for a while the *Bundestag* hesitated to ratify it.

No leader lightly offends the susceptibilities of large masses of his people; and Ben-Gurion, whose personal courage none has disputed, must have trembled at informing the nation of his proposal to open talks with those who in Israel are still identified by many as the murderers of their fathers and mothers, their husbands or wives, or their children. Indeed, from the moment his intentions became known, the Jews ceased being a nation in the impersonal sense. They became a community of mourners, with memories leaping back to the Jewish agony of the thirties and forties, and staid *Knesset* members saw themselves once again with bundles on their backs, trudging through the snow in flight from Belsen and Terezin. Though the world forgot, Jews were remembering.

Those who have risen from the depths of tragedy even to the extent of welding themselves into a political organism complete with a government, a civil service, a judiciary and an army, conceal within their subconscious a pent-up suffering unable to express itself within the strait-jacket of national discipline. For a brief moment Israel came close to civil war. Neither the parliamentary building, nor the Premier's person, was sacrosanct. Men and women were prepared to die to prevent, as they thought, the sacrilege of their dead, and they were prepared to kill. An economic, a political, even a moral case, could be made out for the policy of forcing the Germans to pay—in so far as payment was possible—for their crimes. But respected figures among the clergy, the intelligentsia and in politics, together with less articulate citizens on the farms and in the towns, felt revolted by the principle. And there were those who, because of their hatred of Ben-Gurion or their scorn of parliamentary government, were ready to exploit that revulsion. Of these, Menachem Beigin, the perfect Israel edition of the warped, prison-camp mind turned demagogue, was one, and the most formidable.

The *Knesset* debated the issue in January, 1952. *Mapai*, a few members of the religious parties and some non-socialist Progressives were in favour. The combined forces of extreme Right and extreme Left were ranged against them. Beigin's party, *Herut*, allied itself to the conservative General Zionist group (not within the government), *Mapam* and the Communists. They brought against Ben-Gurion's supporters a case whose ingredients varied from the 'capitalist-imperialist plot' theme and charges of 'insulting the memory of our dead', to grounds of political inexpediency and of unjustifiable confidence in the German's word. Some claimed America was encouraging the negotiations to escape her own payment to Israel of grants-in-aid, others claimed that reparations would bring the industrial enslavement of Israel by Germany, because of the need for technicians and spare parts to go with the goods delivered. The opposition in the House was determined and powerful. But the real opposition was voiced outside it. Monday, January 7th, 1952, dawned as a fateful day for democracy in Israel.

During the afternoon a mass meeting was held in Zion Square, in the centre of Jerusalem, addressed by Beigin and Professor Klausner, an elderly scholar concealing extremist political views beneath his venerable appearance. They declaimed against Germany, against the government, against the police who, armed with shields, batons and gas-mask kits, had cordoned off a section of the city-centre around the *Knesset* building, put up road-blocks and diverted bus routes. To the inhabitants of the Holy City, 1948 had come again: only this time Jew confronted Jew. A crowd estimated at 2,000, the majority of them youths, participated in the demonstration. Some 600 police patrolled the cordoned area. In the *Knesset* Ben-Gurion had already spoken. Yaacov Hazan, of *Mapam*, was replying, and he described the proposed reparations as the spearhead of an attack upon Russia. At that moment a heavy column of demonstrators arrived outside the *Knesset*, having first been informed by Beigin: "I am not here to inflame you, but the police have grenades containing gas manufactured in Germany, that very gas used to kill your fathers and mothers. We shall suffer any torture they may think up for us to prevent a decision to deal with Germany!" Zion Square lay just a few hundred yards below the *Knesset*.

Battle raged for four hours. The mob encountered tear-gas and smoke-bomb resistance, but managed to overpower the police by the use of similar weapons. Some youths jumped from the roof-tops into the cordoned area. Many were wounded, and were smuggled to secret first-aid stations and then out of the city. The debate continued throughout, though *Knesset* windows were smashed and stones hurtled over the heads of those within. Gradually, smoke billowed through the chamber, and as members buried their faces in handkerchiefs, Beigin himself mounted the tribune. He

denied the rioting had been stage-managed, and read out a list of
distinguished citizens who opposed reparations. Ben-Gurion then
rose and pointed to the windows. He had till then sat motionless,
apparently unaffected by the choking atmosphere.

"They are not identified with your hooligans in the street," he
shouted.

"You are the hooligan!" was the angry retort. Uproar followed
in the House and confusion as Beigin refused to withdraw the un-
parliamentary expression. Army reinforcements arrived in the
streets, gradually overpowering the demonstrators. There was not
enough room in Jerusalem's jails to take all the arrested. A hundred
policemen were wounded. Beigin returned to the speaker's stand,
apologised and was suspended till the end of the session. But he had
plans of his own. "We shall go to the barricades, we are ready to die,
drag us to concentration camps if you will, but some issues are
dearer than life!" Members took this as a threat to turn his *Herut*
party into the *Irgun* again, and lead it underground. The debate
continued the following day, and the day after. When the vote was
taken, one *Herut* member, stricken by a heart attack, was carried on
a stretcher to strengthen the opposition vote. A government
supporter flew back from New York to register his vote. In the
streets all was now quiet. By a majority of sixty-one votes against
fifty with five abstentions, a motion was passed, not authorising
the government to enter into direct negotiations, but placing
responsibility on the *Knesset* Foreign Affairs Committee to 'take
action'. In effect it was *Mapai*, and they alone, who were completely
at peace with themselves on this issue.

Ben-Gurion still had his old score to settle with Beigin. He hated
the instability, the impetuosity, the military mumbo-jumbo of
Beigin, who despised socialists for their subservience to Britain and
their apparent stolidity in the face of the burning of Jews in the
European hell. The Premier now addressed Beigin as he would a
traitor, and in a broadcast, so that all the nation might bear
witness.

"I do not underestimate the declaration of Mr. Menachem Beigin
that he is preparing for a war of life or death," he declared, "nor have
I any illusions against whom these threats are directed. I know, too,
that it is not too difficult to carry out acts of murder against members of the Government, of which I have the honour to stand at the

head. Nor am I ignorant as to who is the principal target of Mr.
Beigin's plan in this war 'unto life or death'.

"I consider it is my duty to tell the nation : do not panic and do not
be afraid. There are sufficient forces and means in the hands of the
state to defend the sovereignty and the freedom of Israel, and to
prevent the domination of hooligans, political murderers and protracted acts of terror. The army, the police and the people are the
faithful and effective guarantee that this criminal and insane plot of
the *Herut* hooligans and their Communist supporters will not
succeed. . . . We shall not be turned into a Spain or a Syria. . . .
Fascism in its various guises either of the Right or the Left will not
be victorious. . . . I do not underestimate the physical courage of
these men. . . . It is not my purpose to tell the nation that the danger
is not serious. . . . Mr. Beigin's statement about war is no empty
threat, but a declaration of terror, underground terror.

". . . We have sufficient will, strength, and means, to prevent any
terrorism designed to destroy our democracy. . . . I do not know
what is likely to happen in these days to the chosen representatives
of the nation. But it is our duty to guard above all the rule of law and
the authority of the state. . . . I can guarantee to the nation which
dwells in Zion, to the Jewish people abroad and public opinion
throughout the world that . . . terror against the sovereignty and
the freedom of the state of Israel will, unhesitatingly and uncom-
promisingly, be utterly uprooted."

Everyone knew Ben-Gurion would not hesitate to use the army.
He would proclaim the curfew, declare martial law if necessary, and
many were alarmed lest he should hasten into some premature, disastrous action. But how far would Beigin and his followers go?
With memories of the King David Hotel explosion returned to
haunt them, the people of Jerusalem wondered whether the lunatic
streak in *Herut* supporters really would lead them to blow up the
Knesset or assassinate the Premier. German reparations constituted
an issue so alive and intimate to large numbers of peaceful citizens,
that few of them could not but admit a certain sympathy for the
Beigin policy, even though they feared the Beigin method.

There was no civil war, no assassination. One or two bombs were
thrown, but not at the Premier, and the hysteria passed. Israel agreed
to accept the offer from Germany and to chance her luck that in the
years to come there would still be a Social-Democratic régime in

Germany to honour Adenauer's commitment. The leaky financial dyke, which only just managed to keep the floods of economic disaster out, found another cork. Little more was heard of Beigin, who was made for violence, not parliamentary debate. He returned to his seat in the *Knesset*, to talk and behave like anything but a man of destiny. Nevertheless, those concerned kept a watch on him.

The show of force deeply wounded Ben-Gurion's national pride, for it was a threat to the standard of democratic government he was so anxious to present to the outside world. Israelis are fond of testing their development as a state by comparison with other nations. The one Ben-Gurion takes most frequently as his model is Britain, with whose weaknesses and strength he has come to be intimately acquainted. And Englishmen have never had recourse to the barricade, except to defend their shores from foreign invasion. Perhaps it was their differing assessments of the British character which was the ideological point of departure in the hatred between Ben-Gurion and Beigin.

On the principle that like is attracted to like, Ben-Gurion the socialist and former general secretary of the world's most comprehensive trade union movement sought during his Premiership to relieve Israel's isolation by courting socialist sentiment throughout the world. His success with British Labour, taking account of his bitter years as the protagonist of 'independent' Zionism as against Weizmann's 'Mandatory' Zionism, was prodigious. By some psychological quirk his love for Britain is second only to that of his own land, and it will be recalled that the one holiday abroad that Ben-Gurion allowed himself during his years of office was a week's stay in England, where he went by way of Athens and Southern Greece. It was a completely private visit, spent browsing in Oxford bookshops and reading in his room at the Mitre Hotel, or discussing philosophy (no politics) with Isaiah Berlin of All Souls. With Ehud Avriel he came to sample once more this country's great sense of tradition, which he envies. He considers the Labour Party the most idealistic body of socialists in the world, and Winston Churchill the greatest figure of this age. Truman, on the other hand, he thinks of as a Jewish miracle.

Ben-Gurion set himself one other great foreign task. This was to get his country, despite its unpopularity with the Arab League, accepted by the great Asian land-mass. His frequent allusions to the significance of the new Asia were not the ruminations of a fire-side geo-politician. They were based on his appreciation of the fundamental strength of the many peoples he saw confronted, as were his own people, with the pitfalls of suddenly-achieved independence. This appreciation he sharpened by long study of Buddhism and other Eastern philosophies. The difficulty, he constantly emphasised, was the lack of a common basis upon which to build. The West understands Israel because Jews and Christians share the Bible. The Jews have no cultural possession in common with India or China. "How shall we learn to understand each other?" he would exclaim. He always made a point of receiving Asiatics when they came to Israel, and made copious notes of the interviews.

The formative influence on Ben-Gurion, let it be remembered, is the inter-action of British colonial domination and the inherent nature of continental Asia: a territory where every popular leader has had difficulty in reconciling abstract, and favourable, political pronouncements from London with the puny despotism of the English pukka sahib. This inevitably groups Ben-Gurion with Jinnah in Pakistan, Nehru in India, and Senanayake in Ceylon. All these men said of the English: "They did great things for our country, built roads and harbours, taught us administration, sent us their most conscientious educators. But the best thing they did for us was to leave." Now a large part of Asia has been given over to these men, or their successors, to use as they wish. Ben-Gurion wants them to pool their talents for the development of their continent. They all face problems of magnitude created by the desert, by mass displacement, by antiquity obtruding in the form of religion into contemporary issues.

Ben-Gurion and Pandit Nehru are moderate socialists with a lively appreciation of the power a united Moslem world could wield throughout the East, and within the international scheme. A band of Moslem states lies stretched between them, and even if the more ambitious aspirations dreamed of by Pakistan are discounted, they nevertheless cast a long shadow over both New Delhi and New Jerusalem. Among Western statesmen men like Anthony Eden and Dean Acheson recognised the dangers inherent in the political emancipation of the Moslem peoples at a pace far outstripping their technological advance. Ben-Gurion and Nehru are conscious of a new danger caused by the demands of western strategy—technological acceleration without an equal amount of democratic progress. India's strength will be her safeguard, but for the smaller races of the East, only time can determine whether they can preserve their individuality or whether they are to become tributaries of the Moslem stream.

Unfortunately, Nehru has shown little interest in Israel. This has been another source of regret to the Jewish Prime Minister, and after a series of unsuccessful attempts to forge closer links with India, he has come to be censorious of her leader, regarding him as an opportunist ignorant of the true forces governing their continent. Nevertheless, whenever left-wing groups come together in Asia, as in Rangoon early in 1953, Israeli socialists, because of their comparatively long history as a party, their highly-developed ideological sense and their practical experience of collectivism, are bound to play an influential role.

Now the question arises: has Ben-Gurion's foreign policy been a success? His country has benefited materially from American aid, but this is due to the Truman administration in Washington and the phalanx of Jewish voters in New York, not to the Prime Minister in Jerusalem. He managed to gain current acceptance for his stand against total repatriation of the Arab refugees miserably encamped in their masses along his borders. Here, again, Arab political ineptitude must be thanked. His declared policy of 'non-identification' with either East or West soon crumpled, but it had been little more than a pious hope from the beginning. He fought tenaciously to keep Jewish Jerusalem within the borders of his state, even to the extent of defying a United Nations order to the contrary. This is now a political fact, though not a diplomatically accepted one. His handling of the Jerusalem problem has not been skilful, and from the first he underestimated international sentiment and the power of the Vatican on this harassing question. Since Malenkov assumed the mantle of Stalin, even the tension with the Soviet Union has lessened and once more a Russian envoy sits in Tel-Aviv.

The nature of any nation's foreign policy must flow from the realities of its geography and history. Israel is situated in a region precipitated into modernity as a consequence of the collapse of the Ottoman Empire, the construction of the Suez Canal, and the discovery and exploitation of almost limitless oil resources. Israel was born as the result of a war with the Arab states, and her birth had been impeded by Britain, hastened by the U.S.A., and largely unaffected by the Soviet Union. She is tiny, as regards size as well as numbers, and her natural resources are meagre. Her frontiers are long, grotesque, and vulnerable. These are the realities. The fact that Israel has survived, and without the revolutions so characteristic of change in her neighbour states, must be counted a triumph for the man carrying more of the burden than any other, David Ben-Gurion. Within these realities he was furthermore embarrassed not only by the lack of a tradition in foreign affairs, but also by the paucity of suitable personnel to conduct them. Britain left a large and valuable inheritance to the Jews when they declared their independence in May, 1948. A legal system, an administrative framework, an economic method had all been there before in which the future leaders of the country could serve an apprenticeship. But the country could have no foreign policy as such. Britain had declared war on behalf of Palestine, had entered into commercial agreements for her, had protected her citizens abroad and issued their passports. Before this the Turks had looked to these tasks. Now for the first time Jewish ambassadors represent their government in foreign capitals, and take up positions at the United Nations on a wide range of questions upon which previously the Jewish sector of Palestine was expected to have no opinion. It has all been very strange, and therefore not surprising that mistakes, not merely of tactics, have been made.

Israel had to set up an administrative framework and to organise departments for western Europe, for America, for the British Commonwealth, for Asia and for eastern Europe, in her Foreign Ministry. Who was there qualified to head them? Moshe Sharett was the natural choice for the Cabinet portfolio, since foreign affairs had been his responsibility—jointly with others not resident in Palestine—during the years of the Jewish Agency. But in May, 1948, only a handful of men in the country could qualify as candidates for appointments demanding a long period of training and knowledge of foreign countries. An ambassador, after all, is not to be lightly chosen. In the beginnings almost any Jew from the West, if his intellect were equal to it and he knew the Hebrew language, became an automatic candidate for the Diplomatic Service. The perplexities of the authorities will be even better appreciated when it

10

Prophet in Jerusalem

A man in a hurry – Ben-Gurion's mission – Discarding old loyalties – Religious issues – Cabinet crises – Second General Election – Ingathering of the Exiles – Death of Weizmann – Ben-Zvi becomes President – Coalition at last – The pioneer returns to the desert

BEN-GURION HAD a favourite dictum: "Unlike other nations," he would say, "we have not centuries at our disposal. Israel must accomplish in a few years what has taken others generations." Having established a political state for the Jews, what exactly was it he wished to achieve?

Again, in his own words, his aim was the achievement of Zionism. The term defies accurate definition. At the minimum it means adherence to the principle of a Jewish return to the ancestral home of Palestine; at the maximum the re-creation of the Jewish nation accompanied by the revival of the long-neglected barren soil of that home, the transfer to Israel of millions of people and their own metamorphosis into a homogeneous national unit before the complete dissolution of their Jewish individuality into the *mores* of their adopted countries. At one extremity, therefore, Zionism is purely a spiritual urge, and capable of satisfaction by proxy if a few can keep alight the beacon of Judaism on behalf of the scattered remainder. At the other extremity, Zionism is a revolutionary movement having as its goal the elimination of Jewry's minority characteristics, caused by the concentration of the race in a few large cities around the world where they pursue economic activities which are, essentially, on the surface of, rather than basic to, a national civilisation. This was Ben-Gurion's interpretation. To him, Zionism only began where the political and military struggle for independence left off. He had always thought this from the earliest days, and, consequently, the objective he set himself was fundamentally different from Chaim Weizmann's, whose life-task ended in the legal award of territory by the United Nations in 1947.

To assist him in achieving this revolution within the prescribed

17

period of a few years Ben-Gurion had a people 650,000 strong and an area the size of Wales, only a small part of which was cultivated (or at that time cultivable) and without known natural resources. The communications system was rudimentary, the educational framework uncoordinated and partisan. The 120 members of his parliament subscribed to widely-varying interpretations of their goal, while his Cabinet was composed of thirteen men whose experience and outlook were so limited as largely to disqualify them from the huge task. The Jewish people have throughout the ages produced outstanding political figures, as well as great scientists and thinkers; and today they may be found occupying important roles in many nations. But apart from Selig Brodetsky, of England, whose stay in Israel was cut short by a breakdown in health, not one of them personally identified himself with Israel by immigrating there and thus contributing all his talents to the struggle for national rebirth. This was Ben-Gurion's first great handicap. The second was that the people at home would help him only on their own terms. Neither fact deterred him from carrying out the policy he had set himself. But not unnaturally he was often angry with those offering him advice from outside, and ruthless with his critics at home.

In five years Ben-Gurion went far towards realising his goal. The 650,000 became one-and-a-half millions. New industries were created to employ them, and new towns for them to live in. The army was expanded and every young newcomer baptised by national service into citizenship. The nature of the landscape, no less than the quality and the distribution of the people, changed. With all this Ben-Gurion's position as national leader grew daily stronger as the rivalries of earlier times became more and more academic. All but his constant enemies on the extreme Right and extreme Left accepted him. The General Zionists, though they considered his economic policy suicidal, the Orthodox, though they knew he flouted the *Torah*, and *Mapai*, despite his many heresies, were with him. The masses of newcomers, condemned for years to live in shanty-towns and forced to suffer the rigours of a discipline for which they were wholly unprepared, blessed him for bringing them home. The children, like his army, adored him. He embodied authority, power, decision. And in his simplicity and devotion to the things of the spirit he touched greatness.

Why, then, had he to suffer years of political frustration after the achievement of statehood? Partly because his party's popularity lessened as his own increased. Partly also because he drove the people into their messianic responsibilities too hard. They saw no reason why a small fraction of national redemption should not be sacrificed for a little more material comfort.

Very quickly, under the Ben-Gurion policy of speed in all things the nation divided into haves and have-nots. Ironically, this happened at a time when the trade-union, social-welfare nexus of *Histadruth* was the mightiest organisation in the country, and its own officials the most influential 'haves'. Hence the waning enthusiasm for socialism and *Mapai*. There was the social upheaval caused by a mass-immigration drawn from all social levels, excessive European sophistication side-by-side with the primitive customs of those only recently unearthed from beneath the crust of Moslem oppression in Oriental lands. Not surprisingly, several thousands left during those five years. It was the story of the early colonisation days repeating itself: an immigration-wave, a period of optimism reflected in a fever of activity, then unemployment, deflation of the spirit, and emigration.

Ben-Gurion's is a mind laboriously improved through the study of great literatures. His judgment, like his character, is not tempered by carefully-planned education in childhood and adolescence. He cannot see life in all its subtleties, and understands neither poetry, music, nor painting. Therefore he is spellbound by what he does understand. He shares his admiration equally among Spinoza, the Bible, and Marconi. Having decided that the Jews are now carrying on their national life at the point broken off by the Second Temple, he was continually amazed by the limitations of the beings around him. He spoke like a prophet, they acted like parish politicians. He was repeatedly mystified when given the answer, "You are asking the impossible". This was the case not only with departmental officials but with the foreign experts he invited to plan a new harbour, or set up a new industry, or straighten out his income-tax regulations. To the Premier courage and imagination could throw out no challenge impossible for technology to take up.

Gradually, he broke with the old party loyalties, and was aloof and severe even with the *Histadruth*. It was sad for him to have to chastise the *kibbutzim*. He believed they constituted a unique and successful pattern of community-living, but even they failed to measure up to the needs of the times. Many of them ignored his request that they take in the newcomers, either as hired labourers or as members. With living conditions growing ever more austere, the *kibbutzim* became as calculating and self-seeking collectively as were the bourgeois individualists in the towns. Ben-Gurion, being now less representative of agnostic radicalism, found new popularity with the Orthodox. The *Mizrachi* responded to his streak of mysticism, his apt allusions to the Bible, his love of the Hebrew language, his fidelity to Jerusalem. They harried him within the Cabinet and out; yet he was an inseparable part of what in their belief was primarily a religious act—the resumption of Jewish nationhood. It was their ambition one day to make the state as much a religious as a political organism, with the *Torah* the basis of its laws and ordinances. This must await more propitious times, but meanwhile Ben-Gurion in office prevented his irreligious *Mapai* from turning Israel into a completely secular state.

After the death of Berl Katznelson in 1944, Ben-Gurion had no close friend or confidant. But he found relaxation in the company of Rabbi Maimon, the ageing leader of religious Zionism. In Maimon the Premier recognised that rare phenomenon, the complete Jew, untroubled by the minority complex or inner cultural conflicts. A conservative in political, as in spiritual, affairs, Maimon had one of the finest private libraries in Jerusalem, a favourite refuge for the Premier when he needed to escape from his troubles in that small city.

The religious issue is present in almost every domestic question. It is arguable whether it is capable of solution at all, except by the complete subjection of the synagogue by the state or the reverse. Neither eventuality is probable. So far, open conflict has been avoided by a series of short-term arrangements on matters such as a written Constitution, state education and military service for women. Cabinet crises frequently coincided with the termination of those arrangements and negotiations for their renewal.

Religion has principally confused and bedevilled policy on education. It was immediately apparent to Israeli politicians that many problems would have to await a new generation for their solution. Therefore, how that generation was educated would largely determine the future nature of the state, and it was upon this point that the two opposing views were irreconcilable. A religious Jew cannot conceive of an educational system denying the significance of basic Jewish observances. He refutes the right, indeed denies the possibility, of non-religious educators to teach these precepts. A Jewish socialist suffers similar agonies of conscience when such archaic regulations are advanced as a recipe for modern living. The holy laws, he contends, acted in the past as a preservative ensuring Jewish survival in the Diaspora; today they could become a tyranny, render the state medieval and inefficient and hamper the development of the personality of their young.

During the Mandatory era, when education was not compulsory, there had been a privately-endowed system of Jewish education enabling parents to send their children to the schools of their choice: religious schools for the Orthodox, *Histadruth* schools for the left-wing, non-sectarian schools for those opposed to religious or political indoctrination. The system worked better in practice than would appear possible. It avoided a *Kulturkampf* and was elastic enough to make a common range of subjects available to all trends, with differences only of emphasis. Unfortunately, a further group of schools, sponsored by the ultramontane opponents of Zionism, was allowed to come into existence after independence had been won, and before the newly-established Ministry of Education fully realised the explosive character of its baffling inheritance. The small number of pupils in this group were taught, in the manner of the Jewish Dark Ages, little besides the Pentateuch and Talmud.

Within its limitations this educational formula was able to cope with the first great influx of newcomers, comprising some 200,000 from central and eastern Europe. They were people of developed cultural background, and parents chose whatever schooling they preferred for their children. Not so in 1950, when the European zones of misery were evacuated and Israel brought in new citizens from Moslem countries such as the Yemen and North Africa. For now both father and son were primitive and illiterate, raw human material whose only Jewish characteristic was a devotion to the religious Orthodoxy which had enabled them to survive. They were precipitated into the dazzling modern era, a leap in time from the thirteenth to the twentieth century. Whoever educated them would, as the children reached maturity and parents grew adjusted to their new conditions of life, exercise control over their voting power.

By the latter part of 1950 there were 300,000 of these Oriental Jews, with prospects of many more arriving in the future; enough in fact to transform them into a numerical majority. A struggle developed for mastery of their souls. The interests represented in the *Histadruth* sought to absorb them by eradicating their religious traits. It was possible to convince them that while strict religious observances were important in their lands of origin, they could safely be discarded in the state of Israel.

The Orthodox forces were alive to this move to disaffect a potentially decisive following. They held the scales in the *Knesset* and threatened Ben-Gurion with withdrawal from the Cabinet unless this strategy was stopped. As a result they won important concessions, and not only in the field of education. The waiving of a written Constitution, for example, averted a head-on clash between synagogue and state; school-inspectors of the Orthodox affiliations were sent to protect religion in the immigrant-camps; the importation of cheap non-*kosher* meat was vetoed, even at a time of near-starvation in protein foods. Still the Orthodox were not satisfied. They baulked at resigning office but absented themselves from Cabinet meetings. After one angry altercation with his Prime Minister, Rabbi Maimon left the Cabinet-room in a huff and boarded a plane for London, to continue a conflict approaching tragi-comedy by long-distance telephone.

At this point control of the *Mizrachi* party was lost by the unworldly rabbi to a man from Tel-Aviv who was not only a religious Jew but a banker into the bargain. This man was David Pinkas, and he promptly demanded the portfolio of Trade and Industry. He wanted to ensure that the new regulations which had been made to entice foreign private capital into the country were administered by an adherent of private enterprise. After long haggling over their usual religious demands, Ben-Gurion found this new claim the last straw.

The Premier was prepared to accept the South African Jack Geri, a non-party businessman, but not a confirmed conservative. Once again he turned to *Mapam* and the General Zionists to help him out of his predicament. Neither party would budge from its stated position: the one wanting more socialism, the other more *laisser-faire*. On October 15th, 1950, Ben-Gurion telephoned Dr. Weizmann in Rehovoth to inform the President of the collapse of his government, and to ask him to appoint another Premier. The move caught the Orthodox bloc unawares. Its members, instead of attending Cabinet meetings or the *Knesset*, were in Tel-Aviv planning their tactics. They reproached Ben-Gurion for his rash step. A solution, they claimed, could be found. Why was the Premier in such a hurry?

Of course there was no one else; and Pinchas Rosen, the Minister of Justice and leader of the five-man Progressive Party, used his considerable influence with Ben-Gurion to restrain him from a complete break with his disgruntled Orthodox partners. From London Maimon telephoned Ben-Gurion begging him not to dissolve parliament and force an unnecessary general election. Ben-Gurion's answer was an ultimatum that if no solution was found by the end of the month he proposed going to the country. This would be a risk for everyone concerned. The electorate was swollen by forty per cent and the newcomers' political affiliations were an unknown quantity.

A compromise was reached at the eleventh hour. Geri became Minister of Trade and Industry while the Orthodox were appeased with Under-Secretaryships, both for this department and for the Education Ministry. Pinkas was superseded once again in the *Mizrachi* party by Maimon, who returned to Jerusalem to take over his old portfolio of Religious Affairs. Ben-Gurion extracted from his troublesome colleagues a 'pledge of honour' to accept collective Cabinet responsibility and keep the peace until the natural expiry of this parliament in 1953.

A note of confidence was, however, absent from the Prime Minister's speech when he presented his patched-up government to parliament. In an address largely composed of extracts from the Book of Numbers, he administered severe reprimands all round, reserving the larger part of his anger for *Mapam* and the General Zionists for eschewing their share of the responsibility and problems of statehood. His critics, he said, behaved precisely as did the Wandering Jews when they revolted against Moses in the times of the Exodus. They complained then, as now, of food-shortages: "And the children of Israel wept and said, who shall give us flesh to eat. We remember the fish we did eat in Egypt freely, the cucumber and the melon, and the leeks and the onions and the garlic. But now our soul is dried away." Then there was the matter of the

'arrogance' of Moses, and those associated with him: "And Korah
. . . took men and they rose up before Moses with certain of the
children of Israel, 250 princes of the assembly, famous in the congregation, men of renown. And they gathered themselves together
against Moses and against Aaron and said unto them, Ye take too
much upon you, seeing all the congregation are holy, every one of
them, and the Lord is among them. Wherefore then lift ye up your-
selves above the congregation of the Lord?"

As for the embarrassments of alliance with the Orthodox, these
too were not unknown thirty-two centuries before: "And when
Moses heard it, he fell upon his face. . . . Hear, I pray you, ye sons of
Levi. Seemeth it but a small thing unto you that the God of Israel
hath separated you from the congregation of Israel to bring you
near to himself to do the service of the tabernacles of the Lord, and
to stand before the congregation to minister unto them? And he
hath brought thee (Korah) near unto him, and all thy brethren the
sons of Levi with thee. . . . For which cause both thou and all thy
company are gathered together against the Lord: and what is
Aaron, that ye murmur against him?

"And Moses sent to call Dathan and Abiram, the sons of Eliab:
which said, we will not come up. Is it a small thing that thou hast
brought us up and out of a land that floweth with milk and honey
to kill us in the wilderness except thou makest thyself altogether a
prince over us? Moreover thou hast not brought us unto a land that
floweth with milk and honey, or given us inheritance of fields and
vineyards: wilt thou put out the eyes of these men? We will not
come up."

Sadly, Ben-Gurion offered his commentary on the text: "Moses
never appeared again but Dathan and Abiram are with us still."

It took four dispiriting weeks to gain a semblance of unity and, in
November, 1950, Ben-Gurion judged the situation safe enough for
him to take his holiday in Oxford. Then Municipal elections took
place and the results indicated the existence in Israel of a floating vote
prepared to give the General Zionists a chance. Rokach and Bernstein were jubilant. They would give the government no rest, they
announced, until the House was dissolved. The opportunity soon
occurred. The following February David Remez, then Minister of
Education, made a statement of policy which the Religious bloc
considered contrary to the spirit of their agreement with the Prime

Minister. They voted with the opposition; and the government, which Ben-Gurion had hoped would last another two years, fell. This time there was no question in Ben-Gurion's mind but that the country had to decide. He went to Rehovoth to offer his resignation to the President.

Weizmann's life was all but over, and, as bulletins on the state of his health were telephoned daily to Jerusalem, the government prepared a plan, known by the code-word 'Joseph', for the implementation of the funeral arrangements. During his last lingering years the mutual animosity between him and Ben-Gurion melted away. It had not been so in the beginning when Weizmann arrived from America to respond to the call that he become the first President. Then Ben-Gurion's long-smouldering resentment against the other had gathered new fuel. The Premier equated the Presidency with political catalepsy. Weizmann considered he had been elected to lead, counsel and direct the nation, as did Truman whose guest in Washington he had but lately been. Assuredly, there was no Constitution to deny him such authority, just as there was no law to sanction it. In 1948 and in 1949, he showed his displeasure at Ben-Gurion's monopoly of supreme power in Israel by refusing to accept the state papers sent to him. When he did relent, it was ill-health, rather than the Prime Minister, which persuaded him to bow to the facts.

Almost blind, he hardly saw the man who now came with a story, long familiar to Weizmann's ears, of controversy and conflict in the nation. Formality demanded that Ben-Gurion surrender office; but they both knew that he would have to carry on, at all events until the election. Weizmann received, as was required of him, the representatives of all other parties. The Religious groups, the Progressives, even *Mapam* spoke of the importance of finding a solution to the crisis without recourse to a general election. Only the General Zionists were prepared to test their strength by going to the polls. Ben-Gurion's mind was made up, and his party saw an election struggle with the General Zionists as unavoidable. The sooner it was over, the better.

The President made a final appeal to Ben-Gurion to try to carry on as before. "Following your resignation," he said in a letter, "I called upon the leaders of the various groups in the *Knesset* for consultations on the position thus created. . . . The opinion was

repeatedly expressed that dissolution was likely to have serious consequences for the stability of the state and for the great efforts now
being made to strengthen its financial and economic position. The
representatives of most parties expressed the opinion that it was
mandatory to make another effort to find some way of bridging the
gulfs within this parliament. For many months the state will suffer
the poisoned atmosphere of party strife in anticipation of elections.
The members of the government will themselves be involved
in this struggle, and who can predict what will be the conclusions
arrived at by our friends and enemies abroad? What certainty is
there that the position will be better after new elections have
been held? Conflicts may even be sharpened by factors yet un-
foreseen.

"For these reasons I have decided to appeal to you, before we turn
to the last resort, that of elections, for a renewed effort to find a
solution which would promise stability within the framework of
this parliament, and to form a government that will enjoy the
support of a majority in the *Knesset*. I know this task will, in the
present circumstances, not be easy for you: but it is my duty to ask
you to undertake it."

Ben-Gurion replied two days later, on February 27th. His reply
was a catalogue of his difficulties during the past two years. "I regret
I cannot comply with your request," he wrote, ". . . From the
Diaspora of the past we have inherited an excessive, morbid
tendency to form splinter groups. Twenty-one lists were submitted
for the elections to the first parliament, for a population of 700,000.
There are eight separate factions in the *Knesset* and one of these (the
Orthodox) is in reality a bloc of four separate parties. The Communists and *Herut*, for obvious reasons, could not be taken into
consideration in the forming of a government. Two others, *Mapam*
and the General Zionists, both of whom were in the Provisional
Government, declined to join because the majority would not permit the minority to dictate its policy. . . .

"The activities of neither Left nor Right were limited to verbal
attack, whether in the *Knesset* or outside. Destructive activities were
organised, including demonstrations by unemployed and by members of the 'Peace Movement' on the one hand, and strikes by shop-
keepers, orange-growers and factory owners on the other. Slander-
ous and uncontrolled propaganda was carried on abroad, in a

manner not practised by any civilised country, or by any loyal opposition.

"The tremendous and majestic tasks that have fallen to the state (and the government)—security, the ingathering of the exiles and the forging of a progressive and sovereign nation, were not made any easier by this attitude on the part of the opposition. While we could rely on a stable majority in the *Knesset* we hoped that we might be able to overcome the enormous difficulties—difficulties that probably cannot be matched in any other country—and what has been achieved up to now demonstrates that there were good grounds for such hopes. Our security forces were perfected and enlarged; we admitted more than half a million people, and nevertheless succeeded in maintaining almost full employment; industrial production was developed while agricultural settlement made giant strides; great things were achieved in the building of houses and roads in every part of the country; a beginning was made in the development of the Negev. Israel's name among the nations was given stature.

"Probably no other country in the world can show such rapid progress and dynamic development as our young state. We have not yet overcome the great difficulties in our path, and we are still far from overcoming them, but the two sources of strength on which we have leaned have not failed us—the creative ability of the citizens of the state, and the attachment of world Jewry. I am fully convinced that it is possible to achieve in their entirety the aims we have shouldered. But to do this a stable government is needed, for the government of Israel cannot work on a day-to-day basis. This work calls for carefully thought-out planning over a period of years, and the long-term activation of forces and factors both here and abroad. But it has become clear that the Orthodox bloc is not prepared for such stability, either owing to internal difficulties or for other reasons.

"This 'front', although it had accepted the basic lines of policy laid down by the government, from time to time put forward claims that were not provided for in the agreed plan, and which it was difficult to reconcile with the basic policy that we had jointly accepted.

"The position was made more difficult by the connection of some members of the Orthodox bloc with the right wing, which was not a party to the government, and the origin of the first government crisis in October, 1950, was first caused by the pressure of the right-wing parties on the *Mizrachi*, pressure that was concerned with totally non-religious matters. It was only in order to ensure unity of all Orthodox factions that a religious element was later introduced into the discussions.

"Two weeks ago the Orthodox bloc brought about a new crisis. The pressure on the Orthodox bloc of the right wing continued to make itself felt even after the formation of the present government in November, 1950. As a result of the Municipal elections in the middle of November, the right-wing control of several municipal-ities was shaken, despite the considerable growth of the General Zionist party, and the position of the Orthodox bloc became more precarious.

"A religious pretext was once more found to ensure the solidarity of the Orthodox bloc, and after upheavals, resignation and threats of further crises on the part of members of the Orthodox bloc, the bloc voted against the government together with *Mapam*, the General Zionists, *Herut* and the Communists. The government of Israel, which is carrying a burden that is almost too heavy to bear, cannot be a plaything in the hands of factions and sub-factions, unable to achieve unity and fighting ceaselessly among themselves. I see no way out but an appeal to the people.

"I do not overlook the harm inherent in untimely elections. The chief danger that I see is the unhealthy precedent being created in this young State. And as you point out in your letter, within a few months the country will be enveloped in an atmosphere poisoned by party polemics. However, the atmosphere had already been poisoned by unrestrained party polemics from both the left and the right opposition. When the Religious bloc, *Mapam*, General Zionists, *Herut* and Communists voted against the government, it had of necessity to be presumed that their purpose was not merely destructive, but also constructive, and that they would reveal political courage and a sense of national responsibility in forming a new government. This supposition has not, to my regret, been borne out.

"If you, the President, perceive any prospects of forming a government that will receive the confidence of a majority of the *Knesset* it is incumbent on you to turn to the leader of one of the parties that voted against the government. If any of them should succeed, I would gladly relinquish my post to him and heartily wish him success in his task.

"Despite the immense difficulties that surrounded the work of my colleagues and myself, we have no grounds for regret in the work we have done so far. Faith in the vision of full redemption, both of the Jews and of humanity, trust in the creative capacity and struggle of a pioneering nation, faith in the aid that will come from the entire Jewish people towards the historic aims of the State of Israel, have guided us until now and will guide us in the future."

Ben-Gurion and his fractured coalition remained in office as a caretaker-government. There were no more compromises on the religious issue. On the contrary, the Prime Minister announced new legislation to conscript religious women for national service (hitherto they could object on grounds of conscience), and thus was plunged into a fierce controversy with the Rabbinical authorities. The latter made the serious charge of pronouncing service for women contrary to the *Torah*. This would make it impossible for Orthodox Jews to obey the law, should the measure be passed; and foretold ominously of a coming struggle between synagogue and state.

The Prime Minister angrily retorted: "Jews were among the first to recognise the equality of women. In ancient days at least one Jewish army was led by a woman. Another, Manya Shochet, inspired the first Jewish self-defence movement in this country in modern times!" Psalms were recited in the synagogues of Jerusalem's Orthodox quarters. Animosity deepened. *Mapai* made ready its appeal to the country.

The campaign began in earnest soon after Ben-Gurion's return from his Bond-drive tour in America, which was described in the opening chapter of this book. The first casualty of the poisoned atmosphere to which the President's letter had referred was, indeed, the Religious bloc. As its radical wing demanded a larger share of seats in the coming parliament, the four components separated out, each submitting its own lists to the electorate. *Herut* too lost some supporters, notably Eri Jabotinsky, who retired from politics. Isaac Tabenkin of *Mapam*, making his first speech in two years, had his own tale of woe to tell. Some of the upper Galilee settlements, outposts of the Trumpeldor country, withdrew from his treasured

Hameuchad network to join up with 100 per cent *Mapai* collectives. "What is *Kibbutz Hameuchad* without upper Galilee, or upper Galilee without *Kibbutz Hameuchad!*" he helplessly moaned. Israel Galili was allotted 120th place on the *Mapam* list, a strong hint that he would not be wanted by it in the next *Knesset*.

There were four sets of Arab candidates, one of which consisted solely of Druse admirers of Haifa's *Mapai* Mayor, Abba Hushi. Number two on the Communist party list was also an Arab, the youngest member of the first *Knesset*. Although his Hebrew was perfect, he insisted, as was his right, upon addressing parliament in Arabic. Sixteen lists were eventually approved, but it was clearly to be a tussle between the two giants, *Mapai* and the General Zionists, with the smaller groups weakened by discord.

David Ben-Gurion came back from America fresh and buoyant. He was full of optimism that the flotation of a loan would at last release the springs of economic progress. He toured the country literally from Dan to Beersheba, visiting the encampments humming with cramped newcomers and the old streamlined farm communes. Everywhere, he was accorded the welcome of a hero at the zenith of his popularity. Down the coast, not far from Majdal, the nodal point of his battle with the Egyptians, thousands of new immigrants were being incorporated into a rebuilt Askelon, planned as a tourist and industrial centre. They had little understanding of the party politics of their new-found motherland, but they knew they would vote for the man who had united them with it. Along the Jerusalem corridor, made secure for Israel by the addition of three dozen new villages, thousands more lined the newly-surfaced roadway to cheer him. Speaking to Tel-Aviv's housewives he attacked politicians who made impossible promises. "Even in England there are still food-queues," he pointed out; and, in one of his rare essays at humour: "I will not undertake to find for every woman a husband and a new dress." In Beersheba the pounding hammers of hundreds of Solel Boneh carpenters, prefabricating a township for as yet non-existent industries in the Negev, were silenced by the arrival of the Premier's dust-covered car. "Let's not yearn after the unattainable!" he urged the workers crowding up to him. "Four thousand years ago 600,000 Jews wandered the wilderness for forty years because they yearned for the flesh-pots of Egypt. We brought that number here in three years."

Then on to Galilee: to Acre, with its Turkish atmosphere tantalisingly foreign to the Israelis debarred by the unfinished business of war from travelling across their frontiers; and Naharyah, thirteen years before an unmapped strip of coast, today a thriving holiday-resort favoured by solid, beer-drinking German *émigrés*. In Nazareth, still a wholly Arab town, Sharett electioneered in Arabic, while at an open-air rally of new immigrants nearby he made his speech five times—in Hebrew, French, Yiddish, Turkish and Arabic.

The General Zionists' manifesto declared: "The greatest miracle of this land of miracles is how the private individual, at the mercy of a régime of bureaucracy, red-tape and inefficiency, manages to live at all." Another miracle worthy of mention was the effective conduct of electioneering in the midst of a paper-famine. There were no newsprint stocks in the country, and the daily papers were down to single sheets. *Mapam* circumvented the obstacle by over-printing back numbers of their party journal with a large red M, and pasting them upon any patch of blank wall. The campaign was orderly, though unbelievably noisy. One-half of the electorate was confirmed in its political ways, almost unaffected by the avalanche of oratory and handbills. The other half, composed of those who could not yet speak Hebrew, were without fixed occupations or homes, and were still resentful, unsocial and perplexed, was less predictable. This was the camp-population, exiles ingathered in three years of Ben-Gurion's rule.

The results were announced in August, 1951. The General Zionists trebled their representation, but not at the expense of *Mapai*, which was returned as strong as before. Unless the General Zionists and *Mapam* could be brought in, there would have to be a *Mapai* government again, with Ben-Gurion at the mercy of the bargain-hunting small fry. He for his part was in no mood for surrender. "All moderates elected are welcome to join the government," he announced, "but this does not include *Herut* or the Communists. Seventy-five per cent of the electorate have rejected the General Zionist economic policy, and eighty per cent the foreign policy of *Mapam*. There will be no concession to them on these issues."

This in effect was what they demanded. Ben-Gurion all but brought in *Mapam*, till it insisted upon an assurance that Israel would not vote against the Soviet Union in any debate at the United

Nations. The General Zionists asked for, and were denied, the portfolio of Trade and Industry. After fifty-five meetings with the other parties, Ben-Gurion, with 'mixed feelings', as he confessed, presented a new government, consisting of all the old faces, to the *Knesset*. In order to achieve this result, he agreed not to press the national service of religious women, while an intricate *modus operandi* was found for the education of new immigrants. By the time the various elements in the coalition settled down to administer the country, their capacities for mutual toleration were all but exhausted.

The partnership limped along for a year, a period which saw the completion of 'Operation Ezra and Nehemiah'—the influx of three-quarters of Iraqi Jewry, an ancient community of 120,000 souls. Their arrival tipped the numerical scales against the European elements in the state. Jews the world over blessed the great concept of ingathering the dispersed nation, because of its humanity, self-sacrifice and daring. In contrast the old settlers of Israel, who would have to share citizenship with these bedraggled fugitives from the Moslem world arriving by the plane-load, knew the policy had not come off. Without an equivalent immigration of westerners to help teach them useful skills and the laws of hygiene, and to raise their cultural level, the ingathering was a reckless adventure.

Ben-Gurion heard the rumblings of discontent but was impervious to them. To keep this land, he preached to the *Knesset*, they had first to populate its sparsely inhabited areas. The accompanying sociological indigestion could be dealt with later. In the meantime what doctors there were had to toil heroically with diseases rarely encountered among European Jews, and teachers sought to bring the Hebrew language to old and young. Elders of the established settlements went to live among the newcomers, the women to cope with primitive prejudices on child-rearing, the men to unfold the secrets of husbandry to reluctant bazaar-pedlars grown prematurely old in the slums of Bagdad and Mosul. Ben-Gurion refused to see in the immigrants a menace to the European structure of the state. They were Jews, and his conviction that they would be infected by the collective ideal of Israel so that a unity might be welded from the diverse elements, was unshaken. None was superior to the other, he said. And besides, why necessarily had Israel to be a *European* nation? And what exactly was a European nation? He wanted these rescued derelicts to forget they were Oriental Jews, just as he had forgotten that he was a Polish Jew.

He applauded mixed marriage provided it did not lead to the elimination of Jewishness. Amos his son had brought back an English bride after the war. She was a native of the Isle of Man, a nurse at a military hospital in Liverpool where he had been a patient. She had embraced the Jewish religion in London and the father had accepted the match without protest. Why should not the Orientals intermarry with the westerners, to the improvement of both strains? His colleagues in the Cabinet shook their heads dubiously, but none dared openly to challenge the policy.

The religious issue then came up again to break the peace of the coalition. Ben-Gurion had purchased relief from chronic crisis by leaving the enlistment of religious women in abeyance for a year. Now the year was up, and as he indicated his intention of carrying the measure through, the ultra-clericalists of the Orthodox parties in September, 1952, felt compelled to resign. This gave the opposition 60 votes, exactly one-half of the parliamentary total. The Premier found himself in an impossible situation, with government at a standstill. A two-months' period of arduous negotiation followed, but its outcome was decisive: no less than a minor revolution in the young political life of the state. Ben-Gurion resumed negotiations with Peretz Bernstein of Tel-Aviv for the entry of his General Zionists into the government. Bernstein responded eagerly—the economic situation, the hesitancy of the newcomers to form agricultural collectives, the unwillingness of the old collectives to surrender their treasured ideals so as to cope with the great social and economic problems by which the country was now engulfed, the reaction everywhere against the clutch of the *Histadruth* and the struggle for power within that body itself, all these told him that the moment was now at hand to woo Ben-Gurion away from his socialist loyalties and make possible the termination of his own four years in the political wilderness. The Prague trial, which occurred during the discussions between the two men, removed any doubt from their minds that this was the time for compromise.

"This state cannot become either capitalist or socialist," Ben-Gurion told Bernstein. "Both private enterprise and national control are essential for the fulfilment of Zionism." The other's conditions were: the diminution of the *Histadruth*'s widespread power, a

18

liberal economic policy and the unification of the educational system. The Premier accepted them. Privately, the two men agreed on measures to amend the electoral system so as to eliminate the blackmail which minute party groups could exercise. Thus, during the months when the volcanic issue of national service for religious women became alive again, and a group of three Arab *Mapai* members held the balance of power, it seemed that Israel would be heading for a two- or three-party system, as good as democratic government had to offer in any country.

However, in its solid, cautious way, *Mapai* surveyed the outlook moodily. The party men appeared to be losing their grip and their leader showed no signs of caring. As in 1948, his great love remained not the party but the army; and although he had earlier undertaken to do so, he refused to surrender the Ministry of Defence, to whose affairs he devoted two full days of every week. Under his guidance Igal Yadin, the Chief of Staff, shaped the armed forces into a state of absolute preparedness. It became the chief medium through which an immigrant was turned into an Israeli. Foreign military observers wrote impressive reports of its efficiency. In its way it was also a factory for the new Hebrew language, for it created new words and expressions to fill deficiencies in technical phraseology. The army was an ubiquitous symbol of the dignity and power of the Jews in independence, and as such it was almost the only institution of state which escaped censure. *Mapai* felt it was being blamed for all the inadequacies of the new state while the credit for its achievements went to the army. Along with this a resentment of Yadin's own standing with the Prime Minister grew up among the hardened old Labour pioneers. They criticised him so frequently that ultimately his relationship with Ben-Gurion was affected. Suddenly, he resigned and went to England, to work on a book dealing with his father's archaeological discoveries.

Still Ben-Gurion would not give up the Defence Ministry. He tended now to detach himself completely from party affairs, and was rarely to be found with his old friends except for an occasional rally and at the meetings of the parliamentary committee of his *Knesset* faction. His day began early, but when it was done he preferred spending his evenings alone in his modest official residence in the Rehavia quarter of Jerusalem, once the home of a Manchester Jew, an official of the Mandatory government who had been killed in the King David Hotel explosion. There he and Paula lived in the utmost simplicity, rarely entertaining any but official guests. He slept badly, and would break up the long evenings of writing and study by going down to the kitchen to brew himself a glass of Russian tea. The Ben-Gurions kept no servants. At sixty-six the Prime Minister was still agile, ruddy-faced and in robust health.

On December 9th, 1952, the funeral plan 'Joseph' was put into operation. Both Ben-Gurion and Sprinzak, Speaker of the *Knesset*, addressed Parliament the following day. Sprinzak, the man of *Hapoel Hatzair*, those old non-Marxist radicals who throughout the years had remained faithful to Zionism's great international leader, wept. Ben-Gurion, risen from *Poale Zion*, delivered an unemotional, detached survey of Weizmann's place in their story. Weizmann personified universal culture, to which Ben-Gurion aspired, and the diplomatic Zionism of the Diaspora, which he despised. He described their departed President as the greatest Jew of their generation, but in his private estimation there was one greater—Albert Einstein.

A gesture from Ben-Gurion might have elevated Sprinzak, for five years the President's deputy, to the office he not unreasonably expected would now be his. The gesture was not made. Instead Ben-Gurion addressed an appeal to the man at Princeton University whom he had visited a year and a half before and whose great intellect he revered. To Ben-Gurion, Israel was the highest collective achievement of the Jews after centuries of national oblivion, while Einstein embodied their capacity to reach the summit of individual achievement. He belonged to humanity, not to politics. How better then to crown their national redemption than by reuniting Einstein with his people! Yet Einstein, the European refugee, refused him. This new disappointment accentuated Ben-Gurion's sense of isolation. Israel was not great enough to cast a spell; the Jewish world outside, as represented at its highest and most tragic by Einstein, was unequal to its destiny.

Searching among his parliamentary colleagues for a candidate deserving of their country's highest honour, Ben-Gurion saw 119 men and women, few of whom in his estimation could forget the past, or elude the pitfalls of the ephemeral present. He wished to protect the nomination of Weizmann's successor from party controversy, and therefore his choice fell upon Pinchas Rosen, who up to the general election had been Minister of Justice, and leader of the least partisan of the *Knesset* groups—the Progressives. Rosen was more of a European than almost any other personality in Israel's public life, and more of a German than any other European. This, Rosen confessed, was his failing. The new Israel was a blending of Occidental and Oriental, a European state committed to Asia, a Biblical people in the modern world. He did not fully express that admixture. In Rosen's view only one man fulfilled the role: Isaac Ben-Zvi.

Thus the loose ends of this story were drawn together. Within the councils of *Mapai* the choice was made amidst the stored-up memories of Zionism's early days. Of the few who had smuggled themselves into this one-time Turkish province and changed the course of Jewish history by changing their own lives, three names— Ben-Gurion, Sprinzak and Ben-Zvi—stood out for length of service and steadfastness of will. The victory of Zionism in Palestine is largely the history of their lives, the weakness of Israel an account of their limitations, its strength a reflection of their obduracy. One of them, Ben-Gurion, had the power to decide which of the other two was to be the nation's first citizen. Nearly fifty years before, he had rejected the youths of *Hapoel Hatzair* and joined with *Poale Zion*. Similarly, he now passed Sprinzak over for Ben-Zvi. An old partnership was restored, and Rachel Yanait, their colleague on the earliest *Poale Zion* newspaper *Unity* in 1910, now became First Lady of the Jewish state.

Recalling Ben-Zvi from his semi-retirement proved popular in the end. His nomination, however, was not accepted without some controversy in *Mapai*, nor was it accomplished with the maximum of dignity. Sprinzak was hurt because he had gained the impression that if he indicated his readiness to stand for office, he would be un-questionably accepted, and that Ben-Gurion himself would sponsor him. Instead, the Premier delivered a long speech—which he sub-sequently had published as a pamphlet—extolling Ben-Zvi's merits and not once mentioning the name of Joseph Sprinzak. It was one more stab at the hearts of the guardians of the *Histadruth*'s interests, with which Sprinzak's name was now as closely identified as once Ben-Gurion's had been.

Another cause for grievance soon followed. That December, Ben-Gurion and Bernstein reached agreement and a new coalition government came into being with Bernstein himself occupying the portfolio of Trade and Industry, hitherto so jealously guarded by *Mapai*. The government was further strengthened by the addition of Pinchas Rosen in his old post as Minister of Justice, and by the radical wing of the Religious groups. It gave Israel her strongest executive since the 'Committee of Public Safety' in 1948.

This proved a harmonious team. Under the stimulus of the devotees of private enterprise a capitalist economy was evolved. Luxury goods found their way back into the shops, but unemployment rose as white-collar workers, discarded with all the accretions of an over-administered bureaucracy, fell by the roadside. Hardship and prosperity stood side by side, while the emphasis in plans for development shifted from industry to agriculture.

In this new atmosphere Ben-Gurion grew to be less a Prime Minister than a national guide, always looking to the future, always enjoining Zionism upon the Zionist state. He initiated reforms in the Hebrew language, a vernacular still unequal to all the demands of modernity. Often he would stop business at the Sunday Cabinet meetings to engage in a lengthy semantic debate with Sharett. He wrote prolifically on any subject that appealed to him. The one man able to secure immediate access to him on demand was the Tel-Aviv bookseller issuing his collected speeches and writings. Religious Jews were sure they would one day welcome the Prime Minister into their fold.

He made some aspects of education, which might normally have been the province of a university, his personal responsibility. He considered the Hebrew language in its modern usage to be a unifying influence upon the whole world of Jewry and, after the army, the most potent instrument of nation-building. But it was also an insulating factor, closing the mind of young Israel against the ideas of other civilisations. He met this danger, characteristically, by setting up a department within his Prime Minister's Office for the translation of the world's classics into Hebrew. For Hebrew is so recently-resuscitated a vehicle of social and cultural intercourse that at present the large body of classic literature is outside the reach of the average Israeli. Not all of Shakespeare, very little of the French classic poets or of Augustan Rome can be had in translation. This may seriously warp the cultural outlook of the growing generation in Israel, for unlike its forebears of the Diaspora it is not multilingual. The difficulty, Ben-Gurion discovered, was to find suitable translators, and the search for them still goes on the world over. Jewry is not short of rabbis, but first-class Hebrew scholars are rare.

Politics had been Ben-Gurion's life; now they wearied him. He was depressed by what he read of Israel in the foreign Press (he regularly received the London and New York *Times*, the *Manchester Guardian*, the *New Statesman* and the *Economist*), and was disgusted with the journalistic tendency to concentrate on the blemishes rather than the virtues of his state. Since he put the Arab invaders to flight 350 new points of habitation had been established, mostly by ghetto-bound Jews unversed in agriculture. Israel would one day show the world that these gauche, primitive newcomers, breathing for the first time the air of true freedom, could rise to great achievements. Somewhere among those ragged children saved from a Moroccan *mellah* would rise another Ralph Bunche or a new Spinoza. "I live for the day when a Yemenite immigrant will be elected president of the state," he would say.

He was waiting for an Israeli to scale an intellectual Mount Everest; and while brooding over that intrepid expedition (which served, incidentally, to deepen his admiration of the British) politics dragged him back to the present. Early in June, 1953, the four General Zionist recruits to the coalition resigned. Again, it was a petty brawl over *Mapai*'s insistence on flying the red flag, as well as Israel's own blue-and-white colours, on *Histadruth* schools. Ben-Gurion, vexed by his comrades' lack of adaptability, advised them not to make an issue of the flag. The time would come, and soon, he hoped, when such divergencies would be forgotten in the process of the nation's growing up.

During long meetings he begged his party to surrender the point, for the sake of harmony. But it was not learning as fast as he taught, and soon angry words were exchanged. "Remember what happened to Ramsay MacDonald!" warned one of his followers. The Premier decided to let his party stew in its own juice. Soon the party came round to his way of thinking. "We must keep the coalition going," they agreed. "We are ready to concede the issue." Once more, the Cabinet met each Sunday morning to tackle significant questions of state.

It was Ben-Gurion's final act of reconciliation. He was the common ground upon which Left and Right, Religious and Secular, Oriental and Occidental, could meet. Therefore, he *was* Israel. He enjoyed authority, but loathed despotism; and he saw in his position a possible symptom of great danger. Suddenly, a thunderclap came to end the factious murmurings of Jerusalem politics. Ben-Gurion announced his impending retirement. The nation was stunned. What was their world without its Atlas!

Each of his colleagues, as well as most of the editorials of the newspapers in their sixteen languages of publication, begged him not to desert them. In one sense they were fully justified in their plea. For the course upon which their ship of state was charted had been set by him, and the pilot should not leave the helm before the ship is safely brought to harbour. He chose to quit at a critical stage in the country's affairs, when old friends abroad were deserting it and Arab truculence was on the increase. But he was adamant, and pleaded strain. In reality he was weighed down by his lonely responsibilities. After twenty years of tumultuous struggle, since the Jewish Agency days, the legitimate respite other statesmen enjoy by going into opposition was not within his prospect. Government was impossible without *Mapai*. Therefore, *Mapai* should learn to be without him.

His going was an escape from the confined circle of party warfare by which he was surrounded, and a protest against the negative response of western Jewry to his challenge to join him in resurrecting the long-dispersed nation. Only a national calamity, or perhaps a national regeneration, would bring him back. Having made the decision, he described it to President Ben-Zvi as a 'bitter necessity'. And indeed he made his retirement one of the deeply meaningful acts of his full life. Mystic that he was, he felt called to return to the bosom of the land, to a personal identity with the creed he had preached for a half-century.

On December 7th, 1953, he broadcast his farewell. "We have taken upon ourselves a gigantic threefold struggle," he said. "With ourselves and the acquired habits of exile; with the natural forces of this country, its desolation and impoverishment; with malicious and evil forces in the world, both near and far, who neither understood nor favoured the uniqueness and mission of our people from the day it first set foot on the stage of history. On each of these fronts we have known failure and defeat. But we never retreated and we never surrendered. And our struggle has been crowned with victories and achievements such as our people has never known since the days of the Maccabees." Of that people he said: "Words of mine cannot adequately express what I feel towards the nation for having had faith in me and entrusted me with an exalted and fateful mission. I have endeavoured to fulfil that mission, as far as lay in my power, with devotion and in all humility. But I do not claim to have been free from fault and error. With complete sincerity I can repeat literally the words of the Psalmist: 'Lord, my heart is not haughty, nor mine eyes lofty; neither do I exercise myself in things too high nor in matters too wonderful for me.' "

His creative genius had first flowered in the rocky Galilean colony of Sejera, an outpost of Zionism in the north. Now he responded once again to the same call, but this time where it would have most meaning, in the uncultivated south. Zionism meant physical labour, the nurturing of the wilderness back to life. Anything less than this was the shoddy, the incomplete, the imitative, the persistence of Diaspora. There was still room for Zionism in Israel. In the act of abdication, and as he made ready with his wife to apply for member-ship of a young, non-political agricultural settlement, Sde Boker, he threw out his greatest challenge to *Mapai*, to Israel, to Jewry.

David Ben-Gurion, with Paula still by his side, surrendered the reins of office to Moshe Sharett. Then he took leave of his friends in Tel-Aviv and, seated for the last time in his official motor-car, flanked by outriders, he joined the tiny colony of labourers planted in the desert forty miles south-west of Beersheba. Israel wept at his parting. His advice was not to weep, but to follow.

THE END

Index

269

12/8/55

35496

DS
125.3
B37
L5

LITVINOFF, BARNET
BEN-GURION OF ISRAEL

DATE DUE

GAYLORD

PRINTED IN U.S.A.